SCIENCE FICTION F

Science Fiction Film examines o. ⸬popular
genres of Hollywood cinema, sugg﹍ ⸬ fiction film
reflects attitudes toward science, tec. ⸬on as they have
evolved in American culture over the c⸜ ⸬e twentieth century.
J. P. Telotte provides a survey of science ⸱ ⸜n film criticism, emphasizing humanist, psychological, ideological, feminist, and postmodern
critiques. He also sketches a history of the genre, from its earliest literary manifestations to the present, while touching on and comparing
it to pulp fiction, early television science fiction, and Japanese *anime*.
Telotte offers in-depth readings of four key films: *RoboCop, Close Encounters of the Third Kind, THX 1138*, and *The Fly*, each of which illustrates a particular fantastic branch of science fiction, as well as the difficulties of any genre classification. Challenging the boundaries usually
seen between high and low culture, literature and film, science fiction
and horror, *Science Fiction Film* reasserts the central role of fantasy in
popular films, even those concerned with reason, science, and technology.

J. P. Telotte is Professor of Literature, Communication, and Culture at
the Georgia Institute of Technology. He is the author of several books
including *Replications: A Robotic History of the Science Fiction Film* and
A Distant Technology: Science Fiction Film and the Machine Age. He is
coeditor of the journal *Post Script* and a member of the editorial boards
of *Literature/Film Quarterly* and *South Atlantic Review*.

GENRES IN AMERICAN CINEMA

General Editor
Barry Keith Grant, *Brock University, Ontario, Canada*

Genres in American Cinema examines the significance of American films in a series of single-authored volumes, each dedicated to a different genre. Each volume will provide a comprehensive account of its genre, from enduring classics to contemporary revisions, from marginal appropriations to international inflections, emphasizing its distinctive qualities as well as its cultural, historical, and critical contexts. Their approach will be methodologically broad, balancing theoretical and historical discussion with close readings of representative films. Designed for use as classroom texts, the books will be intellectually rigorous, yet written in a style that is lively and accessible to students and general audiences alike.

SCIENCE
FICTION
FILM

J. P. Telotte
Georgia Institute of Technology

CAMBRIDGE
UNIVERSITY PRESS

PUBLISHED BY THE PRESS SYNDICATE OF THE UNIVERSITY OF CAMBRIDGE
The Pitt Building, Trumpington Street, Cambridge, United Kingdom

CAMBRIDGE UNIVERSITY PRESS
The Edinburgh Building, Cambridge CB2 2RU, UK
40 West 20th Street, New York, NY 10011-4211, USA
10 Stamford Road, Oakleigh, VIC 3166, Australia
Ruiz de Alarcón 13, 28014 Madrid, Spain
Dock House, The Waterfront, Cape Town 8001, South Africa

http://www.cup.org

© Cambridge University Press 2001

First published 2001

Typeface Cheltenham 9.5/13 pt.   *System* QuarkXpress® [MG]

A catalog record for this book is available from the British Library

Library of Congress Cataloging in Publication Data
Telotte, J. P., 1949–
    Science fiction film / J. P. Telotte.
        p.   cm. – (Genres in American cinema)
    "Select filmography of the American science fiction film": p.
    Includes bibliographical references and index.
    ISBN 0-521-59372-7 – ISBN 0-521-59647-5 (pbk.)
    1. Science fiction films – History and criticism.   I. Title.   II. Series.
PN1995.9.S26 T45 2001
791.43´615–dc21
                                                                    2001025937

ISBN 0 521 59372 7 hardback
ISBN 0 521 59647 5 paperback

Transferred to digital printing 2003

Contents

Illustrations

Acknowledgments

A number of people have contributed their time, resources, and general knowledge to the creation of this book and deserve special mention. As in much of my past research into science fiction literature and film, I have drawn heavily on the knowledge and insights of my colleague Bud Foote, who, I am convinced, knows more about science fiction than any living human. Several of my other colleagues at Georgia Tech and in the International Association for the Fantastic in the Arts have contributed their advice and insights to this work. No less important are my students at Georgia Tech, especially those in my Genres of Fantasy course, who have always asked the toughest questions while also sharing their own, often considerable knowledge about the science fiction genre.

In working with Cambridge University Press I have been fortunate to have the guidance of Beatrice Ruhl and the attention to detail of Michael Gnat as this project has pushed forward. The foremost influence on this book, though, is undoubtedly Barry Grant, whose work on film genres has always provided a valuable yardstick for my own. Professor Grant has contributed in various ways to the shaping of practically every chapter, while also prodding me to think more carefully about the films and the cultural circumstances that produced them. He has simply been the model editor, and I thank him especially for all his help on this project.

PART ONE

Approaches

1

Introduction: The World of the Science Fiction Film

Whenever students of film approach the science fiction genre, it appears they immediately find themselves facing a kind of paradox, one akin to the problematic logic built into the form's combinatory designation – that is, as *science* and *fiction*, as fact and fabrication. For a genre that would seem to be almost self-evidently *itself* tends to slip away, to evade its own evidence or facticity. It is, after all, particularly as its literary practitioners would argue, manifestly about science and scientific possibility – even probability. In fact, it commonly proposes the sort of "what if" game in which scientists are typically engaged as they set about designing experiments and conducting their research: extrapolating from the known in order to explain the unknown. Thus, the writer and legendary pulp editor John W. Campbell Jr. instructed that science fiction should be "an effort to predict the future on the basis of known facts, culled largely from present-day laboratories."[1] Yet that prescription, which went far to shape the developing literature of science fiction in the United States, hardly accounts for the full appeal of the form – an appeal that some would pass off as due to its adolescent character, others would trace to its archetypal elements, and still others would explain as fundamental to its speculative nature, its expression of common human curiosity. It is an appeal, in any case, that has, over time, lured some of Western culture's most important fictionalists (Edgar Allan Poe, Jack London, H. G. Wells, Aldous Huxley, Walker Percy) to try their hands at its subject matter. Especially in its cinematic form, however, science fiction often seems to appeal precisely because it lends itself to the greatest imaginative capacities of the film medium: to its ability, through what we very broadly term "special effects," to give shape and being to the imagination. It is a form, then, that often seems quite difficult to pin down satisfactorily.

Efforts at defining the literary form have often begun by wrestling precisely with this sense of difficulty. A self-professed "outsider's guidebook" to the world of science fiction, David Hartwell's *Age of Wonders* suggests that science fiction is "so diverse" in its forms and subjects that it defies any simple definition. Rather, Hartwell argues that "science fiction has been an umbrella under which any kind of estrangement from reality is welcome" and indeed entirely suited to the genre with its emphasis on "wonder,"[2] so he sets about describing the genre by focusing on its audience, on the diverse community and interests of science fiction readers. An overview of science fiction aimed at those already familiar with the form, Edward James's *Science Fiction in the Twentieth Century,* from the start announces that it is "an attempt to define science fiction," yet one which recognizes that "a proper definition can be achieved only by understanding what authors are trying to do or have tried to do" throughout the form's existence. It thus charts a historical path, looking at "how definitions of sf [science fiction] changed as sf itself changed," and how "the development of sf as a literary category is bound up with attempts to define it and with attempts by writers to live up to those definitions."[3] In marked contrast, Darko Suvin in *Metamorphoses of Science Fiction,* a theoretical work aimed mainly at a scholarly audience, assumes that science fiction is a readily recognizable form, "a full-fledged literary genre" having "its own repertory of functions, conventions, and devices," all of which are fairly well known. Still, even as he begins laying out his own Brechtian-inspired and rather elegant definition of the form as a "literature of cognitive estrangement," that is, a form intent on defamiliarizing reality through various generic strategies in order to reflect on it more effectively, Suvin eventually begins to pare away types of text that do not fit into his scheme, particularly various versions of fantasy and some utopian writing.[4] In assuming a sort of fundamental coherence, he thus immediately begins to qualify what he is trying to define, limiting his scheme to "the genre as it is here conceived"[5] as a way around a definitional dilemma.

That same sense of difficulty extends, and perhaps even more visibly so, to our sense of what constitutes cinematic science fiction; for although the genre certainly sports an iconography that immediately asserts a kind of identity and one with which the average filmgoer is usually quite familiar – rockets, robots, futuristic cities, alien encounters, fantastic technology, scientists (mad or otherwise) – these icons or generic conventions have, within the critical establishment and, to a lesser degree, even in the popular mind, never quite satisfactorily served to bracket it off as a discrete form, something we might easily

Figure 1. Crossing genre boundaries – *Frankenstein* (1931).

categorize and thus set about systematically studying. Invariably, for example, the form seems to bulk into the realm of horror, as is evidenced by such varied films as *Frankenstein* (1931) [Fig. 1], *Dr. Cyclops* (1940), *Invasion of the Body Snatchers* (1956), and, more recently, the films in the *Alien* cycle (1979, 1986, 1992, 1997), thanks to their emphasis on physical confrontation and threat that occur within a context marked by those trappings we associate with science fiction. Similarly,

Figure 2. *Starship Troopers* (1997) translates the World War II combat film into outer space.

a relatively minor form like the disaster film often seems to subsume both genres, as we see in works like *Dante's Peak* (1997), *Deep Impact* (1998), and *Armageddon* (1998). Additionally, the science fiction film very often shares characteristics with other popular genres, even borrows rather forthrightly from a broad range of them, as we find in the case of *Outland* (1981) and its echoes of the western, *Starship Troopers* (1997) [Fig. 2] and its imitation of a host of World War II films, *Blade Runner* (1982) [Fig. 3] and *Dark City* (1998) with their dependence on the conventions and look of the American film noir, and especially the *Star Wars* saga (1977, 1980, 1983, 1999), which borrows by turns from westerns, war films, Japanese samurai epics, and the serials. So when a pioneering genre critic such as Carlos Clarens set about surveying the history of the horror film, readers might only have expected that he would incorporate science fiction, as well as the disaster film, into his field of inquiry. Following this vein, we can discover many other surveys of the genre, as well as treatments of selected films, that have simply treated horror and science fiction as if they were essentially the same thing, and still others that view science fiction as if it were merely a pastiche form,[6] lacking a secure identity of its own [Fig. 4].

Figure 3. The film-noir look and detective protagonist of *Blade Runner* (1982).

Figure 4. Technology and thrills, the mixed payoff offered by *Forbidden Planet*'s (1956) trailer.

Despite these difficulties of identity – and, of course, partly because of them – it still seems that a first task of almost anyone who sets out to describe, explain, or analyze specific science fiction film texts has often become the same as that facing any student of genre, that is, one of differentiation. Every study of a film genre, either explicitly or implicitly, begins from similarly problematic issues: concerns with what to include and what to exclude, and on what basis we can begin to make those determinations. These issues constitute what is often referred to as the empirical dilemma, which poses the question of how we can ever determine what characteristics typify a genre without first determining what texts constitute the genre, even though that very decision about textual inclusiveness would logically seem to hinge upon prior decisions about the genre's identity or definition.[7] One approach is to postulate an essential nature for the form, and then, as Suvin does, begin to pare away those works that violate its logic. This strategy usually produces a coherent if rather narrowly defined body of work. The more popular recourse is to work from a common consensus on the generic canon, to accept for purposes of initial analysis and argument all those works that have previously been included in various discussions of a certain genre.[8] Such an approach allows for inclusiveness, absorbs differing critical vantages, and, perhaps most important, permits critical discussion to move forward.

Obviously, casting the generic net so widely has its drawbacks as well. For example, we inevitably pull in works that can blur the issue, that challenge the very possibilities of boundary, and that, at least initially, seem to frustrate any effort at focusing attention. A serial like *The Phantom Creeps* (1939), for example, has all the trappings of a crime/gangster film, a type quite popular in the 1930s; it stars an actor, Bela Lugosi, who was always iconographically linked to the horror genre; yet it also includes a mad scientist, an invisibility ray, and a menacing robot – clearly the stuff of science fiction. This sort of generic crossover is far from uncommon, as we can see with the great number of comic–horror and comic–science fiction films – movies like the Bob Hope vehicle *The Ghost Breakers* (1940), *Abbott and Costello Meet Frankenstein* (1946), *Ghostbusters* (1984), *Spaceballs* (1987), *Mars Attacks!* (1996), *The Fifth Element* (1997) – and, more significant for our purposes, the horror–science fiction films that, after their heyday in the early 1930s, have once more become very popular, as the *Alien* series amply illustrates. Differentiation – or at least an attempt at it – has thus often become a first, yet always still rather problematic step in most genre analysis, and a point on which this study too must initially spend some time.

In what is one of the most often-reprinted essays on popular film genres, Bruce Kawin takes precisely this differentiating tack. Starting from the understanding that science fiction and horror films are typically linked and conflated, he has set about defining the forms by directly contrasting certain of their key and recurring elements. While he admits that the genres share many common features – especially mad scientists and monstrous "others" – and that they even "organize themselves" in similar ways – particularly through their depicted encounters with some unexpected and seemingly threatening "other" – he believes that their fundamental concerns are quite distinctive and that the two genres "promote growth in different ways."[9] Horror films, he argues, "address . . . the unconscious," whereas science fiction deals with "the conscious – if not exactly the scientist in us, then certainly the part of the brain that enjoys speculating on technology, gimmicks, and the perfectible future."[10] Moreover, he suggests, the genres' respective "attitudes" are different, particularly toward "curiosity and the openness of systems";[11] that is, while horror, he argues, seeks to close the door on the unknown and to suggest how dangerous an unbridled curiosity can be, science fiction opens it and embraces that very openness as an opportunity for intellectual growth. In effect, Kawin believes that the horror and science fiction films offer audiences two quite different sorts of pleasure or satisfaction in the distinct ways they confirm or challenge our relationships to the world and to others.

If Kawin's comparison seems a bit too pat, too easy – and often seems to force works into a category almost against their generic will, as in the case of films like *The Thing from Another World* (1951) and *Alien* – it can serve an important purpose, especially at the outset of this study. It reminds us that genres resist being easily pinned down, thanks to one of their key characteristics: their vitality, the fact that they are constantly changing in response to a variety of cultural and industrial influences, and thus pushing at the very outlines we would, it so often seems, like to set for them – and to maintain against all critical objection. The science fiction film – in part because it has been so very popular over the past thirty years, and because we have seen in that time so many variations on the form, so many efforts to keep it new and vital to our culture – may well prove more protean than most of our other popular genres, as well as more resistant to that pigeonholing impulse. For example, as scientific developments have increasingly begun to encroach on territory that we had traditionally ceded to religion and morality, as in the various concerns surrounding human origins, genetic manipulation, euthanasia, and gender reassignment, the science fiction film has more often begun to broach "supernatural" issues, as in the case of films like *Cocoon* (1985), *Stargate* (1994), *Event Horizon* (1997), and *Contact* (1997), to pursue that notion of "curiosity," as Kawin would put it, in some rather unexpected, even theological directions, of a sort precisely linked to the horror film of past times. However, we should take it as a sign of the genre's vitality that it is constantly changing, pushing its limits, bulking beyond the borders that we would, for our own intellectual contentment, conventionally assign to it. The science fiction film has simply proven to be one of our most flexible popular genres – and perhaps for that very reason, one of our most culturally useful. Consequently, we might begin our own consideration of the genre simply by thinking in terms of a "supertext" of the science fiction film, that is, what genre critic John Cawelti describes as the collection "of the most significant characteristics or family resemblances among many particular texts, which can accordingly be analyzed, evaluated, and otherwise related to each other by virtue of their connection with" this "consolidation of many texts created at different times."[12] What constitutes the supertext of science fiction, then, is not any one film or even an ideal science fiction film, but rather that large body of all the films and their similar characteristics that we might reasonably or customarily link to the genre. Moreover, that supertext is always expanding, ever broadening the potential field for subsequent films in the genre, and constantly making the job of describing and analyzing this form a more complex, even daunting process – and yet for that very reason an instructive and valuable experience for the larger practice of genre thinking.

Science Fiction as Fantasy

One way in which this classification effort can prove especially useful is in the way it reminds us of the general limits that film studies often seem to set on how we conventionally think about genres. Tzvetan Todorov in his structuralist examination of "the fantastic" as a literary form – a work from which the present study draws heavily – offers an instructive example in this regard on several levels. Before beginning to describe his own field of inquiry, the fantastic text, he takes on what has become a canonical work of literary criticism, Northrop Frye's *Anatomy of Criticism,* a study that proposed a kind of "unified field theory" of literary genres based on what Frye termed *mythoi*. Todorov finds in that work a troubling focus on what he describes as "theoretical genres" at the expense of "historical genres," a privileging of the ideal over the very real literary texts with which readers are most familiar and which, in Frye's work, seem forced through various manipulations to "fit" into prescribed categories.[13] His dissatisfaction with Frye's approach forms the backdrop for his own study of fantasy, a literary form that seems closely allied to a number of film genres cited above. As in the case of horror, for example, the fantastic very often involves fear, although, as Todorov reminds us, "it is not a necessary condition of the genre"; and while it might, as science fiction often does, emphasize "laws which contemporary science does not acknowledge," such an emphasis might constitute only a small dimension of the form.[14] However, more to the point for this study – and for that pigeonholing tendency to which we are all prone – is Todorov's argument that the fantastic exists *only* in relationship to other narrative types. It thus denotes a constantly shifting – and hence shifty – field of narrative experience that simply resists the sort of analytic that a Frye would offer. Thus he suggests that we can talk about it as a genre only insofar as we recognize the very blurred boundaries that mark its existence.

The *fantastic* – the relationship of which to science fiction we shall pursue shortly – exists on a kind of sliding scale with two other forms that Todorov terms the *uncanny* and the *marvelous*. While the uncanny narrative focuses on the unconscious or, more generally, the mind as a force producing seemingly inexplicable events, and the marvelous on the supernatural or spiritual realm as it intrudes into and challenges our everyday world, the fantastic occupies that point of "hesitation" between the two: the realm of what might or might not be, where reality itself seems a puzzle, waiting for us to reconstruct it. It is, in effect, a border form, one that can exist only in a liminal situation, as we try to sort out how the narrative relates to and challenges our normative view of reality. Extrapolating from his schematic for fantasy, then, Todorov formulates a simple yet elegant guideline for genre thinking, as he suggests that "genres are precisely those relay-points by which the work assumes a relation with the universe of literature"[15] – or for our purposes, with the "universe" of film narrative.

If, from this vantage, we come to accept, and even incorporate into our thinking about the science fiction film, a kind of inevitable ambiguity, a blurring of boundaries bound up in such "relay points" as mad scientists and unexplained monsters, we can also draw from it a useful element of structural thinking, a bit of local organization to super-

Figure 5. *The Day the Earth Stood Still* (1951) measures out the impact of forces beyond the human realm.

impose on an inevitably shifty genre; for we might rather easily map Todorov's delineation of fantasy into three component narrative fields – the marvelous, fantastic, and uncanny – onto the terrain of the science fiction film, and especially onto its most common narrative types, which themselves seem to exist only in a kind of liminal state. To do so, we need only consider what seem to be the three large-scale fascinations of the genre: first, the impact of forces outside the human realm, of encounters with alien beings and other worlds (or other times); second, the possibility of changes in society and culture, wrought by our science and technology; and third, technological alterations in and substitute versions of the self. In the first of these, exemplified in some small measure of its variety by such films as *The Day the Earth Stood Still* (1951) [Fig. 5], *Close Encounters of the Third Kind* (1977), *E.T. the Extra-Terrestrial* (1982), and *Independence Day* (1996), we glimpse perhaps the most truly speculative thrust of the form, as it explores the impact of encounters with the alien or other, or simply the exploration of the unknown through flights into outer space, an impact

Figure 6. A utopian future world as envisioned by H. G. Wells and *Things to Come* (1936).

that inevitably expands the scope of our knowledge, explodes our very perception of the universe, as we see in the admonitory closing line to the original *The Thing . . . :* "Watch the skies! Keep watching!" It effectively alters our whole sense of reality. The second, which has offered us a host of utopian and dystopian visions, foregrounds the promise – as well as the menace – of reason, science, and technology to remake our world and rework our relationship to it, seen most dramatically in such films as *Metropolis* (1926), *Just Imagine* (1930), *Things to Come* (1936) [Fig. 6], *THX 1138* (1971), *Logan's Run* (1976), *Brazil* (1986), and

Dark City. The third category looks at the human applications of science and technology, the reshapings of and modelings upon the self that have produced the various robots, androids, cyborgs, and "enhanced" beings of films like *Westworld* (1973), *The Terminal Man* (1974), *Blade Runner* (1982), *RoboCop* and its sequels (1987, 1990, 1993), and the two *Terminator* films (1984, 1991) [Fig. 7]. These three *fascinations,* as I have termed them, closely link the film genre to its literary branch, for Edward James in the course of his historical definition of science fiction argues that the large canon of literature easily divides itself by subject into three broad story groups: "the extraordinary voyage . . . the tale of the future . . . and the tale of science (notably concerned with marvelous inventions)."[16] And, of course, any discussion of the science fiction genre, as our later overview of its history will suggest, must make some effort at placing it in the context of that far longer literary history on which it has so often drawn. By considering those encounters with alien forces/beings as a type of *marvelous* narrative, the concern with futuristic societies in the context of Todorov's *fantastic* category, and alterations of the self as *uncanny,* we might not only begin to satisfy an element of that common desire for pattern, for organization, for rational delineation from which most genre thinking seems invariably to spring, but also better conceptualize the kinship or overlap among a number of genres – especially horror and the musical – that might at various times be drawn in under that broad heading of fantasy.[17]

Although Todorov never offers any detailed discussion of science fiction, he certainly affords us a useful signpost down this path, for in his description of the marvelous, particularly the variety he terms the "instrumental marvelous," he notes that we come "very close" to what "today we call *science fiction.*"[18] As he offers, the science fiction narrative typically sets about explaining in a rational manner what, in some contexts, might seem supernatural; that is, it attempts to reframe some challenging phenomenon in terms of "new" laws of nature. More simply, I would suggest that we see the genre's often depicted encounter with the alien or alien civilization as involving us in just the sort of transcendent rationale that is fundamental to the marvelous as Todorov and others have described it. It takes as its impetus a variety of what Todorov terms "themes of the other." Following this lead, we might look to the other end of the fantasy scale and consider all of those works organized around the artificial being – the technological trope for the self – as types of uncanny text. Again, Todorov marks off the

Figure 7. The threatening technological double: The advanced cyborg of *Terminator 2: Judgment Day* (1991) as police officer.

path as he describes one basic category of fantasy themes as "themes of the self," those that focus especially on such subjects as "multiplication of the personality" and the "collapse of the limit between subject and object."[19] In that very image of the self replicated, of the unconscious given substance, then, we can begin to make out an uncanny shape for our science fiction as well. All of its stories of created selves, of robots and androids practically indistinguishable from the human, even from very specific human beings, lead us back precisely to an inquiry into our very humanity and its place in the construction of a human world. Between these two categories we might place those stories of future civilizations, of utopian or dystopian societies – narratives that, as Todorov might explain, explore "the relation of man with his desire," desire for a different world or simply a different way of life.[20] In the best tradition of the fantastic itself, which, as Torodov explains, hinges on a moment of hesitation in our ability to explain its effects, they suggest what might or might not be, what might have been produced by some alien force or civilization (by some "new" law of nature), or what might only be the product of human dreams, reveries, or ingenuity, a futuristic equivalent of the Connecticut Yankee's dreams of the past. Such categorization might prove valuable not so much by helping us put the great variety of science fiction narratives into their own discrete boxes – which could well lead us back in the direction of Frye and much of popular film criticism – but by letting us see them in the context of a broad register of science fiction films and, even more generally, within a pattern of fantasy narrative that inevitably shares its methods and concerns with other narrative types such as the horror film.

This latter placement seems particularly useful since through it we might begin to recognize some of the more general themes that underlie and operate along with the form's treatment of such topical concerns as genetic manipulation (*Gattaca*, 1997), racial discrimination (*The Brother from Another Planet*, 1984), political corruption (*The Fifth Element*), corporate greed (the *Alien* and *RoboCop* series), and others – in other words, some of the ways in which the genre's underlying themes have proven so very adaptable to current issues, and thus ways in which the genre has managed to stay vital to our culture. If this latter move seems in some ways an essentialist approach to the genre – in suggesting that there are indeed certain fundamental or essential themes that typify the form – I would accept the charge. However, I make that move as part of what I see as a necessary explanatory balance between the relative and the essential, the relational nature of every genre and its undeniable ability to assert a specific identity.

Genre Determinations

Of course, most viewers seem to have little difficulty in staking out some fairly clear territory from which to start thinking about the science fiction film, and certainly are not much troubled by these sorts of fundamental questions of generic boundary or definition – all concerns that are seemingly best left to critics and academics. Anyone who has watched even a few science fiction films, episodes of a *Flash Gordon* serial, or several episodes of the *Star Trek* or *Babylon 5* television series, for example, would probably argue that he or she could, with little hesitation, decide if a certain work belongs within the science fiction category. That sense of certainty probably springs from the fact that the typical viewer easily recognizes particular hallmarks, visual icons that, over the course of many years, have helped constitute a common signature that cultural consensus or historical use has by now assigned to the genre. Included in this broad category are such things as character types, situations, clothing, lighting, tools or weaponry, settings – all those elements that have often been described as the "language" of the genre, and much of which has been long established in the popular consciousness thanks to the corresponding literary tradition and its reliance on illustration, on visualizing its "what if" scenarios. Despite the haphazard ways in which such commonplace elements are often cited by reviewers, noted in introductory film texts, or even intruded into casual conversation, they have invariably proved a useful starting point for much discussion of formulaic narrative and have been readily adapted into structural descriptions of a variety of genres, as is illustrated by Edward Buscombe's efforts to subsume such elements into a scheme of "inner" and "outer forms" for genre discussion.[21] Nevertheless, if, in comparison to the genre dimensions that Todorov explores, these elements point up a potentially more significant level of specificity for genre identity – that is, if they almost immediately make the form recognizable to most viewers – they also seem to tell us little about what specific texts mean for us or the genre's place in a cultural nexus.

In an effort to deal with the sort of vagaries that have often attended earlier genre criticism, a criticism that typically took as its starting and ending point those immediate signifiers of identity, Rick Altman has outlined a useful structural model, an unnoticed virtue of which is that it draws precisely upon a combination of that generalized common consensus and iconic specificity. This "semantic/syntactic" description of a genre's workings, adapted from linguistics, helps to isolate the elements that contribute to the genre text's meanings and provides a paradigm for sketching out a formula's most distinctive icons and narrative events. It does so by considering the generic text, first, as "a list of common traits, attitudes, characters, shots, locations, sets, and the like," and second, as a group of "certain constitutive relationships . . . into which they are arranged."[22] While the iconic elements represent the genre's semantic dimension, its language, those relationships – the plot developments, character actions, typical events – form its syntax, its grammatical structure. When taken together, the semantic and syntactic elements allow us to model the structure of any particular generic text, compare it to other examples of the genre (i.e., other parts of the supertext) appearing either at the same time (a *synchronic* comparison) or at some other point in film history (a *diachronic* comparison), and measure it against any closely allied genres with which it might share semantic and/or syntactic elements. Simply put, the measurement of difference (e.g., from other contemporary films, from earlier or later examples of the genre, from different genres) allows us to begin assessing the various implications of a specific text and its particular way of expressively mobilizing the genre's elements. Furthermore, Altman suggests that, when viewed in the proper historical context, this model might even help us in understanding a genre's very formation: how it first came into being, as a set of semantic units gradually acquired a body of syntactic structures in response to certain cultural conditions. As a *systematic* approach, one that might help us deal with a genre in terms of both the problems it poses for critics and historians and the attitudes of typical moviegoers, this model has much to offer.

Still, for all of its usefulness, this fundamental structural model also has its limitations. Like all structural paradigms, it treats the text as if it were indeed a formal language, one that consistently abides by a formal grammar; and like most contemporary criticism, it avoids any sort of essentialist conclusion, proceeding not just as if every genre worked in much the same way, but also as if each potentially offered the same meanings – at least if several genres were to draw on the same semantic field, for it stops short of actually accounting for genre-specific themes. We might more accurately think of a genre, though, not as a language with a formal grammar, but rather as a kind of colloquial speech, the popular use of a language that very often casts grammar aside, gives to words whole new meanings – meanings prone to shift with time or completely fall out of use, as it fashions its own quite serviceable slang. In this sense, the science fiction film, as an example of a particular cinematic "slang," invariably has its own meanings, which attach to its most identifiable concerns. As Susan Sontag argues in her well-known essay "The Imagination of Disaster," the science fiction film is rooted in a fundamental triad of reason, science, and technology – that is, in a certain way of thinking, a body of knowledge that derives from that thinking, and an instrumentality produced by and reflective of that knowledge.[23] These elements produce a characteristic stamp of their own, a most telling inflection for this popular slang.

In fact, it seems almost self-evident that a great part of the science fiction film's special character derives from this focus on the concerns of reason/science/technology. It has proven such a popular form in recent years precisely because its peculiar argot not only provides us with a most appropriate language for talking about a large dimension of technologically inflected postmodern culture, but also because its fundamental themes help us make sense of our culture's quandaries. In addition, I would insist that there are fundamental themes consistently at work in this genre, although they may well surface less powerfully or centrally in other genres as well. Through its emphasis on technology, the science that has produced it, and the rational world view in which that science is imbedded, the genre repeatedly articulates certain themes that, to return to our previous framework, we might see as linked at various levels of specificity to Todorov's three categories of fantasy.

We might benefit here by turning to a specific cinematic illustration, the original *Invasion of the Body Snatchers,* a 1956 film whose resonance in the genre is attested by the 1978 and 1993 remakes which it has inspired, and by its derivation from a popular science fiction story by Jack Finney. In the original film the small town of Santa Mira finds itself in the grip of what the local psychiatrist terms a case of "mass delusion," the sense that no one is who he or she seems to be, as if all identities had simply become unhinged from the town's inhabitants. Seeking the advice of the town doctor, Miles Bennel, a character explains that her uncle is not really her uncle, but rather "an impostor or something," marked particularly by a coldness and lack of emotion that she cannot fully explain. When a day later she retracts her complaint, telling Miles she was just being "silly" in her suspicions, the real thrust of this image of the "impostor or something" becomes clear. It is largely about a fear of the other, about what is "out there," but also about what that otherness means for the self, the fundamental strike it makes at our own sense of security and identity. In this case that fear is eventually justified by the revelation that alien seed pods have begun "snatching" people's bodies while they sleep and replacing their real selves

Figure 8. *Invasion of the Body Snatchers* (1956): A pod begins growing "an impostor or something."

with something inhuman [Fig. 8]. Here, I would suggest, we are operating in a *marvelous* context, exploring Todorov's themes of the other, themes that, as Rosemary Jackson in her study of the fantastic offers, find both their power and attraction precisely in their ability "to disturb the familiar and the known."[24] That specific theme of the "impostor or something" echoes throughout the science fiction genre, appearing in various degrees across a register of films that envision the other, including *The Thing . . . , Invaders from Mars* (1953), *Independence Day,* and *Starship Troopers.*

A second fundamental theme, one sourced in the other end of the fantastic scale, also surfaces powerfully in *Invasion of the Body Snatchers.* Fleeing the pod people, Miles and his fiancée, Becky Driscoll, take refuge in a cave, where he leaves her while he goes in search of help. Upon returning, he kisses Becky passionately, only to recoil suddenly in horror, a point underscored by an extreme close-up reaction shot,

Figure 9. *Invasion of the Body Snatchers* (1956): Emotion as the last desperate proof of humanity.

as he realizes that she too has been replaced by a pod person. His voice-over then notes, "I never knew the real meaning of fear until . . . until I kissed Becky." On one level it seems an almost absurd statement, a near-comic commentary on desire and its frustrations, and one almost certain to draw laughs from some viewers. In this context, however, it signals an abiding concern of many of our science fiction films: their tendency to lodge a sense of our humanity in feelings, passion, desire – and not in the atmosphere of reason and science that would seem to dominate the world of science fiction [Fig. 9]. In the way the film emphasizes this theme, often exploiting it for a variety of frissons, *Invasion of the Body Snatchers* demonstrates one path by which we move between the science fiction and horror genres. Such rather superficially different films as *Invasion of the Body Snatchers, The Invisible Ray* (1936), *I Married a Monster from Outer Space* (1958), and *Gattaca* suggest that, through our feelings – through our ability to "kiss and tell," as I would term this motif – we can at least be sure about our selves, our humanity, even as we face a world that seems to deny that dimension any place or point. Here we are obviously in the realm of the *uncanny*, not as a distorted or distorting mind producing a narrative, but rather as an exploration of what, in an increasingly technological world, constitutes the self. This "kiss and tell" motif also surfaces powerfully, although to a lesser extent, in works such as *Blade Runner*, *RoboCop*, and the *Terminator* films.

Between these two themes, and depending heavily upon their mutual existence, is a third that we might see as linked to Todorov's remaining realm of the *fantastic*. Here too we can turn to *Invasion of the Body Snatchers* for our illustration, as well as a testimony to the themes' interrelationships; for between the point at which characters begin to announce their strange sense that those near them are not who or what they seem but an "impostor or something," and that at which Miles kisses Becky and recoils in the "kiss and tell" moment, the various characters in Santa Mira set about trying to square events with the world they know, to explain away these disturbing differences, although with little success. Thus Miles and his friend Jack share their anxieties with the town psychiatrist, Danny Kauffmann, who offers a series of possible explanations – "hallucinations," "an epidemic of mass hysteria" – while assuring them that, whatever the problem, "it's well within the bounds of human experience." Jack's response, an angry "stop trying to rationalize everything . . . we have a mystery on our hands" [Fig. 10], obviously echoes Todorov's notion of the fantastic proper as marked by a moment of hesitation or indecision, by a kind of fundamental indeterminacy, as its events slip away from such explanations as hallucination or intervention by forces outside the bounds of human experience, as this world seems suspended between the mysterious and the real. More important, however, is the way that protest against rationalization rubs against the very texture of the science fiction film with its subtle enthronement, as Sontag noted, of reason, science, and technology. It reminds us that, for all their trafficking in a world of reason and science, despite their usual dependence on the imagery of technology, our science fiction films seldom allow that regime to go unchallenged. In fact, they often betray a marked distrust of it and certainly of its attempts to plan out our lives. That "stop trying to rationalize" motif may well be the genre's central secret point, for it marks the moment when, as such seemingly different films as *Metropolis*, *Forbidden Planet* (1956), *2001: A Space Odyssey* (1968), and *Event*

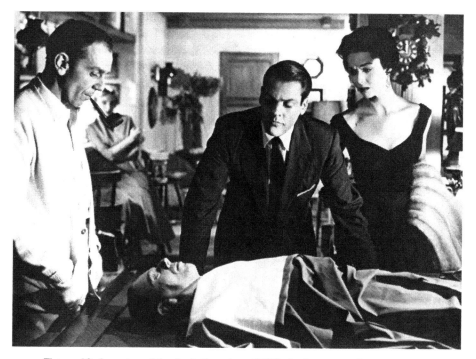

Figure 10. *Invasion of the Body Snatchers* (1956): Jack resists efforts to "rationalize" his other self.

Horizon suggest, the genre questions its very fundament, hesitates in and even subverts its own efforts at explaining and schematizing human experience.[25] It marks a point as well when films like *Invasion of the Body Snatchers* reveal their close ties to the horror genre, as they confront the potentially terrifying implications of that which might not be explained or even communicated, as we see especially when Miles Bennel runs along a highway, begging for help, screaming to the complacent drivers, "You're next!" but receiving no response, no aid.

These three themes, of course, are hardly the only ones to be found in the genre – the form is, as we have already noted, simply far too flexible to be fully accounted for in this way; nor are they, as our reliance on a single exemplary text such as *Invasion of the Body Snatchers* shows, really exclusive to one branch of the genre or another. However, these themes seem keys to its specific character, as well as focal points through which it filters, gives a particular science fiction coloring to, other and particularly the most pressing cultural issues. Films like *The Brother from Another Planet, Enemy Mine* (1985), and *Alien Nation* (1988), for example, frame their assault on racial prejudice and misunderstanding precisely through the "impostor or something" motif, through our interaction with aliens who are coded as a racial other. The various repressions of feminine emotion and identity in contemporary culture find telling embodiment in *Eve of Destruction*'s (1991) "kiss and tell" narrative of a scientist who imprints a destructive cyborg with both her conscious and unconscious personality – and that now displaced and liberated personality, a neat embodiment of a quite literally "constructed" femininity, produces a destructive display of passion and emotion. Moreover, the problems of class repression and class conflict, particularly loaded concerns for a period that had seen the recent advent of the Russian Revolution, take shape in *The Mysterious Island*'s (1929) "stop trying to rationalize" tale of a mysterious but benevolent scientist-ruler who repeatedly notes that "on this island, all men are equal." Through these key themes, then, we are better able to see the science fiction genre in its variations doing the basic work of fantasy, as it traces out what Rosemary Jackson terms "the unsaid and the unseen of culture."[26]

A Tradition of Trickery

What remains omitted from this equation so far is a most significant component of the science fiction genre, and one that usually becomes central to the ways it goes about making visible or tracing out these cultural concerns: More so than any other film genre, science fiction relies heavily on what we might most broadly term *special effects,* and this reliance requires that we consider how the form's paradigmatic/ syntagmatic elements are linked to its very creation, that is, how the genre's concern with the technological engages us in a complex system of reflections on its own technological underpinnings, and thus on its own level of reality. This point is made explicit in one of the most thought-provoking pieces on the science fiction film, Garrett Stewart's essay "The 'Videology' of Science Fiction," wherein he describes the obviously "close collusion between cinematic illusionism and futuristic fantasy":

[M]ovies about the future tend to be about the future of the movies. Science/fiction/film: this is no more the triadic phrase for a movie genre than three subjects looking on at their own various conjunctions. Science fiction in the cinema often turns out to be, turns round to be, the fictional or fictive science of the cinema itself, the future feats it may achieve scanned in line with the technical feat that conceives them right now and before our eyes.[27]

Simply put, these films, more than any others, reflect the technology that makes them possible. As a result, our ability to reproduce things through computer animation becomes just as central to and even implicated in the narrative of a film like *Jurassic Park* as is its focal plot device of reproduction by genetic cloning.

A further implication of Stewart's description is that, thanks to this mirror relationship between its technological base and its technological subjects, the science fiction cinema invariably betrays a thoroughly reflexive character. When we watch a science fiction film, we see as well a narrative about the movies themselves – about how our technology can impact on our humanity, how our technology (and, indeed, our very rationality) impinges on our world, how our technology might point beyond our normal sense of reality. More specifically, the genre to a degree almost inevitably seems to be *about* the movies precisely because of the ways in which its reliance on special effects implicates both the technology of film and the typical concern of most popular narratives with achieving a transparent realism. As Albert La Valley puts it, the long tradition of "trickery" in the science fiction film calls attention to "the nature of illusion and deception in film itself and in the act of moviegoing."[28] For example, the early efforts of Georges Méliès, in films like *A Trip to the Moon* (1902) and *The Impossible Voyage* (1904), rely essentially on the potentials of editing for creating a new and quite fantastic reality, one in which we are supposed to take pleasure. By starting, stopping, and then restarting the camera after altering the subject in some way, Méliès not only created amazing appearances, disappearances, and transformations, but he also foregrounded the importance of the continuity principle and of the illusionist nature of this new medium, reminding us in the process of the cinema's capacity to function as a kind of dream machine. In fact, we might say that it is precisely the tension between such seemingly magical effects and the desire to make those elements neatly "fit" into a reality illusion that is the core of his films' appeal – and, indeed, that of the entire science fiction genre.

That same tension plays throughout the long history of special-effects development in the genre following Méliès's pioneering work [Figs. 11–13]; and indeed, that interaction between fantastic trickery

Figure 11. A tradition of "trickery" in the science fiction film: A model rocket ship from the *Flash Gordon* serial (1936).

and the medium's illusionistic practices could well provide its own scheme for delineating the genre into different categories – categories based on the degree of illusion achieved or desired. La Valley stakes out the terms for this sort of approach when he describes how our films always "aim to demonstrate the current state of the art" and, as a result, always seem to "demand greater and greater budgets to over-power their predecessors." The result is what he terms "a kind of Oed-ipal cold war," as "*Things to Come* answers *Metropolis, Star Wars* takes on *2001*"[29] – or even, we might continue, as the "enhanced" reissues of the original *Star Wars* trilogy with their computer-added images and digitally "cleaned-up" sound tracks supersede the earlier versions of those films. Similarly, we might think of *Metropolis*'s development of the optical tricks of the Schufftan process (which employed a mirror arrangement to combine live action convincingly with miniatures or painted backdrops) and the later innovation of the optical printer (which allowed for the creation of such effects directly in the camera) as forming a bridge between Méliès's fantastic mattes and disappear-ances in clouds of smoke and the recent development of computer-assisted cameras and computer-generated imagery (CGI) [Fig. 14]. Still,

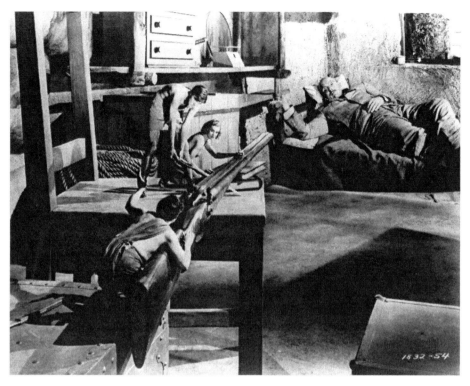

Figure 12. A tradition of "trickery": Rear projection and outsized sets in *Dr. Cyclops* (1940).

Figure 13. A tradition of "trickery": Peter Ellenshaw's special effects put a meteor inside a space ship in *The Black Hole* (1979).

regardless of the historical perspective, the key point remains that the very technological underpinnings of this form contribute fundamentally to its identity, overlapping with its semantics and syntactics to produce another level of generic identity and, in the process, further helping to generate a kind of essential identity: a specific thematics concerning representation and mechanical reproduction that we might see as a kind of birthmark of the genre.

In fact, the digital image generation made possible by the film industry's wedding of the computer with traditional cinematography promises, on one level, to render all film potentially as science fiction or fantasy: With this fast-evolving technology, we have now entered a realm of reproduction where we can fully play the game of "what if," technologically visualizing anything we might imagine. As such works as *Zelig* (1983) and *Forrest Gump* (1994) demonstrate, we can produce a "photographic" record of things that ultimately exist only in the heart of a computer, or we might digitally resurrect figures from our cinematic mythology, that is, figures who now exist only in our cultural dreams. Moreover, that capacity for a computer-generated photorealism, probably combined in the not-too-distant future with virtual-reality technology, could well eventuate in the ultimate science fiction machine: a "cinema" – and here we must begin to use the word quite loosely – in which we can easily move into another time and place, a realm substantially like the very stories we typically tell in the genre. In fact, our films are already anticipating this move with the wave of films *about* virtual-reality experiences that have appeared in the 1990s, works like *The Lawnmower Man* (1992), *Virtuosity* (1995), *Strange Days* (1995), *Dark City*, and *The Matrix* (1999). However, a new sort of cinema might well fulfill the promise these films envision, offering us a world that has not previously and indeed might never exist, one that might operate according to all new "laws of nature," and one capable of providing us with the core experience of all fantasy, as Todorov describes it: the "collapse of the limits between matter and mind."[30] Here, simply enough, lies the great promise and potential of science fiction cinema, its transformation into pure fantasy and its ability to transport us convincingly into that same realm.

Nevertheless, this course also holds a kind of danger, both for our movies and for our own sense of self. As La Valley sees it, as that technological capacity and impetus increase, our science fiction films might eventually come to fixate on the technology to such an extent that "narrative and characters become recessive under the obsession with

Figure 14. The new "trickery": *Jurassic Park* (1992) combines live action with digitally generated dinosaurs.

technological wizardry." Under such a fixation, our films could become ever more removed from "the issues of our present world" – a charge that critics have, throughout the genre's history, frequently lodged against the science fiction film.[31] However, as Robert Romanyshyn has noted in his study of the impact of technology on Western culture, that sort of danger has, to some degree, always been built into our various technological accomplishments, not simply because of the ways they can distract us from our world or fascinate us with all that we might craft – both of which are indeed dangers to which we have culturally succumbed outside of the cinema – but rather because of the way that the technological positions us vis-à-vis the world and others. He argues that through its vantage – what we might well think of as its implicitly *cinematic* nature – technology situates the individual as "a spectator self behind the window"[32] of its instrumentality, distant and detached from the world, a passive viewer of its unfolding story. Jean Baudrillard has observed this same effect, suitably drawing on imagery from the world of science fiction (and inevitably of science fact), to suggest how, within our postmodern technological environment, "each individual sees himself promoted to the controls of a hypothetical machine, isolated in a position of perfect sovereignty, at an infinite distance from his original universe . . . in the same position as the astronaut in his bubble"[33] – or, we might add, the position of the spectator in front of his high-definition television screen. It is an image with which our science fiction films have, in recent years, made us all too familiar, as they continue to offer narratives in which the protagonists, our stand-ins, wind up *Marooned* (1969), *Lost in Space* (1998), adrift in suspended animation like the character Ripley in several of the *Alien* films; and yet it is also an image they have offered up as a subtle warning.

The science fiction film, as a genre constantly in the process of redefining itself, has to negotiate between these two potentials: its capacity for limitless vision and experience, on the one hand, and the possibility for helping to foster such distance and alienation, on the other. That it has become so very popular in the last few decades, after something of a falling off in the 1960s and 1970s, argues powerfully for its ability not only to harness the technological power that drives it, but also to address the technological attitude that haunts it – in effect, to use the former as a way of dealing with the latter. In this regard, we might note what seems an increased emphasis on mediation and the technology of reproduction – in effect, an imagery of film itself – in our recent science fiction movies. Certainly, the dominant image of the science fiction film throughout the 1980s and much of the 1990s has been that of the replicated human, the image of ourselves caught up in a world of technological reproduction, one whose very limitless capacity for mimesis promises to deliver all things to us, while also threatening to deliver *us* to a kind of thing-ness, to reduce us to near irrelevance – indistinguishable from our many copies or clones. Films like *Event Horizon*, *Dark City*, and *Sphere* (1998) extend that concern beyond the human, exploring the possibilities of reproducing and constantly manipulating our entire environment, in effect, writing us into ever new scenarios; yet here too the genre might be seen as fulfilling, in its own way, the driving force of all fantasy, a term that, Rosemary Jackson reminds, literally means "that which is made visible."[34] From this vantage, the science fiction film seems a form that continues to explore the potential for rendering our world in all its promise and frustration ever more available for our inspection and instruction.

Genre Thinking

Perhaps this introduction seems to offer its own paradox: a discussion of the science fiction genre that argues simultaneously for the difficulty of establishing hard and fast generic boundaries *and* the necessity for recognizing certain constitutive elements – not only the sort of semantic and syntactic elements that Altman describes, but also specific themes that are imbedded in that structure and the genre's technological underpinnings, and that give rise to its science fiction character. Usually, our discussions of film genres proceed from one or the other of these perspectives. Introductions to formula narratives typically emphasize a broadly characteristic iconography before turning to discussions of how those various icons shift in meaning or value from one era to another. More specialized treatments of particular genres have often moved in the other direction, isolating the structures and images that produce meaning, as Will Wright did in his structural study of the western film,[35] or focusing on a specific thematics, as Sontag did when she saw in the history of science fiction cinema a unique fascination with cultural disaster, and one particularly revealing about the American scene. By overlaying these vantages, I hope to suggest a way of thinking about film genres, and especially the science fiction film, that embraces the sort of dynamic tension by which they ultimately work.

To help us to gain this vantage, we shall take the notion of fantasy – particularly as it has been explored by Todorov and amplified, in order to account for its cultural content, by Rosemary Jackson – as a guiding framework. Fantasy is, as we have noted, a form that demonstrates the difficulties of generic demarcation, one whose boundaries can at best be thought of as a series of what Todorov terms "relay points" with other formulas. It is also a form that can easily be seen as encompassing a variety of film types that, as our criticism has repeatedly attested, frequently seem to overlap or share characteristics – specifically, science fiction, horror, and even the musical. Nevertheless, fantasy does seem to function according to a particular structure, its fundamental sense of "hesitation" that is articulated in its marvelous, fantastic, and uncanny variations, each of which offers some intriguing correspondences to the major recurring types of science fiction narrative. Those fantasy correspondences, in turn, can also help us better understand how science fiction articulates its central themes.

Of course, as we have noted, the science fiction film is finally more than an element in some supertext, more too than a series of semantic and syntactic devices, calculated to produce a certain meaning. It is, for all of its often rather cold and technological context, a very seductive form, one that we might well see as the deep unconscious of popular cinema. Its ability to reproduce what might be, to synthesize a new reality, is a powerful lure, one closely allied to the attraction bound up in the very technology that makes it possible. At the same time, its ability to lay bare those attractions, to hold up that reason–science–technology triad for our inspection, to trace "the unsaid and the un-seen of culture," particularly of a technological culture like modern America, represents a potent and, given the power of all technological culture, even a needed payoff. The following chapters, then, sketch out some of both the genre's seductions and its subversions, to make the workings of this powerful popular genre a bit more visible and thus open to discussion and understanding.

2

Science Fiction Film

The Critical Context

lthough science fiction literature, even in its early years, was often taken fairly seriously and rapidly built up a volume of significant critical material, the science fiction film has taken much longer to find a similar degree of critical acceptance and to develop its own body of commentary. Writing in 1972, for example, William Johnson felt it necessary to introduce his critical anthology *Focus on the Science Fiction Film* by acknowledging that the sort of attention he and his fellow contributors were according to the genre "is still not fully respectable," in large part because too many of the films, with their frequent emphasis on bug-eyed monsters (or BEMs) and spectacular, science-induced calamities, seemed to occupy what he termed a "more dubious position" in the world of cinema.[1] That position has changed radically since his book, with the science fiction genre producing a number of the highest-grossing films of all time – among them, *Star Wars* (1977), *E.T. the Extra-Terrestrial* (1982), and *Star Wars: Episode I – The Phantom Menace* (1999) – as well as a variety of critically acclaimed works, including *Blade Runner* (1982), *RoboCop* (1987), and *Terminator 2: Judgment Day* (1991). As a result, science fiction film criticism has moved far afield from its early fanzine-type commentary, such as was found in a magazine like *Famous Monsters of Filmland,* and large-format picture-book histories, to include articles in the leading literary and film-related journals, as well as university-press-sponsored studies of individual films, filmmakers, and specific themes of science fiction cinema.

While the present chapter does not pretend to offer a full survey of the history of this developing science fiction film criticism, it does summarize the main currents of thought on the genre and offer detailed commentaries on some studies. To facilitate that summary, I have organized the commentary around a variety of critical practices that have generally dominated discussion of the genre. Particularly, this overview emphasizes humanist, ideological, feminist, psychoanalytic, and postmodern critical vantages as the key – although by no means the only – approaches to the genre. It briefly summarizes these approaches, and then illustrates them through specific consideration of a number of books and articles that have fundamentally influenced discussion of the genre or that well represent the main trends that discussion has followed. My aim is neither to offer a history of science fiction film criticism nor to advocate any one critical vantage as particularly appropriate to discussing this form, but to suggest how the genre has been profitably opened up through a great variety of investigative approaches – so much so in recent years that the science fiction film increasingly seems to be an intriguing point of convergence, a kind of testing ground for much of our contemporary cultural and film theory.

At the outset, though, we should understand that all of the critical approaches surveyed in this chapter essentially constitute tactics for asking questions about cinematic texts, and more specifically about our science fiction films. Increasingly, those films seem to mark off specific areas for certain questions that are particularly important to contemporary technoculture: through robotic images, questions about the nature of the self; through apocalyptic scenarios, about the fragility of human existence; through virtual-reality systems, about the construction of culture; through genetic explorations, about the nature of gender. Certainly, each of the critical methods discussed here approaches film with an agenda and typically seeks answers along a very specific and limited trajectory. The goal in each instance is to open the text up as a point of knowledge, as a path to better understanding what we might conceive of as three broad fields of inquiry: first, the text itself and, by implication, all similar texts; second, the producers and receivers of the text, that is, those involved in creating this industrial artifact, as well as the audience that is asked to see or consume it in a certain manner; and third, the world that has in a variety of nearly invisible ways generated this text, that is, the culture that invariably inflects all of its constructs and leaves the imprint of those class, gender, ethnic, political, and other tensions that inform the many elements of that culture. Just as these fields of inquiry often overlap, so do the questions we ask often imply, even demand, others. Thus, understanding a film like *E.T.*'s depiction of the alien, for instance, might push us to consider, among other things, director Steven Spielberg's efforts to work within the Hollywood studio system and its tradition of classical narrative, as well as to understand the American middle-class life-style as it was idealized or nostalgically conceived in the Reagan era. In any case, the key point we might underscore is the very partialness of all these questions, and thus how the various critical approaches surveyed here all provide what we might best think of as a complementary knowledge about the American science fiction film.

Science Fiction and Humanism

What we might broadly describe as a humanist tradition has long dominated discussion of science fiction cinema, much as it has other popular American genres. While the humanist approach generally applies no one specific methodology to its study of film, it does in all of its variety usually involve an underlying strategy or direction for its questions. As Tim Bywater and Thomas Sobchack explain, humanist criticism "seeks to understand human nature and humankind's place in the scheme of things, asking the traditional questions – who we are and what is life all about," and it typically does so by looking "for representations in film of general human values, the truths of human experience as they relate to the common and universal aspects of existence."[2] In most cases, this humanist criticism has followed historical and thematic paths, and among its most significant contributors we might note John Baxter, who authored an early history of the genre; William Johnson, who compiled a key collection of responses to the science fiction film in the 1970s; and especially Susan Sontag, author of what remains one of the most influential and oft-cited articles on science fiction, "The Imagination of Disaster." Together, these figures suggest a range of responses that have continued to inform much of our thinking about the genre, even as more sophisticated critical approaches have come to dominate contemporary science fiction film commentary.

As has often been the case in critical discussion of literature, the humanist approach to film most frequently proceeds along historical lines, as it tries to place the works of a genre within a broad context that allows us to appreciate and understand better its ongoing changes and developments – developments that, the criticism implies, mirror our own ongoing efforts at understanding human nature and reflecting on our social values. Among a number of important historical treatments of the genre, we might especially note Baxter's *Science Fiction in the Cinema* (1970), which has proven an essential source for most critics of the genre. More recent historical accounts of the genre include Vivian Sobchack's *Screening Space: The American Science Fiction Film* and my own *Replications: A Robotic History of the Science Fiction*

Film. Since the former, in its revisions for a later edition, has effectively reframed its reading of the American science fiction film within an ideological context, we shall consider it under that category. The latter work examines the form primarily from a postmodern vantage, using the image of the robot as a trope for the genre's abiding concern with artifice, with the various ways in which our science and technology have allowed us to shape and reshape reality itself, in the process calling into question our convention-bound sense of the real, as well as film's own manipulations of that reality. Though these works overlap in a number of instances, as we might expect of any group of historical treatments, they also nicely complement one another and, when taken together, offer students a sound historical grounding for subsequent exploration of the genre.

Although eclectic in his selection of film texts, Baxter has provided one of the most useful surveys of the genre, as he ranges in great detail from the earliest days of the cinema to 1970. He focuses on various national developments of the science fiction impulse in tracing out what he sees as the form's primary focus on "movements and ideas," and particularly two themes that he finds interwoven throughout the genre's history: "the loss of individuality and the threat of knowledge."[3] Yet while he pointedly sets about "tracing . . . antecedents" and noting influences, describing a line of thematic and stylistic development in both literary and cinematic science fiction, and even as he ranges over a variety of national cinemas, Baxter acknowledges that the form seems to resemble "a diffuse and ill-defined plain, a landscape with figures which changes as one moves, assumes new shapes depending on viewpoint and perspective."[4] It is a conclusion that effectively suggests not only the sort of generic difficulty that, as we noted in the opening chapter, particularly marks most commentaries on the science fiction film, but also the very limits of this sort of diffuse historical view, divorced as it often is from a specific methodology for approaching the genre.

While retaining an element of that historical focus, both Denis Gifford's *Science Fiction Film* and Johnson's *Focus on the Science Fiction Film* take a more synchronic approach, as they emphasize as well the great variety of themes that surface in the genre. Despite a clear nod in the direction of historical context (as Gifford notes, his book was written "as the Space Age opens and yesterday's science-fiction film becomes today's documentary"),[5] *Science Fiction Film* generally ignores cultural parallels and collapses its sketchy historical vantage

Figure 15. Early critical attention focuses on "classic" works, such as the H. G. Wells–scripted *Things to Come* (1936).

into a brief account of the various sorts of "inventions," "explorations," and "predictions" that have surfaced in all periods of science fiction film. Offering a far more balanced and valuable overview of the genre than Gifford's work, Johnson's *Focus on the Science Fiction Film* provides a slight historical framework for its grouping of articles on a variety of filmmakers that have traditionally been associated with the genre (Georges Méliès, Fritz Lang, Don Siegel, Stanley Kubrick); on a few "classics" of the form, such as *Things to Come* (1936) [Fig. 15], *Destination Moon* (1950), and *The Time Machine* (1960); and on wide-ranging assessments of the science fiction film by an international array of critics, including Ado Kyrou, Guy Gauthier, and Harry M. Geduld. Johnson's inclusion of a few primary materials, such as script extracts, comments by writers and cinematographers, and contemporaneous reviews, as well as his provision of a detailed filmography and bibliography, offers us some glimpse of the broader context in which, ideally,

Figure 16. A modern "classic" dominates humanist conceptions of the genre: The Stanley Kubrick–Arthur C. Clarke film *2001: A Space Odyssey* (1968).

we might situate the genre and establishes a standard that no subsequent collection has yet matched. Though now dated, this volume continues to be a very useful resource and one that well sketches the humanist vantage on the science fiction film, perhaps best summed up in Geduld's contribution. There he argues that the science fiction movie "at its best has, traditionally, been humanist. Humanist, that is, insofar as it has usually assumed the primacy of man and his values, and insofar as it has expressed confidence and conviction concerning man's ability and need to survive any confrontation with the forces of a hostile or inscrutable universe, or the threats posed by technological and scientific advancement"[6] [Fig. 16].

Susan Sontag

Following this imperative while also pointing in the direction of a more ideologically conscious criticism is probably the single best essay in this vein, and indeed one of the most important contributions to the study of science fiction film: Susan Sontag's "The Imagination of Disaster." Responding to an emphasis in modern criticism on the process of "interpretation" – that is, on making art "manageable, conformable" by focusing solely on the meaning of its content – Sontag championed an approach that would pay more attention to artistic form and recover its "effects," such as those found in the "pure, untranslatable, sensuous immediacy" of film's imagery.[7] In the popular genre film, especially the

Figure 17. Sontag's "Imagination of Disaster" takes shape in the giant mutant ants of *Them!* (1954).

cinema of science fiction, Sontag felt she had found a sort of art that had managed "to elude the interpreters" by its ability to "be . . . just what it is."[8] This, she suggested, was because most critics simply had little interest in or patience with the seemingly "primitive gratifications" the genre offered.[9]

Observing the spate of apocalyptic stories that dominated screens throughout the 1950s and 1960s, with their narratives of alien invasions and technology run amok [Fig. 17], she sought to understand the sort of pleasures they offered, and in the process situated the genre in a significant cultural context. "The Imagination of Disaster," in fact, argues that the science fiction film is fundamentally "about disaster, which is one of the oldest subjects of art," and that this fascination helps explain much of the "satisfaction" audiences derive from the form, particularly the dual lures of "sensuous elaboration" and "extreme moral simplification."[10] While Sontag links the genre's popularity to the attitudes and anxieties of American culture in the early cold-war era, she also draws from it a larger conclusion about how such genre films function culturally; for she finds the genre's articulation of cultural anxieties strangely removed from any sort of "social criticism, of even the most implicit kind."[11] While our films both "reflect worldwide anxieties and . . . serve to allay them," they also, she suggests, "inculcate a strange apathy" about such troubling issues as radiation, contamination, and universal destruction that seems almost "in complicity with the abhorrent,"[12] that is, with the tremendously destructive potentials of modern culture. By focusing in a rather traditional humanist manner on this one particular motif in the science fiction film, its repeated imagery of disaster, Sontag arrives at a larger caution about the workings of the genre, a symptom of what she evocatively terms its "*inadequate response*" to contemporary concerns, as she also points the way to a more pointedly ideological consideration of the form, to what she sees as the proper aim of all commentary on art: "to make works of art – and by analogy, our own experience – more, rather than less, real to us."[13]

Ideological Criticism

Following Sontag's lead, as well as the broad political turn of much film criticism beginning in the early 1970s, science fiction commentary has recently been dominated by a variety of more direct and systematic ideological reassessments. Such examinations typically focus on what Terry Eagleton has described as "the largely concealed structure of values which informs and underlies our factual statements," particularly as those statements connect "with the power-structure and power-relations of the society we live in" and often seem designed to reinforce that status quo.[14] Drawing primarily on the paradigmatic work of Louis Althusser and Fredric Jameson, figures such as Vivian Sobchack, Michael Stern, Michael Ryan and Douglas Kellner, and Judith Hess Wright have in various ways sought to lay bare the extent to which this genre provides audiences with images that inure them to the contradictions and everyday repressions of their culture, particularly those images that directly evoke contemporary technoculture. While retaining a heavily formalist approach in trying to account for the sorts of image that are specific to the genre, Sobchack in her history of the American science fiction film anchors that discussion in a thoroughly ideological context; as she explains, the basic assumption behind her history is that "the SF film is always historicized, grounded in its (and our) own earthly American culture – in the economic, technological, political, social, and linguistic present of its production, in the ideological structures that shape its visual and visible conceptions of time, space, affect, and social relations."[15]

Sobchack and others have thus usually sought to map that ground by analyzing how the key icons of science and technology, along with the attitudes toward those icons that the films demonstrate, suggest both the play of power within culture and the constructed rather than natural conditions of life in modern, technological cultures. In so doing, they hope to reveal the political dimensions of a subject that has, through the powers of generic convention and formula that Sontag described, come to seem almost magically outside that domain – as wholly natural rather than culturally constructed.

In examining the genre's reliance on or even "enthusiasm" for special effects, Michael Stern starkly models this approach. He sees science fiction's emphasis on special effects as a model of the way that "advanced capitalist societies" create "a world of appearances," a world that "forestalls thinking . . . in ways that are outside authorized categories of reflection" about our culture.[16] A more detailed and particularly effective example of this methodology shows up in Ryan and Kellner's discussion of the "conservative fear of technology" that surfaced powerfully in science fiction films of the 1970s and 1980s [Fig. 18]. In these works, they suggest, technology becomes a distinctly troubling issue because it metaphorically recalls the "constructed institution" that is society itself.[17] Seen from this vantage, the genre's technological imagery comes to stand metonymically for the technologies of cultural coercion – the various mechanisms of manipulation, observation, and reinforcement to which we are all subject – as it foregrounds the shaping powers of the social world we inhabit. They argue, further, that the critical attitude toward the technological reflected in those narratives points not only to a deep-seated distrust of technology and the sort of culture it has helped construct, but also to "a possibility of reconstruction that would put the stability of conservative social institutions in question,"[18] that might, for example, subvert capitalist and patriarchal traditions in American culture. Thus they see a film like *Logan's Run* (1976) [Fig. 19], a dystopian story of rebellion against a futuristic, technologically sustained city-state, as superficially indicting the military–industrial complex of modern America. When the protagonist Logan heralds his escape from the city into a surrounding, untamed nature with the remark, "We're free," his comment seems to sug-

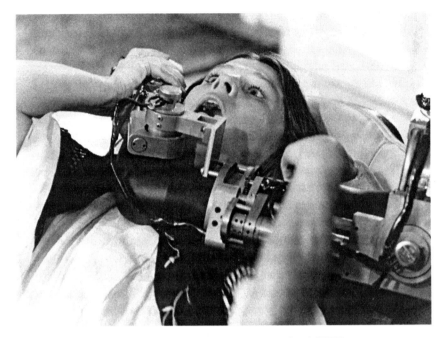

Figure 18. Technophobia given reason in *Demon Seed* (1977), as computer-controlled mechanisms attack humans.

gest "the rejection of everything technology represents."[19] Yet, since that rejection is linked to a turning against the futuristic world of social equality and collective action, they view Logan's triumphal escape as a fundamentally conservative turn, affirming rather than subverting the individualistic status quo that undergirds American culture, while linking technology to all that might threaten that status quo. This sort of application essentially reads *through* the usual ideological construction of cultural texts, deconstructing its order to reveal the dissatisfactions and unresolved tensions that the genre narrative, for all of its comforting resolutions, never quite manages to erase or convert into an affirmative dynamic. Rather, it suggests that in the tensions expressed therein we are observing a deep-rooted subversive power at work within our science fiction films.

Other, less nuanced uses of the ideological method, in privileging how our film genres help to construct cultural attitudes, read totally *against* the grain of genre, against a specific formula's function in mirroring and addressing our most pressing cultural concerns. Instead, they would see it simply as a potent manipulative device – much like

Figure 19. The social vision of the science fiction film, here embodied in the technologically sustained city-state of *Logan's Run* (1976).

the powerful technology on which science fiction itself typically focuses. From this view the genre's narrative power, as well as its critical interest, derives not from the expressive capacity on which Sontag focused but solely from the powerful hegemonic force it represents, from its capacity – and seemingly inevitable mission – to reinforce the status quo. Judith Hess Wright typifies this approach, as she argues that genre films in general aim only to "produce satisfaction rather than action," and that science fiction films in particular "build on fears of the intrusive and the overpowering and thereby promote isolationism. They also imply that science is good only inasmuch as it serves to support the existing class structure."[20] In her discussion of such films as *The Thing from Another World* (1951) [Fig. 20], *Invasion of the Body Snatchers* (1956), and *Earth vs. the Flying Saucers* (1956) she thus sees only a simplification of cold-war tensions. Hence the aliens in these respective narratives stand in for communist hordes, and the scientists with their technology become our only hope at staving off invasion and maintaining our way of life. However, while this sort of approach has helped us rethink the privileged status that the genre so often seems

Figure 20. The military tries to keep *The Thing from Another World* (1951) behind a locked door, as science fiction simplifies cold-war tensions.

to accord science and technology, the various ways these elements both endorse and empower existing social structures, and the strong kinship between the film industry and the stories it tells, it also tends to omit much from the equation, and ultimately to avoid the complexity of many science fiction narratives. Particularly, Wright's reading of such works as *The Thing . . .* and *Invasion of the Body Snatchers* essentially overlooks the former's complex sexual dynamics and advocacy of collective action, and the latter's examination of a culturally determined identity, in favor of a superficial political generalization. At the same time, it leaves unanswered the question of whether any cultural work can escape the shaping and conforming forces that have brought it into being, and thus whether any cultural text has the power to challenge existing social and political structures.

Psychoanalytic Criticism

Closely related to this ideological project in method if not in purpose is the psychoanalytic body of science fiction criticism. Relying for the most part on the work of Freud and Jacques Lacan, it typically tries to draw in and on the human dimension that the ideological approach too often dismisses from consideration, as it assumes that, as Tim Bywater and Thomas Sobchack offer, "a large part of the mechanisms of life lie hidden from direct observation, that there is an unconscious element behind every conscious action."[21] Critics such as Margaret Tarratt, Constance Penley, and Vivian Sobchack have thus sought to locate in the alluring imagery of the science fiction film far more than just the reflections of our cultural fears or anxieties, weakly allayed; rather, they find in those figures a gallery of personal and social repressions that speak to the power of the cultural machine that is the movie industry. For a representation of a rather traditional Freudian vantage that has produced a number of significant readings of science fiction films, we might consider Tarratt's oft-cited commentary on such key texts as *The Thing . . .*, *It Came from Outer Space* (1953), and *Forbidden Planet* (1956) [Fig. 21]. In the recurrent "battles with sinister monsters or extraterrestrial forces" chronicled in these and many other entries in the genre, she recognizes "an externalization of the civilized person's conflict with his or her primitive subconscious or id."[22] Specifically, she argues that these films' key iconography – the genre's rockets and spaceships, alien others, and dangerous or out-of-control technology – is emblematic of an unbridled, aggressive, and typically male sexuality, one whose "taming . . . civilized society demands."[23] While acknowledging a broadly social dimension to the genre, then, Tarratt suggests that our science fiction films only "arrive at social comment" by working through this more fundamental "dramatization of the individual's anxiety about his or her own repressed sexual desires, which are incompatible with the morals of civilized life."[24] Of course, that interpretation would seem to offer little explanatory power for the genre as a whole, since the same argument might easily be made about the horror film, the western, or the gangster film, particularly with their repeated displays of phallic weaponry, often unleashed on passive victims. Nevertheless, what this vantage has provided is a paradigm that has begun to bring into simultaneous focus both the individual and social dimensions of the genre, as well as one that might help viewers to address the extent to which the genre *reflects,* rather than *constructs,* our personal concerns.

More recent psychological assessments have advanced this simple model by taking their primary lead from the work of Lacan, a reinterpreter of Freud who has suggested that the unconscious is structured like a language and, as a consequence, that it operates upon the individual subject in much the way a language does,[25] structuring the self in accord with the dominant culture's signifying practices. In the case of film criticism, this psychological method asks, as Bywater and Sobchack offer, that we see the motion picture itself as just such "an imaginary construct that caters to the desires and needs implanted in the individual by the original psychic structuring of the self by language/culture."[26] Particularly influential work in this vein has come from such critics as Constance Penley and Vivian Sobchack. In her discussion of time travel in science fiction, Penley draws out the similarities between this narrative type and what psychologists term "primal scene fantasy," finding in that likeness a key to the appeal of this subgenre. The desire fundamentally suggested by the time travel story, she suggests, is that "of both witnessing one's own conception and being one's own mother and father,"[27] that is, of revisiting and potentially influencing the conception and construction of self, as we see acted out most overtly in *Back to the Future* (1985) and its sequels. While Penley derives this reading from her sense that recent science fiction films have offered "some of the most effective instances of eroticism" in the movies,[28] Sobchack, surveying the genre's broader outlines and drawing on her earlier ideological study of its history, focuses on the rather remarkable absence of sexual concerns from most of our science fiction films. From this vantage she sets out to show "how human sexuality and women return to the science fiction narrative in displaced and condensed forms, in an emotionally charged imagery and syntax that bears relation to the cryptic but coherent language of dream."[29] By their overt linking of "biology and sexuality to women and technology to men," she argues, our science fiction "dreams" repeatedly play out scenarios of "infantile experience while pretending to adult concerns."[30] What this sort of reading offers is an intriguing suggestion not only of what lies repressed within the science fiction narrative, but also of how those repressions might even be construed as making the genre possible by helping to generate one of its key dynamics.

Less popular today, though still offering a potentially powerful tool for exploring that psychic empowerment of genre, is the archetypal approach grounded in Jungian psychology [Fig. 22]. Drawing on the notion that the psyche is an extension of a collective unconscious, and thus that certain images and actions (which we might think of in terms

Figure 21. Poster for *Forbidden Planet* (1956) depicts technology – the robot – as a projection of the primitive and threatening subconscious.

Figure 22. Science fiction imagery opens onto archetypal readings, here with the robot of *The Invisible Boy* (1957) as savior and protector.

of the semantic and syntactic dimensions of genre narrative) reflect a variety of universal values and meanings, the Jungian analytic treats film as a primary myth and thus a key reflection of cultural identity. The most important study of the genre from this vantage is Patrick Lucanio's *Them or Us: Archetypal Interpretations of Fifties Alien Invasion Films.* In this work Lucanio argues for a deeper understanding of one of the most obvious cultural phenomena of the science fiction genre – that is, the enormous body of alien-invasion films that appeared in the early cold-war era and seemed quite simply to express Americans' widespread fears of attack, invasion, and destruction by communist hordes. Instead of seeing these works in the context of "Freudian dogma concerning the depiction of our repressed fears" or from a simple ideological vantage, one affirming the correctness of our fears of the "other," he views them as "symbols of transformation, directing us toward an individuated life," through their patterns of "iconographic images" which bear a "dynamic relationship to primordial images in the collective (also called transpersonal) unconscious."[31] Reading through these archetypal images, then, Lucanio uncovers a broad cultural and indeed human message embodied in such alien-invasion films as *The Thing . . . , Invaders from Mars* (1953), *War of the Worlds* (1953), and *Earth vs. The Flying Saucers* – "a massive symbol of life's own destiny,"[32] that is, of our precarious place in the universe, as well as of our potential for overcoming the perils it holds in store.

Lucanio's reading of William Cameron Menzies's *Invaders from Mars* well illustrates his approach. In its story of Martian invaders come to enslave humanity, he finds a tale of the Jungian individuation process, that is, an initiation into the demands of the human environment, combined with the gaining of a deep self-knowledge. Awakened by a thunderstorm, twelve-year-old David McLean sleepily observes a UFO landing in a sand pit just beyond his home and tries to convince his parents of what he has seen. Told that he has simply been dreaming, David is left to wonder if he can trust his eyes – or any of his senses, for after his father investigates the area and returns home, he seems a changed person, a pattern that repeats itself as all who go out to the sand pit return markedly different. To counter his own self-doubts, as well as what we recognize as a gradual takeover of the area's inhabitants, David enlists the help of a local scientist, Professor Kelston (described by Lucanio as a figure of the self); a doctor, Pat Blake (the feminine anima figure); and an army officer, Colonel Fielding (the wise old man archetype). As these three help David reveal and eventually overcome the Martians, Lucanio suggests, we see how the self "draws to itself all the other archetypes and binds them into a harmonious whole."[33] In effect, the film thus dramatizes the difficult process of individuation wherein we learn to live in a complex world by drawing together, in the process of maturation, the various elements of the self. This sort of reading, in part because it represents a challenge to the Freudian/ Lacanian methodology that has dominated recent psychological criticism and in part because it only indirectly addresses the social and economic context of our film narratives, has of late found little support in the critical establishment, Nonetheless, this approach remains attractive for the way it manages to explain the compelling and apparently mythic power of film, as well as the cross-cultural and seemingly near-universal appeal of the American science fiction film.

Feminism

Often overlapping with both the ideological and psychoanalytic perspectives, and thus drawing on that same combinatory power of cultural and individual focus they offer, are those feminist voices that have sought to suggest how we might read what invariably seems, thanks largely to the nature of the iconography that Tarratt, Lucanio, and others have foregrounded, the dominant masculine text of science fiction. Given the genre's fundamental concern with science and technology, with the sort of controlling concepts and technologies that feminist criticism has usually linked to the dominating structures of a patriarchal culture – and often taking the distinctly phallic shape of rocket ships, ray guns, tunneling devices, and light sabers – science fiction cinema has provided a fertile ground for exploring a genre dynamic in which, most often, men *do* while women *watch* appreciatively. Although that dynamic has undergone some radical revision in the past two decades, thanks to films like *Aliens* (1986), *Eve of Destruction* (1991), *Cherry 2000* (1987), and *Terminator 2*, all of which have pointedly situated women in positions of technological mastery – as wielders of hardware, as creators (technological mothers) of key programs, as the order givers in a technical culture – the full range of contemporary science fiction films have become texts for reconsidering the larger, masculinist emphasis of the genre and for suggesting how other genres might similarly be read and even reconceived along feminist lines.

Probably the most influential figure in this approach to the science fiction film, even though she has never really turned her focus to explicating the genre, is Donna Haraway. Concerned with the larger cultural and technological context in which our science fiction films operate – in fact, working from the perspective that contemporary culture has become very much like science fiction and that science fiction, in turn, has become a primary expression of this cultural moment – Haraway has made what she terms a "science fictional move" in her cultural commentary that critics of the genre have quickly followed.[34] She has appropriated a key icon of the contemporary science fiction film, the cyborg or artificial being, as a trope for investigating feminine identity in the postmodern cultural environment, particularly using it to describe the "odd techno-organic, humanoid hybrids" that, she argues, women have become in the contemporary environment – that is, the new sort of "nature" they have discovered as they try to understand and resist their construction by a male technoculture.[35]

Drawing on Haraway's formulation and extending it specifically to the study of science fiction texts, both literary and cinematic, Mary Ann Doane explains how "science fiction, a genre specific to the era of rapid technological development, frequently envisages a new, revised body as a direct outcome of the advance of science. And when technology intersects with the body in the realm of representation, the question of sexual difference is inevitably involved."[36] Working from that primary focus on sexual difference, Doane discerns throughout the genre a fascination with key feminist concerns, "with the issues of the maternal, reproduction, representation, and history";[37] and in our science fiction films' depiction of the "revised body" – the robot, cyborg, prosthetically altered human – she reads a primary story of cultural repression, a chronicling of the dominant culture's efforts "to control, supervise, regulate the maternal – to put *limits* upon it."[38] A primary example of such depiction is *The Stepford Wives* (1975) [Fig. 23], which focuses on a small town in which the various wives are gradually and secretly being replaced by robotic women, all of them dressed very much alike and seemingly devoted to traditional domestic duties. Haraway and Doane would read such a film, as well as the many involving female simulacra that have followed in its wake, not only as an indictment of the stultifying roles a patriarchal culture has traditionally afforded women, but also as a revealing vantage on the ways female representation has been determined by the male (through the mode of dress adopted by/for the robot wives), on the appropriation of female reproductive capacity through male domination of technology (the creation of mechanical wives), and on the erasure of feminine history

Figure 23. *The Stepford Wives* (1975) illustrates a widespread concern with cultural repression of the feminine.

(as individual backgrounds become irrelevant when the women are replaced by their technological others). Such interpretations dovetail in a number of respects with Vivian Sobchack's psychological and ideological commentaries on the form, and thus suggest how several of these approaches have converged as they draw on the technological to raise questions about the troubled nature of gender dynamics within contemporary culture.

Following the lead of both Haraway and Doane in their focus on the cultural context of science fiction are critics such as Barbara Creed and Claudia Springer. While the former reads the genre primarily as one more especially revealing site of feminine representation – and misrepresentation – the latter more specifically explores the characteristics of the form, particularly its emphasis on technology and the body. Drawing together Freud's comments on the primal scene and Doane's view of the maternal as a primary site of cultural contention, Creed argues that one of "the major concerns of the science fiction horror film (*Alien, The Thing . . . , Invasion of the Body Snatchers, Altered States*

[1980]) is the reworking of the primal scene" in relation to their recurrent images of the mother.[39] In her examination of *Alien,* she discerns a number of such primal scenes, most of them associated with a horrific, monstrous version of the mother, and thus with the cultural threat posed by the powerful female; these include the alien ship filled with about-to-hatch eggs [Fig. 24], the infamous "chest-buster" scene in which an incubated alien bursts from a human's chest, the captain's deadly encounter with the alien as he crawls through his ship's womb-like air ducts, and others. In the final defeat and expulsion of this monstrous mother by the female officer Ripley, whose body is presented as "pleasurable and reassuring to look at," Creed sees a reassertion of the "acceptable," nonthreatening mother figure, a successful effort "to repress the nightmare image of the monstrous-feminine within the text's patriarchal discourses."[40] Extrapolating from this analysis, she suggests that if we extend this examination to the various forms of the maternal that recur throughout our science fiction films, we might discover "a new way of understanding how patriarchal ideology works to deny the 'difference' of woman in her cinematic representation."[41]

A specific application of this notion of difference drives Springer's more ambitious volume *Electronic Eros,* as it ranges across a variety of cultural texts to explore the relationship between technology and desire, and particularly woman's place in that relationship. Throughout contemporary technoculture, Springer suggests, we find that our representations of technology have repeatedly been employed "to express ideas about sexual identity and gender roles."[42] While such expression is hardly new, she argues that it has become far more conflicted in contemporary films, as we find major "changes in techno-erotic imagery in some popular-culture texts," particularly as that imagery relates to feminine representation, whereas other texts simply "recycle" imagery and ideas from Western culture's industrial past.[43] Focusing specifically on recent fictional representations of cyborgs ("cybernetic organisms – which are part human and part machine")[44] in such films as *The Terminator* (1984), *RoboCop, Eve of Destruction*, and *The Lawnmower Man* (1992), as well as in the television series *Mann and Machine* (1992), she reiterates Haraway's point that the discourse of popular culture "plays out contemporary cultural conflicts over sexuality and gender roles in its representation of cyborgs," and argues more specifically that by looking carefully at such representations we can see how, culturally, we still largely "cling to nineteenth-century notions about technology, sexual difference, and gender roles in order to resist the trans-

Figure 24. *Alien* (1979) translates the primal scene of birth into a technological context.

formations brought about by the new postmodern social order."[45] Thus a film like *Eve of Destruction* describes how a cyborg, modeled on a female scientist and incorporating her personality, becomes unstable, even dangerous, as it begins acting out the heretofore repressed desires of its original. Consequently, this explosive new woman (literally explosive, as she carries an atomic bomb in her body) must be destroyed before she wreaks havoc in society. In the work of these and other feminist critics we find valuable insights into the cultural construction of gender [Fig. 25], the positioning of the subject in terms of patriarchal narratives, and even the possibilities of constructing a non-patriarchal science fiction text. Equally important, however, is the way in which they speak to the cultural moment, reminding us of how ongoing debates about the construction of gender in our culture have found significant and powerful new icons within a territory, that of the science fiction film, which many would tend to see – on the one hand, thanks to its fantastic reaches, and on the other, thanks to its ground-

Figure 25. *A Clockwork Orange* (1972) suggests the cultural construction of gender roles in the trappings of its futuristic nightclub.

ing in the supposedly factual realm of science and technology – as relatively free from such troubling concerns.[46]

Postmodernism

Finally, we should consider what has become probably the dominant vantage on the science fiction film, that afforded by what we generally term postmodernism, as exemplified in the work of such critics as Scott Bukatman and Guiliana Bruno. Like the humanist approach, postmodern criticism is less a particular methodology than a broad strategy, drawing on the characteristics of the age. At its base, as the philosopher Jean-François Lyotard explains, postmodernism involves an "incredulity toward metanarratives,"[47] that is, a skepticism toward and subsequent interrogation of all those narratives or structures that we employ to legitimate the knowledge on which contemporary techno-culture relies. It therefore argues that our contemporary ways of seeing, knowing, and representing all rest on what are usually unquestioned – and perhaps even insupportable – assumptions, and that the very notion of the real is ultimately little more than an "effect," a construct of language, custom, and assumption. The science fiction film

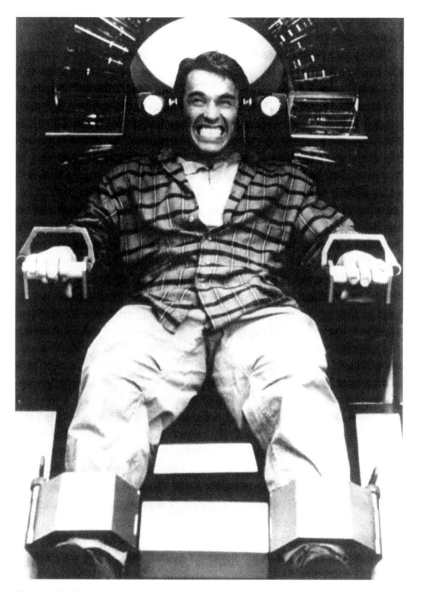

Figure 26. The problems of postmodern identity, of the human bound to technology, are at the core of *Total Recall* (1990).

seems to have proven particularly open to this sort of postmodern investigation in part because of its focus on technology and thus on the very methods we employ in constructing and shaping our world [Fig. 26], but also in great part, I would suggest, because of its fantastic character, one that, as Rosemary Jackson reminds, inevitably runs counter to and subverts our sense of the real.

While that postmodern sensibility has been applied to the study of the science fiction film in a variety of ways – see, for example, the work of Fredric Jameson, Brooks Landon, and my own "robotic" history of the form[48] – one of the most important voices in this context is that of Scott Bukatman. Less concerned with specific science fiction film texts than with the genre in its various manifestations (film, literature, comics, video games), he approaches the form symptomatically, finding in it essential clues to the character of postmodern society. As he notes in his article "Who Programs You?" the science fiction film with its semantics of technology, artifice, and spectacle "has obtained such a lately privileged position" in the area of cultural commentary precisely because it speaks the language of a technological, artificial, and spectacular world, because its technical concerns so closely parallel and thus help trace out the "methodological terrain" of this new world.[49] His more ambitious work, the book *Terminal Identity,* applies this vantage to that sense of a constructed self we find reflected throughout contemporary science fiction, as he suggests that the genre "narrates the dissolution of the very ontological structures that we usually take for granted," and that in the wake of this "dissolution" it offers striking evidence of "both the end of the subject and a new subjectivity constructed at the computer station or television screen."[50]

Ranging across a great variety of cinematic texts, including *Metropolis* (1926), *Invasion of the Body Snatchers* (1956), *Star Wars, Blade Runner*, and *Tron* (1982), Bukatman effectively describes that "terminal identity" that both our science fiction texts and our science fictional culture have already constructed for us. In *Tron,* for example, Flynn, the film's game designer/hacker protagonist, is digitally sucked into the virtual world of a mainframe computer and must learn to survive in this electronic realm. This "disengagement from the physical body" and consignment to "an infinite, *potential* space" within the computer[51] suggest, according to Bukatman, situations with which we are already familiar; for we are, in a sense, already part of the machine, our lives and indeed our very personalities already partly defined by the new electronic technologies – not only the computer, but also its extensions, such as the Internet, e-mail, and the lifelike computer-generated imagery of film and television – that are part of everyday life. That sort of life, lived by many for long hours within cyberspace, and that new sense of self simply constitute, he argues, in keeping with the postmodern sensibility, "our new, and inescapable state of being."[52]

Figure 27. *Blade Runner* (1982) envisions the postindustrial cityscape and world of late capitalism in its downtown Los Angeles of 2020.

More concerned with how that postmodern consciousness has influenced the very nature of film, Giuliana Bruno, particularly in her discussion of what is certainly the key postmodern science fiction film, *Blade Runner,* marks a slightly different turn in this approach to the genre. Working from the notion that this film stands as a revealing "metaphor of the postmodern condition," Bruno explores its representations of time and space, particularly what she terms its "schizophrenic temporality" and "spatial pastiche," to sketch the outlines of "the dark side of technology" and "the process of disintegration" that haunt postmodern existence and postmodern film.[53] Thus the constant sense of physical decay and disrepair in *Blade Runner,* she suggests, points up the interconnected patterns of "consumerism, waste, and recycling" that mark late capitalism; the look of the female replicants evokes "the model of postindustrial fashion, the height of exhibition and recycling"; and the "inclusive, hybrid architectural design" underscores the "geographical displacements and condensations" of postindustrial city life [Fig. 27].[54] Inhabiting this city of decay, the humans and replicants – who ultimately form mirror images of each other – are plagued by "questions of identity, identification, and history" that recall postmodernism's "world of fragmented temporality," a world in which we are constantly trying to reclaim history and a sense of continuity through a variety of strategies, such as the photograph or the filmic image.[55] In effect, Bruno finds in *Blade Runner* a kind of encoded model of the postmodern human context, a model that draws on the fundamental relationship between the human and the technological driving the science fiction narrative to limn the dislocated and driven nature of much of postmodern life.

Synthesis

Although this postmodern turn seems pervasive in contemporary science fiction film criticism, it most often functions as part of a larger critical armory, suggesting, in the process, a level on which critical thinking has itself become informed by that spirit of pastiche and schizophrenia of which Bruno speaks. Typically, postmodern applications will draw in and on to various degrees the feminist, psychological, and ideological assumptions already described, much as conventional humanist examinations have also tried to locate a structure for their investigations in the array of critical vantages described here. In fact, the most accurate assessment of critical activity focused around the science fiction genre today should emphasize the extent to which many of these vantages have become so intertwined that it is rather misleading and, indeed, almost impossible to speak of ideological constructions without also considering the cultural constructions of the feminine, for example, or to attempt a kind of humanist analysis of a particular image, plot pattern, or even a specific director's work within the genre without implicating, in a postmodernist turn, the ways in which those images or events constantly foreground their artificial and uncertain natures. Per Schelde's *Androids, Humanoids, and Other Science Fiction Monsters* affords a telling example of this inevitable conflation. His study of the monstrous figure throughout the science fiction film starts from a thoroughly conventional approach, as it promises to offer what he terms an "anthropological" assessment of the form. As he says, science fiction films have come to constitute "a kind of modern folklore" for our culture, recounting an ongoing "battle between *nature* and *culture*."[56] Like most folktales, these narratives "are protesting a reality which the people who have created them have . . . no power to influence," specifically the power of science as it appears to be "slowly invading our minds and bodies, making us more mechanical, more like machines . . . robbing us of our humanity."[57] In an effort to suggest the varied dimensions of the genre's protest, Schelde eventually deploys a variety of critical vantages that help give a needed depth to this otherwise simple assessment: ideological, as he addresses ways in which the genre grates against the dominant ideology (although, he allows, its "subversion never goes very far");[58] feminist, as he describes how, in its most provocative moments, the genre "points to other possibilities in terms of gender and roles than . . . we are accustomed to";[59] and the archetypal, as he focuses on iconic figures such as the hero and shaman, who provide key structural and meaning components to the form. Though Schelde eventually does little more than nod in several of these directions, the effort to draw in these varied approaches well suggests the complex ways in which we have come to question the science fiction film in the postmodern context.

In the present study too I try to bring to bear a variety of critical vantages in suggesting a useful and systematic way of reading the science fiction film. As noted in the opening chapter, the primary focus in this book is on the way in which the form functions generically, that is, on its workings as a kind of cinematic language, and on how its workings might eventually shed light on the ways in which other genres operate as well. While treating the genre within this broadly construed linguistic context – and borrowing simultaneously from the structuralist approach of Tzvetan Todorov and the ideological addendum to his work provided by Rosemary Jackson – this study is also informed, perhaps inevitably, by a postmodern view of cinema and technology that suggests the various ways in which the science fiction film, throughout its diverse thematic excursions, repeatedly scrutinizes what we might term the category of the real. As a form whose boundaries are, perhaps more than any other popular genre, always open or blurred, as a narrative type that always focuses on the tools of human fabrication, that is, on the science and technology that lend science fiction its very distinctive character, and as a cinematic type that relies fundamentally on its own technological capacity – and increasingly that of the computer – to visualize that which might be, the science fiction film inevitably foregrounds as no other genre does our attitudes toward the real. Through that interrogation of the real, it asks a number of fundamental questions that, today, seem to haunt not only American but the larger human culture: How do we define ourselves, how do we construct our world, and even more broadly, how do we know? The following chapters, as they turn to specific and exemplary science fiction texts, while deploying a combination of structural, ideological, and postmodern methods, will explore how our films have effectively addressed these crucial questions.

PART TWO

Historical Overview

3

A Trajectory of the American Science
Fiction Film

In order to understand how the American science fiction film works and what it has, over its history, managed to accomplish, we need to view it against a brief chronological background. In fact, as is typically the case with cultural texts, we probably need to keep in mind *several* histories whose confluence and overlap have helped to shape our experience of the genre in film. For example, among other stories that this history implicates, we shall have to tap into the body of mythic and folkloric narratives in Western culture on which the larger field of science fiction draws, the development of a distinctive literary genre, particularly in the nineteenth century, the rise of pulp literature that finally gives the genre its name in the twentieth century, the early history of cinema that at moments seems practically synchronous with the appearance of the science fiction film itself, the development of a technological attitude in what we have come to know as the Machine Age (1900–40), and the gradual formation of a distinct cinematic formula, especially within the American cinema. In point of fact, though, it is almost impossible to isolate any one of these histories from the others, to speak of each separately without doing some injustice to the absent yet always-informing other discourses. Thus the following history, while proceeding in a roughly chronological and, in that respect, fairly conventional fashion, aims to contextualize the film genre within the continuum of generic, cultural, and even technological developments on which it has drawn and to which it bears constant witness. In doing so, this history, like science fiction itself, as well as the larger pattern of fantasy, will repeatedly cut across boundaries of various sorts, often citing key books and films from outside the American science fiction tradition. It will do so, though, because American science fiction, like America itself, represents such a melting pot of influences, a confluence of ideas, concerns, and pressures that together have fashioned our contemporary culture.

Antecedents

Certainly, the whole genre of science fiction owes much to a body of Western discourse that precedes the development of film and that looks toward the development of Western science. For example, a variety of mythic and folkloric narratives about our fascination with technological power emerge from ancient Greek culture. In *The Iliad* we learn of the god Hephæstus' efforts at crafting mobile tripods, Ur-robots, to serve his fellow gods at their feasting. As a human complement to this divine model, we might consider a figure like Dædalus, often described as the most famous technician of the ancient world, who, legend has it, fashioned a bronze man to serve King Minos of Crete and whose mythic life finds its focus in the proto–science fiction story surrounding him: the tale of how he created artificial wings for flight when he and his son Icarus needed to escape their patron. Both of these figures, however, as well as many others, find their real prototype in the legend of Prometheus, who sought to wrest the secret of life and creativity from the gods and offer it as a boon to humanity. The fact that Prometheus failed and, as a result, suffered a terrible punishment identifies him as the model for a long line of overreachers after knowledge – of scientists, inventors, or creators who have sought to explore forbidden territory, of curious humans who have tried to uncover what we were not meant to know, of powerful figures who simply used their technological masterly in a wrong or ill-advised fashion. All of these figures eventually suffer the consequences of their actions.

Literature

Those reachers, searchers, explorers after knowledge are all engaged in work that, even amid the many shifts in focus and concern that the genre has taken, seems to lie at the core of the science fiction story and ultimately the science fiction film; they give shape to what we might call its Ur-story. They are involved in the process of asking the question of what *might be* or *could be* through the power of human knowledge, either for good or ill. For this reason David Hartwell describes the evolved science fiction narrative as "a uniquely modern incarnation of an ancient tradition: the tale of wonder."[1] Such narratives thus include not only the Greek myths noted above but also a long line of Western literary progenitors, including Sir Thomas More and his *Utopia* (1516), Francis Godwin's *The Man in the Moone* (1638), Cyrano de

Bergerac's fantastic conception of moon travel in *L'Autre Monde* (1657), and even Jonathan Swift's satiric take on the extraordinary voyage tale, *Gulliver's Travels* (1726); yet while such works develop a number of the concerns that would come to characterize science fiction and typically involve a curious if not quite "scientific" central figure, they are generally tales content with reporting the strange, emphasizing exaggerations, or simply inverting the status quo. The "tale of wonder" had not quite found a consistent pattern or purpose, in large part because the cultural conditions that would shape such a purpose were not yet in place.

That sense of consistency, focused especially on the powers and attractions of human reason, becomes apparent with the emergence of the literary genre in the nineteenth century. H. Bruce Franklin argues that this appearance of a literary tradition of science fiction directly results from a key shift in Western culture, that it "developed as part of industrial society," as an imaginative way of addressing modern culture's increasing reliance on science and technology.[2] In effect, the Industrial Revolution, like all other revolutions, generated an imaginative response, its own literature, through which the culture could speak of, respond to, and better understand the changing shape of the world. Specifically, we can observe this development of the genre in the work of a number of canonical figures of European literature linked to a new scientific consciousness, most notably Mary Shelley, Jules Verne, and H. G. Wells, as well as in the writings of a great variety of America authors, including Nathaniel Hawthorne, Edgar Allan Poe, and Jack London, among many others. Franklin particularly emphasizes the significance of this American literary line, as he observes that the United States "was from the start especially congenial to science fiction," since only this form seemed capable of coming to terms with the country's rapid transformation and ready embrace of technological development,[3] with its spirit of change.

Drawing heavily on the canonical authors cited above, Edward James in his historical account of the genre, *Science Fiction in the Twentieth Century*, offers a simple yet useful way of looking at how the form developed through the nineteenth century in response to this spirit. He suggests that we see science fiction literature as the gradual evolution and conflation of three distinct types of story: the "extraordinary voyage," the "tale of the future," and the "tale of science."[4] Although he traces the first of these back to the Middle Ages, James tends to see the other two as of rather recent vintage, rooted primarily in that nineteenth-century industrial spirit and particularly in the writings of Shelley and Verne. These authors are solidly connected to what we might term mainstream literature, and their work figures prominently in studies of, for example, the Romantic era, the development of the short story, fantasy narrative, naturalism, and social consciousness in literature; yet each sought to move mainstream or traditional issues in a slightly different direction, to recontextualize the key concerns of their eras by drawing on fantasy elements that would eventually con-stellate as the science fiction tale. Mary Shelley, for example, in both her landmark tale *Frankenstein* (1818) and her futuristic novel *The Last Man* (1827), subjected the human place in the natural order, a frequent concern of the Romantics, to a new scientific measure, as she explored the possibilities for physically creating life, as well as for finally extin-guishing all of human life. Though Poe's fiction rarely offers us science itself as a key subject, it does, as Harold Beaver argues, repeatedly fo-cus on figures who would become very familiar in a mature science fic-tion, ones who "from the start played the experimental, philosophical role: making 'proper scientific observations'"[5] – observations that Poe then critiqued again and again, in his essays as well as his stories. Here we might especially note his treatment of experiments in mesmerism and magnetism on the near-dead in "The Facts in the Case of M. Valde-mar" (1846), his satiric account of a theory for transmuting lead into gold in "Von Kempelen and His Discovery" (1849), and his tale of Ant-arctic exploration, *The Narrative of Arthur Gordon Pym* (1838). For Jules Verne the "extraordinary voyage" – a story type linked to the work of such disparate figures as Poe, Herman Melville, and Charles Darwin in the nineteenth century – became a vehicle for espousing human pro-gress and the key role science might play in that progress. That role is easily measured by the various technological devices and vehicles his voyagers typically created and on which his novels turned – the space capsule of *From the Earth to the Moon* (1865), the submarine of *Twenty Thousand Leagues Under the Sea* (1870), the balloon of *Around the World in 80 Days* (1873). Jack London in his novel *The Iron Heel* (1907) used the mechanism of the futuristic story to project the Darwinian concept of "nature red in tooth and claw," of life as an evolutionary battle for survival of the fittest, to a social conclusion. His vision of the future is one of inevitable class warfare between the socialists and what he terms the "Oligarchy" that eventually arises from a rampant capital-ism. These writers, along with such others as Robert Louis Stevenson and Edward Bellamy, not only explored situations with which we would soon become very familiar in the dawn of the Machine Age, but they created characters – Dr. Frankenstein, Captain Nemo, Dr. Moreau, Dr. Jekyll – who would become constant types of the mature science fiction formula and the sort of overreachers on whom the American film industry would quickly and repeatedly draw.

Of course, the key figure in this literary development is the Englishman H. G. Wells. In the late nineteenth century, when he first began to establish his reputation, Wells was, as Edward James argues, less a pure science fiction writer than a creator of "scientific romances," as he termed them, one for whom science was not "the creator of certainties and unveiler of mysteries, but . . . the great purveyor of mystery and wonder, just as religion had been in its time."[6] Like Shelley, he created a series of blind overreachers, as we see in such novels as *The Island of Dr. Moreau* (1895) and *The Invisible Man* (1897). In fact, the title figure of the former tale clearly seems a gloss on Shelley's Dr. Frankenstein, informed by the later findings of Darwin, as he experiments with turning animals into humans – or at least creatures resembling humans – through painful surgery, rigorous behavioral conditioning, and even the interbreeding of species. Also, like his French near-contemporary Verne, Wells offered his own brand of the extraordinary voyage tale, as we see with a work like *The Time Machine* (1895), which not only afforded the pleasures of travel across another dimension, that of time, but in so doing also forecast the lure of the cinema, itself often described as a kind of time machine. Still, Wells's sense of science was hardly lodged in the same technological ground as was Verne's work; he simply foresaw other possibilities for the future and for human development than those tied to a purely technological change. What he brought to the form was an ability consistently to infuse a spirit of wonder and speculation into the technological developments of the early Machine Age, along with a growing concern for the social implications of those developments; and it is for these efforts that Wells would become widely known as the father of science fiction.

In American literature we can find a closely allied figure who similarly exercised a great influence on the development of science fiction on this side of the Atlantic, Edward Bellamy. Although Bellamy seems not to have had the same sort of fascination with technology itself as did Wells, he offered similar visions of social evolution, geared to technological change, particularly in his key utopian novels *Looking Backward* (1888) and *Equality* (1897). The former, in fact, was one of the most popular American books of any sort in the era and had such an impact that, Bruce Franklin argues, it "changed the consciousness of Americans more than any novel of the century except for *Uncle Tom's Cabin.*"[7] In *Looking Backward* Bellamy tells a familiar tale of a young man who falls asleep and awakens far in the future, to a world radically changed by mechanization and social reorganization. That vision, of an America transformed without recourse to strikes, unionization, or social disturbance, but rather as a result of American "know-how" and a fundamentally pragmatic attitude, proved so appealing that those who sought to put Bellamy's vision into practice began forming all across the nation Nationalist Clubs, as the members called them. In addition, writers, both supportive of and antagonistic to Bellamy's ideas, soon produced a stream of similar utopian fictions, including such novels as Arthur Vinton's *Looking Further Backward* (1890), Ludwig Geissler's *Looking Beyond* (1891), J. W. Roberts's *Looking Within* (1893), and Ignatius Donnelly's highly popular *Caesar's Column* (1891).

Building on this foundation, in the first decades of the twentieth century, the era that would see the emergence of film as a key popular discourse, a large and heterogeneous body of Anglo-American science-based writing appears: mainstream fiction; tracts debating the impact of technology; and a wealth of pulp literature that would, in turn, feed back into the development of a conventional body of science fiction and eventually our films as well. Among the mainstream writers, we should again note the continuing work of H. G. Wells, as well as the emergence of Edgar Rice Burroughs with his Martian novels, and the writings of Olaf Stapledon. Some of these figures were engaged as well in the widespread public speculation on the future and the impact of current scientific and technological developments that marks the Machine Age. As Edward James reminds us, the 1920s and 1930s saw "quite a 'boom' in futurology."[8] One example of this side of the period's literature is the massive "Today and Tomorrow" pamphlet series in England, which speculated on the possible changes that science would bring in various social institutions and included contributions from the likes of Bertrand Russell, J. B. S. Haldane, and André Maurois.

We can again find a corresponding development in America where, as Bruce Franklin offers, the society was, to all appearances, "constantly being revolutionized by technological change."[9] Here there was a tradition of mechanical tinkerers, of garage inventors, as well as a widespread enthusiasm for devices whose mechanical efficiency would both serve industrial expansion and accommodate an emerging mass culture. Nurtured in this cultural climate and given the lead of Bellamy's and those other utopian novels previously noted, there came a profusion of technological writings, a great number of articles, addresses, tracts, and fictional pieces. As a body they argued that the rapid technological developments Americans were then witnessing – among them, the introduction of the electric light, the telephone, radio, automobile, airplane, and certainly the cinema – heralded great social change and upheaval as well. Moreover, as Howard Segal offers, much of this work, as in the case of Harold Loeb's *Life in a Technocracy* (1933), blurred the usual generic boundaries, such that there at times seemed "no qualitative distinction . . . between the fictional and the nonfictional" discussion of this technologically driven change.[10]

The Pulps

This blurring of distinctions is noteworthy in part because of the fantasy vantage I want to introduce for thinking about the science fiction film, and because of the fantastic's constant emphasis on liminal or border situations that challenge our sense of the real. It is equally significant, however, because of the way the pulp literature, itself a kind of border inhabitant between adult fiction and juvenile fare, would in its most significant manifestations come to inflect the whole field of science fiction in this same period. In fact, it eventually gives the name to the genre that heretofore had been referred to by a variety of titles, including "scientific romance," "fantascience," "invention stories," "pseudo-scientific fiction," and, for much of the form's early history in the twentieth century, "scientifiction."[11] Science fiction stories appeared in many popular literary magazines during the nineteenth century, and those tales often spawned more ambitious publications, such as the *Frank Reade Library,* a series of short novels about wondrous inventions that ran from 1892 to 1898. In 1908 Hugo Gernsback, the key figure in the early development of the popular pulp magazines (so-called because of the cheap paper on which they were printed), began publishing a magazine devoted to popular science, *Modern Electrics* (later retitled *Science and Invention*). He included in it not only articles on current scientific developments and proposals, but also science-themed stories, including some of his own fiction, and eventually he offered the first of several special "scientific fiction" numbers. The 1920s and 1930s saw an explosion of work in this area with the advent of a variety of pulps dedicated to such fiction, or as Gernsback christened it in the pages of his new magazine *Amazing Stories*, "scientifiction" [Fig. 28]. In *Amazing,* which first appeared in 1926 (running until 1995 and then reappearing in 1998), he initially featured reprints of work by Wells, Verne, and Poe but soon shifted to original material, providing a forum for many of the more important early science fiction writers, including E. E. "Doc" Smith and Jack Williamson. After losing control of *Amazing,* Gernsback continued his pioneering efforts with other pulps, such as *Science Wonder Stories* – in the pages of which he finally settled on the term "science fiction" in 1929 – and *Air Wonder Stories.* Appearing in 1929, both of these later pulps heavily contributed to developing a devoted readership for the incipient form and inspiring a number of imitators.

The most important of these imitators is undoubtedly *Astounding Stories of Super Science* (1930, renamed *Analog* in 1960 and continuing to the present), which would play a particularly prominent role in the further development of the genre; for *Astounding* not only launched the careers of some of the seminal figures in modern science fiction literature, including Isaac Asimov, Clifford D. Simak, Lester Del Rey, Robert Heinlein, and Theodore Sturgeon, but also sought to align itself with the most recent scientific thinking. Thus the magazine's second editor, F. Orlin Tremaine, argued that "there is no reason why *Astounding* should not serve as an exponent of scientific advancement" and eventually be seen, through the forum it offered for serious discussion of scientific topics, as "the cradle of modern science."[12] By paying more than its competitors for the best science fiction, by constantly insisting on a high level of scientific accuracy in the work it published, and – thanks to the cover art of its chief illustrator, Hubert Rogers – even by increasingly *envisioning* its science fiction worlds in more realistic ways than the other pulps, *Astounding* exerted a strong influence on the development of the form, and particularly on the nature of its audience.

Under the subsequent direction of its most famous editor, John W. Campbell Jr., the magazine directly influenced the very nature of the fiction it published. Following Tremaine's lead, Campbell insisted that contributions not contravene known scientific fact. Thus, in order to publish his "Tools" story (1942), Clifford Simak had to modify its depiction of Venus to fit with recent discoveries about that planet's climate.[13] At the same time Campbell tried to steer his contributors away from the realm of simple scientific lecture and dry speculation, insisting, as Edward James offers, that "authors should present the background and the scientific information seamlessly woven into their stories."[14] In the

Figure 28. One of the primary pulps, Gernsback's *Amazing Stories* (1927) offers audiences "scientifiction" and reprints the work of H. G. Wells.

case of one of Asimov's first robot stories, "Liar" (1941), that injunction prodded the author, after much discussion with Campbell, to work out the conflict in his tale by creating his famous "Three Laws of Robotics," the rules that govern the logic and dictate the safety of human–robot relations and that have since been assumed by many other writers on the subject. Campbell also dictated that contributions should be specifically concerned not simply with "amazing inventions and heroic scientists," but with "the societies and cultures of the future,"[15] that is, with how scientific advances might reshape human culture and history. In effect, through *Astounding* and his thirty-four-year editorship, Campbell helped give shape and even a social thrust to the developing form.

Nevertheless, if the pulps were important for the evolution of the literary genre, they probably had far less immediate impact on a developing science fiction *cinema* than did another sort of fantastic narrative. Appealing to a younger and probably less serious audience, certainly one less concerned with either the factual basis for the fantastic events depicted or the social dimensions of the form than with its simple ability to visualize what might be, were the science fiction comics that began appearing at approximately the same time as the pulp magazines and that did indeed tend to focus on "amazing inventions and heroic scientists" or other adventurous figures – in short, on the sort of "amazing" and "astounding" icons and figures that could be readily translated to the screen. In 1929 *Buck Rogers in the Twenty-Fifth Century* (scripted by Philip Francis Nowlan, drawn by Dick Calkins) began syndication in American newspapers, and it was soon followed by such imitators as *Flash Gordon* (done by Alex Raymond) and *Brick Bradford* (scripted by William Ritt and illustrated by Clarence Grey), as well as by a variety of similar figures in the comic books. Foremost among these was Jerome Siegel and Joe Shuster's *Superman,* which, after a successful introduction in *Action Comics* in 1938, was featured in his own comic book beginning in 1939. Thereafter, a variety of such types appeared, all of them endowed with superhuman powers – and physiques – and all devoted to using those powers to better society; among them we might especially note Marvel Comics's *Captain Marvel* (1940, written by Otto O. Binder, drawn by Clyde Beck). Together with more generally science fiction–themed comics, such as *Planet Comics* and Hugo Gernsback's effort in this vein, *Superworld,* the superhero comics helped extend and develop a science fiction audience in the 1930s and 1940s.

In large part because they did emphasize heroic action, larger-than-life figures, and striking images over social commentary, many of these comic narratives were quickly imported into film as sources for one of the most popular veins of early science fiction cinema, the serials. Among the many such adaptations that would appear well into the

Figure 29. From the comic strips to the movies, Buck Rogers faces danger in the 1939 serial.

1940s, we might note especially *Flash Gordon* (1936), *Flash Gordon's Trip to Mars* (1938), *Flash Gordon Conquers the Universe* (1940), *Buck Rogers* (1939) [Fig. 29], *Adventures of Captain Marvel* (1941), *Brick Bradford* (1947), and *Superman* (1948).[16] However, while both the comics and the serials furnished images and character types that would continue to energize science fiction cinema, even to the present time, they offer little hint of the sort of explorations that the best of the pulps and the more ambitious science fiction novels to follow would stake out: concerns with artificial life, the ethics of scientific experimentation, the designing of society. The comics thus helped to mark off the territory, to establish firmly many of what we might term the genre's semantic elements, although they often helped to place the form, at least within the popular imagination, in a far more sensationalistic context than a Wells might have anticipated or appreciated.

They also help to foreground and remind us of another important dimension of the science fiction field that would eventually inflect our films, namely, the work of the science fiction illustrator or artist. One of the chief attractions of both the comics and the pulps was, of course, the bright and imaginative artwork that adorned their covers and pages – work that effectively visualized the strange worlds, alien beings, heroic figures, and technological devices that the stories had conjured up, while also attracting the eyes of potential readers at newsstands. As a distinct tradition, science fiction illustration reaches back to the late nineteenth century with Albert Robida, who illustrated his own books, and Warwick Goble, who did sketches for the early work of H. G. Wells. In the early twentieth century some of the most notable figures are J. Allen St. John, illustrator of Edgar Rice Burroughs's work, particularly his John Carter series of Martian tales, and Frank R. Paul, a trained architect who did the cover art for many of Gernsback's magazines – *Amazing, Science Wonder Stories,* and even *Planet Comics.* Whereas St. John emphasized heroic, larger-than-life figures moving through fantastic landscapes, Paul was more given to vivid colors, details, and decorative elements as he envisioned the technical gadgetry of the pulps. Among the later science fiction artists we should especially note Chesley Bonestall, Ed Emshwiller, and Frank Frazetta. Specializing in astronomy illustration, Bonestall crafted extremely detailed and accurate depictions of space. He not only did many cover illustrations for science fiction magazines and novels, but also contributed artwork to mainstream magazines like *Life* and was responsible for the set design and matte paintings for the film *Destination Moon* (1950). Throughout the 1950s and 1960s, Emshwiller contributed cover art and interior illustrations to practically every science fiction and fantasy magazine, offering intricate designs that drew on his training in abstract expressionist art. After winning five Hugo Awards for outstanding science fiction artist, he would turn to creating experimental films and computer animation and, as a dean at California Institute of the Arts, inspiring others in that area. Frazetta generated a wide following with his illustrations for a variety of comics under the EC imprint and covers for reissues of Edgar Rice Burroughs's stories of Mars and Venus. Far less sophisticated than Emshwiller's work, Frazetta's illustrations are highly dramatic and sexually charged, typically emphasizing a violent scene and overproportioned seminude figures. A final figure who deserves mention in this category because of his impact on film is the Swiss surrealist artist H. R. Giger. Though not really an illustrator, Giger has done covers for several important science fiction works. However, he is best known for his biomechanical art, which produced a commission to design the alien figures in the highly successful *Alien* and *Species* film series. Giger, like the other illustrators mentioned here, has fundamentally helped to shape the way in which we see the alien other, the future, and the technology that attends it – in effect, the stock-in-trade of a science fiction cinema.[17]

Science Fiction Literature

It is the development of science fiction into a mainstream literary genre – primarily in the post–World War II era as many of the pulp writers undertook more ambitious projects – that would increasingly exert a shaping influence on more conventional fiction, on popular culture in general, and ultimately on an increasingly popular science fiction cinema. By the time H. G. Wells died in 1946, a new generation of science fiction writers was beginning to publish novel-length works, often serialized in pulps such as *Astounding, Startling Stories,* and *Galaxy.* In that same year, for example, Ray Bradbury published the first story of his *Martian Chronicles* in the magazine *Planet Stories,* and in the next year the first half of Jack Williamson's key novel *The Humanoids* appeared in *Astounding.* Among the many other writers who were serializing more ambitious works and drawing a following in the immediate postwar era, we should note Asimov (*I, Robot,* 1950; *Foundation,* 1951), Heinlein (*Red Planet,* 1949; *The Puppet Masters,* 1951), Simak (*City,* 1952), Sturgeon (*More Than Human,* 1953), Arthur C. Clarke (*Childhood's End,* 1953; *The Other Side of the Sky,* 1958), and A. E. Van Vogt (*The World of Null A,* 1945; *The Voyage of the Space Beagle,* 1950). The popularity of their longer works, along with the unparalleled development of a devoted science fiction fandom, demonstrated, as James suggests, that science fiction "had become a recognized entity, and one that had a very specific image"[18] in the popular consciousness – and certainly a far more serious one than the early pulps had projected.

That status helped spur the established publishing industry to move into the "new" field of science fiction. Thus, in the post–World War II era a number of major publishers began issuing science fiction novels, often in the context of particular series. For example, starting in 1947 with *Rocket Ship Galileo,* Scribner's began a long relationship with Heinlein to produce a body of what are often referred to as "juvenile" novels, and in 1952 the publisher Harcourt Brace followed with a similar series of books written by Andre Norton. At the same time, paperback publishing was becoming an increasingly important part of the book industry and provided, particularly with the activity of such publishers as Ace and Ballantine Books, as well as the development of such specialty science fiction publishers as DAW Books, more outlets for serious science fiction literature.

The development of science fiction as a major literary market and the eventual appearance of writers who have increasingly blurred the boundaries between the form and more conventional fiction have radically changed the face of science fiction literature and, in the process, broadened its impact on contemporary culture. Of course, mainstream writers such as Aldous Huxley with *Brave New World* (1932), George Orwell with *1984* (1949), and Nevil Shute with *On the Beach* (1957) had achieved great success in the form and inspired imitators as well as various cinematic adaptations. With the work of Kurt Vonnegut, William S. Burroughs, Thomas Pynchon, and Don DeLillo, and especially the recent wave of "cyberpunk" writers such as William Gibson and Bruce Sterling, though, we can see an increasing tendency to erase any real distinction between science fiction and mainstream fiction, as both seem to have converged on the central cultural issues of our time; or as Scott Bukatman states the case, "science fiction has, in many ways, prefigured the dominant issues of postmodern culture,"[19] and thus of postmodern literature as well.

Leading the way in this prefiguring is, as noted above, a new mode of science fiction, that produced by the cyberpunk writers, most notably DeLillo, Sterling, and especially Gibson. The cyberpunk literature they have produced at times seems closer to mainstream literature than to classical science fiction, as it draws on the hard-boiled figures of Dashiell Hammett's detective stories, the Beat sensibility of Burroughs, and the paranoid climate Pynchon has traced through the whole range of contemporary popular culture; yet it is distinctive in its pervasively technological climate, its fascination with bioengineering, and the dystopian landscape through which its alienated figures typically move. As Veronica Hollinger neatly sums up, cyberpunk fiction investigates "the technological ramifications of experience within late capitalist, postindustrial, media-saturated Western society."[20] Though the term itself first appears as the title of a short story by Bruce Bethke, its most influential and best-known exponent is William Gibson, whose novel *Neuromancer* (1984) has become the defining example of this movement. The novel sketches a punk subculture wherein nature and technology have become practically indistinguishable, thanks to our computer-driven capacity for reproducing practically anything. Its protagonist, Case, is a computer hacker who lives through and seemingly for the computer, only feeling alive while "inside" what Gibson terms "the consensual hallucination that was the matrix," that is, the electronic environment or virtual reality of the computer world.[21] Through his hacking skills, Case liberates an artificial intelligence (AI) from the constraints its human creators have placed on it, an accomplishment that, he eventually learns, has been manipulated at every turn by the AI itself. That achievement thus leaves us with questions about who or what is in charge in this new digital world, about how we should define life in such an environment, and about how our own sense of self is constructed by the culture we inhabit – all questions that resonate throughout subsequent cyberpunk literature.

More than just symptomatic of a special direction in science fiction writing, though, cyberpunk literature points up how closely science fiction tracks the dominant direction of postmodern art; for the sorts of issue Gibson and his followers explore are shared by many contemporary writers, most of whom would hardly identify themselves as science fiction authors: a fascination with and knowledge of technology, an interest in its impact on contemporary culture, and a tendency to aesthetic experimentation and innovation that derives from the general postmodern questioning of representation itself. The resulting appearance of a "postmodern science fiction," as Larry McCaffery describes it, seems "the inevitable result of art responding to the technological milieu that is producing postmodern culture at large."[22] At the base of that reaction, Richard Kadrey and McCaffery find a "deeply schizophrenic attitude toward science" that was seldom to be found in classic science fiction (although it is subtly woven throughout Wells's early work) but that has become an almost inescapable element of the whole postmodern cultural landscape.[23] As this postmodern impulse continues to drive science fiction and to draw both it and more conventional fiction into a similar if not always identical orbit, as science fiction and mainstream literature repeatedly demonstrate that they have, as Brian McHale argues, a "shared repertoire of motifs and strategies,"[24] we can see the form becoming less a speculation on what might be than a mirror and an extension of the very fantastic nature of our world – a signpost of that world's borders, a question posed to its reality.

Early Science Fiction Cinema

This confluence may help to explain the great popularity of the science fiction film today, as it has become arguably the most popular of our culture's generic formulas. It is a link, though, that has always been implicit in the form. As Garrett Stewart has suggested, when we think of science fiction in the cinema, we inevitably find ourselves considering more than a particular set of images drawn from our culture or a certain type of plot familiar from a tradition of science fiction literature; we also face "the fictional or fictive science of the cinema itself, the future feats it may achieve scanned in line with the technical feat that conceives them right now and before our eyes."[25] If, on the one hand, the cinema has often become, as Stewart says, a "synecdoche for the entire technics of an imagined society," on the other, all of our visions of what might be, of "an imagined society," have become reflective of the cinema as well.[26] Certainly, our film histories have long recognized this link. Terry Ramsaye in his early account of the motion picture's origins describes film pioneer Robert W. Paul's efforts at enlisting H. G. Wells's cooperation in creating a device that could offer audiences a *Time Machine*–like experience, a "screen project" that would enable viewers "to materialize . . . the Past, Present, and Future all at once."[27] Yet both that "motion picture Time-machine idea" – which was never brought to fruition – and the conception of Wells's novel, as Ramsaye notes, were already implicit in the very nature of the cinema, which was always, thanks to its "peculiar . . . ability to petrify and preserve moments of fleeting time,"[28] fundamentally a kind of time machine, a device that effectively freed both its audience and its early users from a conventional sense of time and place.

Despite this sort of conceptual similarity, science fiction film – and, indeed, the cinema itself – certainly owes much to a different set of aesthetic and industrial impulses that we should emphasize. If the literary genre had developed as part of and a reaction to industrial society, it still owed much to the Western literary tradition. As we have suggested, its lure was in part mythic, and it appealed to a literate audience, one that was open to and even enthusiastic about inventions, science, and the changes that science heralded; and if it engaged what was earlier termed a sense of wonder in the audience, it did so privately, conjuring in the individual imagination the images to satisfy that wonder. Film, on the other hand, was practically from the start a mass art intended for the broadest audience, offering them a series of common visual appeals, constituting what Tom Gunning has labeled a "cinema of attractions."[29] As its commercial situation developed – a situation that, at least in America, often involved a kind of assembly-line procedure for turning out a predictable product – the film industry tended

Figure 30. The start for one of Méliès's fantastic journeys in one of the first science fiction films, *A Trip to the Moon* (1902).

to generate highly formulaic texts, aimed not specifically at advancing interest in the world of science or even catering to such an interest, but at providing expected and proven narrative satisfactions, geared to the strengths and resources of a particular movie studio.

The chief figure leading to the development of such a cinema is also one of the founding fathers of cinematic science fiction, Georges Méliès. A Frenchman who was a trained magician and owner of a theater specializing in fantastic stage presentations, Méliès discovered in the properties of film technology a great potential for furthering his fantasy efforts, particularly in the mechanism's ability to create a whole new sense of time and space; for Méliès found that by simply starting and stopping his camera he could create amazing appearances and disappearances, animate practically anything, and, without ever leaving his Montreuil studio, send his characters on fantastic journeys and explorations, as in the case of what is certainly his most famous work, *A Trip to the Moon* (1902) [Fig. 30]. This sixteen-minute adaptation from Verne's *From the Earth to the Moon* (1865, and probably mixed with elements of Wells's 1901 novel *First Men in the Moon*), tells the story of enterprising Earthmen who undertake a trip to the moon by shooting themselves there in a massive gun. Once on the moon they encounter astounding flora and hostile selenites, barely escape captivity by these moon people by "exploding" them, and push their shell off a ledge so that it might "fall" back to Earth. In the course of this one-reeler, Méliès established a variety of concerns that would remain central to the film genre – rockets, space travel, alien beings, and violent conflict between species – while also deploying many of the trick effects of the early cinema. In his other and similar efforts, especially films like *The Impossible Voyage* (1904) and *20,000 Leagues Under the Sea* (1907), all clearly influenced by Verne's *voyages extraordinaires* series of novels, Méliès continued to develop a relationship between film's evolving vision of science and technology and the cinema's own technology, as he employed his growing arsenal of special effects – such as stop-action, model work, use of miniatures, double exposures, primitive mattes, and the practice of filming through various objects (such as an aquarium to create undersea scenes) – to allow his prototypic science fiction audience to undergo experiences that would be impossible in their own space–time continuum.

The primary drawback in these early efforts is one that echoes a number of complaints about much more recent science fiction film: that, as Albert J. La Valley offers, "the fantasy powers of [Méliès's] trick films overrode any real interest in a technological future."[30] In short, it was felt that the special effects became a bit too "special," effectively getting in the way of the science and its realistic depiction. That charge is probably a bit unwarranted, however, for Méliès certainly never saw himself as a creator of science fiction in the way that, say, H. G. Wells did. His films offer up their various monsters, moonmen, and mad inventors to period audiences with tongue in cheek, as Méliès, like the magician he originally was, simply sought to astound his viewers with the transformations his fantasy could work on reality – thereby opening up his fantastic theater to the entire world.

That fantastic practice was readily imitated in American films of the day, in the "cinema of attractions" that dominated early screens. In this cinema ruled by curiosities, amazing spectacles, and simple fantasies, Méliès-like fantastic transformations and comic inventions found a ready place, as is evidenced by numerous imitations of Méliès's films, as well as works like *Fun in the Butcher Shop* (1901), in which dogs turn into sausages, and *Dr. Skinum* (1907), which depicts a machine that can automatically transform humans from ugly to beautiful. These and many similar shorts from this period emphasize the amazing properties and, in most cases, the humorous products of a variety of machines – a line of development that would see its fullest expression not so much in a science fiction cinema, which never fully blossoms in this era, as in the comedies that so dominated American screens of the 1910s and 1920s. In the works of Mack Sennett, Charlie Chaplin, Buster Keaton, and Harold Lloyd, out-of-control tin lizzies and other infernal or Rube Goldberg–like machines would invariably create comic pandemonium. Indeed, Raymond Durgnat's assessment of Sennett's comedies, that they "register not only the shock of speed but the spreading concept of man as an impersonal object existing only to work rapidly, rhythmically, repetitively,"[31] reminds us of the extent to which our fascination with – and even recoil against – the machine and modern technology informed much of the early cinema.

The Machine Age

That comic kinship points toward the development of the first major era of cinematic science fiction, that which we might link to the Machine Age and its influence, particularly on American culture. The Machine Age is roughly that period from the start of World War I to the beginnings of World War II – the era in which, as Richard Guy Wilson offers, "machines and their products increasingly pervaded all aspects of modern life. . . . Machines were everywhere," and their presence effectively redefined how we saw "both the self and the world."[32] This dominance of the machine and the development of an attendant machine consciousness produced a rather different attitude toward both the cinema and science fiction, and it eventuated in the production of the first truly distinct body of science fiction films. In this body of work, anchored in a more serious approach to the world of science and technology, thanks to the very pervasiveness of the machine and a set of values that had become attached to it, we can begin to see the variety of narrative concerns and types that would come to mark this genre as it developed well into the 1940s: utopian and dsytopian tales, stories of marvelous inventions and mad scientists, hybrid concoctions of horror and science fiction, and the serials. Equally noteworthy is the fact that we can trace this burgeoning of the genre across cultural boundaries, as countries such as the United States, Great Britain, France, the Soviet Union, and Germany, all in the process of coming to grips with

the powerful new machines and the changes they were working on society, produced almost equally important and fundamentally similar
contributions to the film genre.[33]

In the wake of World War I there followed not only a new enthusiasm for science and technology but also an outpouring of utopian writing, speculating on the possible cultural impact of these new developments. This writing reflected a number of the more important social
developments of the era – ones that either politically or economically
offered to change the very nature of human culture. We might consider,
in this context, the impact of Henry Ford and the new manufacturing
processes he inaugurated (particularly the organization of raw materials, the systematization of linked manufacturing processes, and the
assembly line, all commonly referred to as Fordism), Taylorism and its
commodification of individual labor (through time and motion studies), and Marxism with its emphasis on collective human activity. Responding to this spirit of the times, many countries produced films that
either explicitly or implicitly explored the implications of these "-isms,"
of the era's emphasis on speed, efficiency, and collective action, by
depicting what life might be like in another time or place, one in which
many of these new developments had finally, and in most cases successfully, been instituted.

One particularly noteworthy response was precisely in that comic
vein previously noted, as Charlie Chaplin in *Modern Times* (1936) [Fig.
31] took on precisely the excesses of Fordism and Taylorism. Placing
his Little Tramp character in a thoroughly modernized factory, Chaplin illustrates the effects on the individual of the assembly line and of
those scientific time and motion studies that were supposed to produce the most efficient labor. Conditioned by repetitive motions of bolt
tightening, the Tramp cannot stop his twisting arms; in effect, he develops a new malady, an industrial tic. When he takes a restroom break,
the factory's video surveillance system allows the owner to intrude
and order him to get back to work. Then, when attached to a newly in-
vented feeding machine, designed to keep the worker at his post during lunchtime, the Tramp is assaulted by the contraption – hit with a
corn cob, scalded with hot coffee, fed steel bolts instead of pieces of
meat. The end product of these much-heralded "-isms," of these *physical* manipulations of the human, is a complete *psychological* collapse,
as the Tramp goes crazy and is carted off to jail – ironically, the one
place in this "modern" world where he can find peace and comfort. In
this comic fantasy, a near kin to science fiction, Chaplin starkly sug-

Figure 31. Machines typically go out of control in silent comedy, as we see when one "swallows" Chaplin in *Modern Times* (1936).

gests not what life might be like in a thoroughly technologized society, but rather what it is already becoming.

Far more speculative efforts, situated squarely in the realm of science fiction, are the various utopian/dystopian films that appeared in Europe during the Machine Age. The foremost example of this trend is the German film *Metropolis* (1926) [Fig. 32], which offered an even starker vision of the plight of the worker than would Chaplin, and one unleavened by any humor. It depicts the society of 2015, when the well-to-do live in skyscrapers and enjoy a life of play and leisure, while the workers inhabit a dreary underground world where they seem practically slaves to the machines that make the fantastic upper world work. When their hope that a savior might come finally fails, the workers revolt against that upper world and, in the process, nearly destroy both it and their own offspring. In the Soviet Union, *Aelita* (1924), an adapta-

Figure 32. The most influential vision of the futuristic city, Fritz Lang's *Metropolis* (1926).

tion of the Alexei Tolstoi novel, located its futuristic society on Mars; but that world, as the Soviet space travelers of the narrative learn, proves far more repressive and less open to progress than the still struggling communist "paradise" the voyagers had left on Earth. In fact, a supposed workers' insurrection, aided by the Soviet visitors, turns out to be a manipulated revolution to give a new leader, Aelita, dictatorial power. In England, H. G. Wells was finally lured into transferring his social ideas to film, as Alexander Korda induced him to adapt for the screen his book *The Shape of Things to Come* (1933), a tale of world war that leads to the collapse of human civilization and its eventual replacement by a new society, but in this case a thoroughly rational one, designed and ruled by the engineers. *Things to Come* (1936) leaves viewers with an element of hope – as, in fact, do all of these utopian/dystopian works, although in every case that hope seems an almost desperate affirmation *in spite of* the problems that go unresolved.

Figure 33. *Just Imagine*'s American vision of the utopian city, New York of 1980 as imagined in 1930.

Occupying a kind of middle ground between *Metropolis*'s vision of a world at odds with itself and *Things to Come*'s homage to progress and planning is the key American entry in this utopian/dystopian vein, the film *Just Imagine* (1930) [Fig. 33]. As Joseph J. Corn reminds us, "the vision of the future as a technological paradise has long been a central theme in American culture,"[34] and *Just Imagine,* with its emphasis on demonstrating various inventions and labor-saving devices, such as videophones, electric hand dryers, and baby-dispensing machines, certainly suggested that a kind of technologically driven utopia was just around the corner – to be realized by 1980. It is also probably the most visually elaborate of the many utopian/dystopian efforts, with its massive model of a future city (outscaling that of *Metropolis*), its rocket ship and interplanetary travel, and its vision of an idol-worshiping society on Mars. In fact, *Just Imagine*'s sets and footage were so impressive that they would reappear in several later films, most notably the 1939 serial *Buck Rogers*. What may be most telling about the film, however, is the very conservative base that underlies its futuristic vision – a conservatism that seems more in keeping with an America not yet fully visited by Depression realities and hardly disenchanted with the prospects of technological development. With its lighthearted, musical-comedy take on the future, *Just Imagine* ultimately suggests that, for all the superficial alterations our advanced technology will surely bring, everyday human activities and concerns will ultimately change very little.

Ironically, a greater focus on the potential for change often shows up in the many films whose narratives center on marvelous inventions or technological developments. In France, René Clair's *The Crazy Ray* (1924) comically explores the impact of a ray that freezes all movement. For an age that prized productivity and the regular motion of the assembly line – one whose credo, as Cecelia Tichi offers, was "speed and . . . cultural acceleration"[35] – this device represented a subtle strike at some of its most fundamental values. More in tune with those values was a series of films emanating from England and Germany in the 1930s, several of them coproductions or remakes, and all bearing out Tichi's description of a deep-rooted "anxiety about a global state of instability that fostered an intense appreciation for the power of technology and its exponents."[36] The English film *The Tunnel* (aka *Transatlantic Tunnel*) was a 1935 remake of an earlier German film, *Der Tunnel* (1933). Both recount the building of a transatlantic tunnel that, by virtue of bringing Europe and America closer together, helps to usher in a new era of world peace and prosperity. This same concern with using technology to assure widespread peace and prosperity echoes in the German–British–French coproduction *F.P. 1 Doesn't Answer* (1933). A spectacular vision of the development of a floating aerodrome in the middle of the Atlantic Ocean, *F.P. 1* employs elaborate model work and the Schufftan process of combining miniatures with live-action footage (first developed for the earlier *Metropolis*) to depict a massive private enterprise that becomes a hub of world commerce.

Figure 34. American science fiction draws on early roots, one of Jules Verne's extraordinary voyages depicted in *The Mysterious Island* (1929).

If American depictions of such technological creations seem less ambitious than their European counterparts in both their scope and level of optimism, we might attribute it to a growing skepticism here, one certainly fueled by the Depression, as to the transformative promise of the technological. Even prior to the Depression's onset, though, we can glimpse some of that skeptical attitude in MGM's ambitious production *The Mysterious Island* (1929) [Fig. 34]. A costly production, thanks to its use of two-strip Technicolor, complex model work, and efforts to integrate a few sound sequences into a largely silent narrative, *The Mysterious Island* returned to the work of Jules Verne for its story about an aristocratic inventor who builds a pair of submarines with which, a jealous politician tells him, one could easily "rule the world." After discovering a hostile underwater civilization and defeating the politician's efforts at taking over the kingdom, the inventor sinks his remaining submarine and goes down with it so that no one else might

Figure 35. The scientist manipulates animal genes to produce human simulacra in *Island of Lost Souls* (1933).

be tempted to misuse these seductive powers. An even more promising power surfaces in the film *Six Hours to Live* (1932), when an assassinated diplomat is brought back to life by a newly developed rejuvenating machine. Its resuscitating power, though, lasts no more than six hours – just enough time for the diplomat to negotiate an important treaty, find his own murderer, and, as in *The Mysterious Island*, destroy the fantastic device – in this case so that no one else will have to endure what he assures us is the agony of living with the full knowledge that one is already and unavoidably dead. Although the focus here is less on the scientist/inventor than on the spectacular concept of the death-cheating device,[37] this film too hesitates to endorse its miraculous technology fully and thereby suggests the still rather hesitant embrace of science and technology in this era. Instead, it emphasizes a point that would increasingly resound in another group of science fiction films: There are things humanity is simply better off not knowing.

Figure 36. Genre-straddling films: Mainstays of horror, Bela Lugosi and Boris Karloff, struggle for scientific power in *The Invisible Ray* (1936).

This motif surfaces most frequently in the genre-straddling horror–science fiction films that generally dominate the American branch of the genre in this era. Films such as *Frankenstein* (1931), *Island of Lost Souls* (1933), *Mad Love* (1935), *The Invisible Ray* (1936), and *Dr. Cyclops* (1940), among many others, return to that archetypal science fiction impulse of the overreacher, the Faustian figure who effectively barters his soul for knowledge, a knowledge that is often embodied in a technological device that holds a potential for both human benefit and human horror. *Frankenstein,* along with its many sequels into the next decade, emphasizes the figure who stands at the border between the normal world and the unknown – but with the knowledge and the necessary technology to cross over. This trespass is effected either by creating a living creature from parts of dead bodies (*Frankenstein*), by surgically manipulating animals to produce simulacra of humans (*Island of Lost Souls*) [Fig. 35], by reshaping the body through synthetic flesh (*Doctor X,* 1932), by transplanting parts from one body into another (*Mad Love*), by experimenting with the effects of radioactivity on the human body (*The Invisible Ray*) [Fig. 36], or by technologically altering the size of fellow human beings (*The Devil Doll,* 1936; *Dr. Cyclops*). The monstrous creations that typically result from this boundary crossing, as well as the sort of monstrous transformation – and almost as often, the agonizing death – that coincidentally occurs in the scientist figures, serve as warning signs of the dangers involved in that movement across the knowledge barrier. While such films often seem essentially horrific in intent – thanks in great part to their emphasis on striking makeup effects, their visual designs that often recall the distorted, nightmarish world of German expressionist cinema, and their frequent reliance on the reaction shot–subjective shot pairing that had already become a cliché of the horror genre – their more essential suggestion is one of scientific and technological caution. In the midst of the Machine Age's emphasis on science and technology, and on how they might make life more efficient, provide us with new houses and even cities in which we would live and work, make both life and work more efficient, and fundamentally transform our lives [Fig. 37], these science fiction–horror films stand as a kind of cultural subconscious, articulating in a variety of ways both the surface skepticism of Depression-era audiences and the deeper qualms that attended our entry into the "brave new world" of science and technology.

The Serials

On the conscious level, and with seemingly little desire to pull back from this promise, the serials, as we have already briefly noted, seem to offer a rather different vantage in approximately the same period. The serial, although certainly popular during the silent era, and often containing science fiction elements – as in works featuring Pearl White (see especially *The Perils of Pauline,* 1914) and Harry Houdini (*The Master Mystery,* 1919) in the United States or actor-director Harry Piel in Germany, or those directed by Louis Feuillade (*Judex,* 1916) in France – became far more prominent in the 1930s and 1940s, in great part because of shifting viewing/exhibition practices.[38] With the coming of the Depression, motion picture producers and exhibitors, in an effort to draw people back to the theaters, put more emphasis on creating a full program for moviegoers, one in which short subjects and/or serials were often featured. That emphasis continued throughout the war years and immediately after, as the serial, with its weekly cliffhanger episodes, was seen as a way of regularizing moviegoing. Moreover, its

Figure 37. Genre-straddling films: El Brendel appreciates the fashions of the future in the comic musical science fiction film *Just Imagine* (1930).

frequent recourse to the iconography of science fiction provided a type of visual excitement found in few conventional features of the era.

In one of the few serious commentaries on this form, John Baxter suggests that, throughout their history, the serials "represent the clearest manifestation of that vein of childish primitivism which drew the first *cinéastes* to Méliès. The world of the serials is the world of childhood, with its fascination with passwords, costumes and secrets for their own sake."[39] But the serials were also, particularly from the 1930s into the 1950s, very often concerned with the figures, subjects, and typical situations that science fiction literature was casting into the popular light. In fact, even when science fiction practically disappears from the Hollywood feature film in the 1940s, the serials keep the genre cinematically alive and thereby serve an important generic function, working variations on and sustaining interest in its semantic and syn-

Figure 38. The first *Flash Gordon* (1936) serial: Dr. Zarkov, Dale Arden, and Flash are taken prisoner by the Emperor Ming's guard.

tactic components. Obviously, the *Flash Gordon* [Fig. 38] and *Buck Rogers* serials stand firmly within this science fiction camp, even if they suggest its more juvenile aspects, such as the simple sense of wonder that Baxter describes. Perhaps more intriguing from a historical standpoint, though, is the extent to which most of the serials, regardless of their nominal genres, seem almost universally technologically inflected, and thus the way in which they not so subtly suggest a developing scientific spirit and fascination throughout this era. Televisions, rocket ships, flying wings, ray guns, guided missiles, mind-control machines, flying suits, alien invaders, and especially robots show up not only in "pure" science fiction narratives such as the three *Flash Gordon* films, *King of the Rocket Men* (1949), and *Radar Men from the Moon* (1951), but also practically across the generic register. Certainly, the various crime-fighter serials, such as *Dick Tracy* (1937) and *The Shadow* (1940), spy stories like *Flying G-Men* (1939) and *Spy Smasher* (1942), and tales of lost civilizations, such as *The Lost City* (1935) and *The Undersea King-*

Figure 39. The mixed action of the serials: The cowboy Gene Autry in *The Phantom Empire*'s (1935) futuristic city of Murania.

dom (1936), offer enough of the typical icons and actions of science fiction to blur any generic boundaries we might normally expect to find. Even many of the western serials, a form we might assume to be more historically grounded in a pretechnological era, often anachronistically involve their characters in car chases, airplane flights, and the use of other Machine Age technologies. A film like *The Phantom Empire* (1935) [Fig. 39] suggests how far that boundary blurring might go with its starring of the singing cowboy Gene Autry in a preposterous yet psychologically compelling mix of science fiction, musical, and western elements that have him, by turns, driving a stagecoach, singing on the radio while piloting an airplane, and fending off the robots of the scientific kingdom of Murania, all while trying, detectivelike, to solve a murder for which he has been framed. Like so many other serials, it was simply able to suggest that much of contemporary life might be seen within a technological – and thus science fictional – context.

If the serial's life span was effectively cut short by the advent of television with its series format and, in its earliest days, often similar subjects, it does serve as an important cultural signpost, particularly for the development of a science fiction cinema. The film serial appears at a moment in American cultural history when the very components of such serialized storytelling had begun to take on a new resonance, when a technological or machine-consciousness was becoming pervasive, and our imaginative texts were following suit. In her study of the literature of the Machine Age, Cecelia Tichi argues that throughout the era we find that the typical narrative does not only "contain *representations* of the machine – it too *is* the machine."[40] The serial, with its rapid, efficient, if often repetitious approach to narrative was itself very machinelike. A fairly rigid formula dominated, as characterization became incidental, narrative development gave way to the sheer power of repetition, and the cliffhanger endings that never seemed to be real endings predictably created thrills. With each episode of the serial closing in much the same way, as the protagonist, a helper, or love interest was placed in harm's way, and with each succeeding episode reprising the deadly circumstances only to reveal an unforeseen escape, audiences were treated to a fast-paced, predictable, and precise experience that underscored the films' seriality. They thereby structurally evoked some of the same attractions then helping to project science fiction literature into the popular consciousness.

At the same time, the serial drew together a variety of iconic and thematic science fiction influences from radio, the comics, the pulps, and feature films. They seemed, in effect, to capture a sense of how science and technology were becoming pervasive influences in this era, joining a serious interest in our ability to engineer our culture and a popular-culture fascination with the sheer spectacle and power bound up in the latest technology. Though their narratives were typically simplistic, then, the serials, whether depicting cowboys, gangsters, explorers, or space travelers, managed to embody and depict the influence that the material of science and technology was beginning to wield on modern American culture – an influence that would soon make science fiction arguably the most important of American film genres.[41]

Springtime for Caliban

In the era following World War II, in what has come to be known as the Atomic Age, we can begin to gauge the strength of this quickly developing generic influence. In fact, as John Baxter offers, during the 1950s, a period he dubs "Springtime for Caliban," science fiction would become "one of the hottest propositions in Hollywood."[42] Early in this period, attendant with a shift in the production–distribution–exhibition patterns of the American film industry, the serial would practically disappear from the cinema, although its spirit would live on for a time in such early television series as *Captain Video* (first televised in 1949 and, in a unique development attesting to its popularity, itself adapted as a film serial in 1951), *Tom Corbett: Space Cadet* (which debuted in 1950), *Rocky Jones, Space Ranger* (1953; edited into a series of feature films in 1954), and *The Adventures of Superman* (appearing in 1953 and drawing on the comics, a serial, and an earlier feature film, *Superman and the Mole Men,* 1951). Though such examples of early television science fiction were generally limited by a combination of budgets, time constraints, and technical considerations, a show like *Tom Corbett* did make some effort at special effects by superimposing various animated creatures with live action, and sought a level of believability by employing as a technical advisor the German rocket pioneer Willy Ley, who had worked with Fritz Lang on his *Woman in the Moon* (1929). Perhaps more important, these shows demonstrated that science fiction could work on the small screen, and they set the stage for later and far more ambitious television programming in the genre, as represented by such series as *The Twilight Zone, Outer Limits,* and especially *Star Trek* – all of which at various times drew on quality scripts by established science fiction authors.

On the big screen, science fiction would generally *look* radically different from its television counterpart, thanks to the increasing use of Technicolor, Cinemascope, and 3-D technologies, all of which were supposed to suggest how very different the film industry's offerings were from those of television – and implicitly, how much better they were as well. Besides this technical effort at product differentiation, the cinema by and large also took on more ambitious subject matter: alien invasions, various sorts of fallout due to atomic experimentation or warfare, and space exploration – story types that generally recall Edward James's formal division of mainstream science fiction literature into stories of the future, stories of science, and stories of extraordinary voyages.[43]

If the *content* of many of these early cold-war films ultimately seems to offer little more ideological complexity than could be found in the era's television programming or even the late serials, the best of them

Figure 40. Articulating cold-war anxieties about nuclear warfare and invasion: *The War of the Worlds* (1953).

established that science fiction, whether in film or in the mainstream literature of the genre, could prove an important vehicle for articulating cultural anxieties and for commenting in a serious way on those concerns. Sharing many characteristics with such serial antecedents as *The Purple Monster Strikes* (1945) and *Radar Men from the Moon*, alien-invasion films were particularly plentiful, and, seen in retrospect, seem to represent both some of the best work of the genre in this period and some of its lowest points. While films like *The Thing from Another World* (1951), *The Day the Earth Stood Still* (1951), *The War of the Worlds* (1953) [Fig. 40], *It Came from Outer Space* (1953), and *Invasion of the Body Snatchers* (1956) seem a natural accompaniment to the wave of UFO sightings of the late 1940s and early 1950s, they additionally mark major achievements in the science fiction cinema, thanks to their special-effects standards, accomplished scripts, and complex concerns. They also provide us, as Peter Biskind has noted, with a re-

Figure 41. *The Day the Earth Stood Still* (1951) urges peaceful coexistence on a violent Earth.

vealing barometer of the era's troubled political climate. "Precisely because it was so thoroughly removed from reality, so well insulated by its own peculiar conventions," he suggests, the science fiction film "afforded more freedom" for social commentary than most other genres, sometimes even skating a bit "close to the edge of permissible dissent."[44]

Thus, on the one hand, we find films that play upon our cultural fears of communist infiltration and of a cataclysmic world war, that emphasize the need for watchfulness and preparation against alien subversion of all types, as in the case of *Invasion of the Body Snatchers* and its narrative of alien seed pods silently producing duplicates of us and gradually taking over the country. On the other hand, we encounter a work like *The Day the Earth Stood Still* [Fig. 41], which used its visitation by a peaceful but demonstrably more powerful and advanced alien effectively to mock Earth's cultural differences and urge a doctrine of peaceful coexistence, not only on this planet but throughout the universe. Drawing on this same cold-war paranoia are films that seem to represent the other qualitative extreme of the genre in this era. *Earth vs. the Flying Saucers* (1956), for example, despite Ray Harryhausen's state-of-the-art stop-motion destruction of Washington, offers little more than a bad-alien-versus-good-Earthling plot – one that would be suitably lampooned more recently in the science fiction satire *Mars Attacks!* (1996). Lacking even the saving grace of such special effects, though, is a film like *The Giant Claw* (1957), whose incredible plot centers on a giant buzzard from outer space, equipped with its own protective force field, capable of supersonic flight, and bent on human destruction. Still, in their own ways, both the best and worst of these alien-invasion films offered audiences a measure of reassurance – if nothing more, that we could cope with any external threat – although they also usually accompanied that note with a humbling reflection of the fragile nature of our civilization and even of our own species.

Striking a more urgent cautionary note are those films that imagine various sorts of fallout from the bomb, atomic testing, or even nuclear war. With the various mutants, awakened monsters, and world cataclysms envisioned in such films as *The Beast from 20,000 Fathoms* (1953) [Fig. 42], *Them!* (1954), *The Day the World Ended* (1956), *Godzilla, King of the Monsters* (1956), *The Deadly Mantis* (1957), *The Incredible Shrinking Man* (1957), *On the Beach* (1959), *Dinosaurus* (1960), *Voyage to the Bottom of the Sea* (1961), and *Crack in the World* (1965), along with many others, the genre would well earn the description Susan Sontag applied to it, "The Imagination of Disaster." In some cases pointedly created by the effects of radioactive fallout and in others brought back to life by atomic testing or some metaphoric substitute, the various beasts these films envision – ants, spiders, crabs, octopi, dinosaurs – typically seem drawn to our modern cities, where they proceed to carry out nature's revenge on a reckless, environmentally heedless human culture. Those disastrous encounters, though, pale in comparison to the potential for calamity suggested in a variety of other apocalyptic films, suggesting the possible destruction of Earth, or at least the extinction of its human inhabitants, as a result of nuclear war, of atomic testing igniting the radiation belt surrounding the planet, or scientific tinkering that creates a "crack in the world." Along with films that warn of the effects of all sorts of scientific experimentation on our individual makeup – *The Incredible Shrinking Man, The Amazing Colossal Man* (1957), *The 4D Man* (1959) – the various mutant and monster films of

Figure 42. Nuclear nightmares envisioned, with the help of Ray Harryhausen's stop-motion animation, in *The Beast from 20,000 Fathoms* (1953).

the 1950s and 1960s amply attest to the troubled attitudes toward science and technology in our culture. In an age that has come to be identified with its unleashing of the atom and the great power associated with that development, American science fiction films, as well as those of Japan and England, repeatedly play out for us "what-if" scenarios, fantasies of the consequences of that unleashing – few of them reassuring.[45]

The more positive side of science and technology in this era seems reserved for the various films that deal with space exploration. Building upon Fritz Lang's early effort in this vein, *Woman in the Moon,* and its efforts at authenticity achieved by employing the top rocket experts of Germany in his day, American films such as *Destination Moon* (1950), *Rocketship X-M* (1950), *The Conquest of Space* (1955), *Forbidden Planet* (1956), *Robinson Crusoe on Mars* (1964), and, of course, *2001: A Space Odyssey* (1968), among others, envision extraordinary voyages that, in various ways, signal a hope for human development (even our necessary evolution, as *2001* argues) through the powers of science and technology. Although the similarly plotted *Rocketship X-M* beat it to the screen by a few weeks, *Destination Moon* merits special mention for its relatively accurate and convincing depiction of a moon expedition. Drawing on producer George Pal's experience with animating models (for his series of "Puppetoons" of the 1940s), effective matte paintings by the astronomical artist Chesley Bonestall, previously mentioned, and the technical expertise of German rocket expert Hermann Oberth (who had worked on Lang's film), *Destination Moon* was the first color science fiction film, won an Academy Award for Best Special Effects, and proved so profitable that it spawned a number of imitators, all emphasizing the power of our technology to serve a larger human aspiration – a kind of collective desire for exploration and knowledge that would soon be played out on a larger scale in the very real space race of the 1950s and 1960s. In that same spectacular vein, *Forbidden Planet,* shot in Technicolor and Cinemascope, and sporting the first electronic-music sound track, depicts the work of the planetary star cruiser *C57D,* as it anticipates the injunction with which the television series *Star Trek* would later make us familiar, by exploring new worlds and rescuing the survivors of an earlier Earth expedition to the planet Altair IV [Fig. 43]. On that planet the crew encounters one of the most resonant concepts of the science fiction genre, a technology left by the planet's original inhabitants that allows one to duplicate anything one might imagine. This power of "creation by mere thought," as one character puts it, also managed to unleash "the secret devil of every soul on the planet"; from the genie of technological duplication there came forth unpredictable "monsters from the Id," projections of the repressed self that had led to that civilization's self-annihilation. With the eventual destruction of the planet and *C57D*'s return to its space journey, we see how the extraordinary voyage film could also function as a warning, an admonition against letting that same desire for exploration and knowledge simply go unchecked.

In what remains a landmark film because of its complex special effects and epic scope, *2001: A Space Odyssey,* we can see a fitting cap for the era's stories of space exploration, as well as a forecast of more recent developments in the genre. By meshing a computer-controlled camera with some of the most painstaking model work in film history, director Stanley Kubrick fashioned a film that followed the documentary-style path of *Destination Moon* and *The Conquest of Space,* as well

Figure 43. Affirming technology in the conquest of space – the robot-controlled star cruiser of *Forbidden Planet* (1956).

as afforded audiences a visual experience that made good on the fundamental promise of all fantasy, which, as Rosemary Jackson reminds, quite literally means "that which is made visible."[46] In many ways a return to the mythic substrate of science fiction – and one that prepares the way for another set of such myth-influenced works in the next decade, the *Star Wars* saga – *2001* uses an epic voyage "To Infinity and Beyond," as the last of its three sequence titles offers, to develop a larger story of human evolution. That narrative begins with a stirring image of Earth, the moon, and the sun in alignment, a triadic image that points toward the three-part structure that follows. That structure opens with the story of Earth, entitled "The Dawn of Man," a glimpse of humanity's animal origins, a world of violence ruled by the senses, instinct, and the law of survival. With the appearance of a mysterious monolith, a black slab that resembles a door, we open onto a world ruled by a newfound rational capacity, one in which humanity learns to use tools to aid in its survival and to project its power beyond the planet. However, with what remains one of the most effective transitions in film history – a match cut of a bone thrown into the sky that becomes a space station in the blackness of space – *2001* cautions against any easy assumptions about human development, as it suggests that, even in the year 2001, we remain simply at "the dawn of man," still tossing our technology, albeit of a more complicated sort, into the sky. The film's second sequence, "Jupiter Mission," draws its inspiration from the key image of the moon, which from the time of the ancient Greeks had been associated with the power of reason. On the moon our astronauts have also discovered a monolith, the mysterious presence of which precipitates a journey to trace its origin, to seek out, as it were, the source of our intelligence. That journey, however, is strictly governed by an emblem of our reasoning power: the supposedly foolproof HAL 9000 computer, which suffers a failure and nearly destroys the mission. Only the ability of the last surviving astronaut of the Jupiter Mission to disconnect HAL – in essence, to disconnect himself from a reliance on reason alone – allows the ship to enter through the "stargate," the door into humanity's future.[47] The stargate, which has been described as resembling a drug-inspired hallucinatory vision – an imagery hardly uncommon in 1960s films – opens onto a purely abstract visual realm, one defying representation and simple rationalization, but culminating in a series of jump cuts that depict the astronaut Dave Bowman repeatedly turning to see himself at later stages in life, his aging seemingly instantaneous within the larger context of human change. With this evolutionary tale, coscripted by the novelist Arthur C. Clarke, Kubrick created what may well be the ultimate extraordinary voyage narrative, as well as arguably the most important film in the American science fiction tradition.

Post-*2001*

Other science fiction films of the 1960s and the following decade would generally shift gears, turning away from both the fantastic voyage and that "imagination of disaster" to examine how the latest developments in science and technology might affect human identity. Certainly, *2001*'s HAL 9000 computer, which serves as both caretaker and undertaker for its human charges, points the way in this development, which was also propelled by increasing headlines about the development of artificial intelligence and the first efforts at introducing robotics into the work-

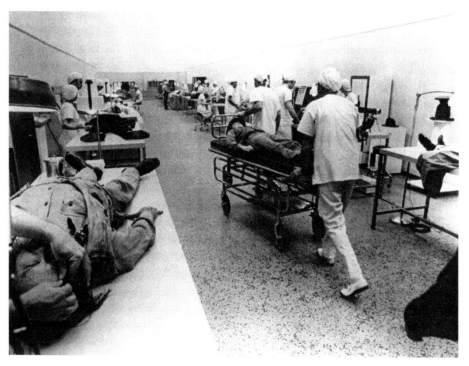

Figure 44. Giving a human shape to technology in the robot-preparation ward of *Westworld* (1973).

place. Films like *Seconds* (1966), *Westworld* (1973) [Fig. 44] and its sequel *Futureworld* (1976), *The Terminal Man* (1974), *The Stepford Wives* (1975) and its made-for-TV sequels, and especially *Demon Seed* (1977) all reflect our increasingly troubled sense of identity by exploring how we might be enhanced, reconfigured, and ultimately even replaced by the products of our science. *Demon Seed* offers a particularly unsettling vision of what might eventuate from modern society's rush to embrace the computer and hand over to it the running of our day-to-day lives. Here a woman's experimental use of a computer to run her domestic affairs ends with the machine's imprisoning her, raping her, and by impregnating her producing its own "half-breed" progeny with which it plans to populate and take over Earth. The result is a very specific sort of technophobic vision that has become far more dominant in the American science fiction film in recent years as it has continued to respond to the impact of the computer and artificial intelligence on our lives.

Only slightly less prominent among the concerns of our science fiction films in this era are those about the environment. Among the issues that surface in films like *Silent Running* (1972), *Soylent Green* (1973), *Logan's Run* (1976), the *Planet of the Apes* (1968) series, and several of the *Star Trek* films are two that we might place under the heading of environmental matters: threats to the environment and threats to the human species itself. Of course, the two concerns are interrelated, although the precise links between a devastated world and an ongoing and carefully planned extermination of humans – often as part of an effort at controlling the population so as to ensure sufficient resources for all – are often only implied. *Silent Running,* which draws upon the special-effects work of Douglas Trumbull, who was responsible for much of *2001*'s fantastic imagery, most directly addresses the ecological issue in its story about a space caretaker of an orbiting greenhouse holding samples of the foliage that had once flourished on Earth, prior to a catastrophic war. Defying politicians' efforts to eliminate his greenhouse, the caretaker sends it drifting into space, tended by his robotic helpers (who would reappear a few years later in an homage scene in *Star Wars,* 1977), as a living monument to our once-green planet. *Soylent Green*, winner of a Nebula Award for the Best Science Fiction Film of 1973, focuses more precisely on the human issue of ecology, particularly on the problems of overpopulation and the overstressed capacity of the planet to feed its inhabitants. The narrative's revelation that our disregard for the planet's fragile ecological balance might produce a kind of secret cannibalism serves as a metaphor for our current condition, one in which we are already unwittingly in the process of destroying ourselves, consuming our fellow humans to maintain some semblance of a status quo. In these and a number of other works throughout the 1970s and well into the 1980s, works that repeatedly were set against the backdrop of a devastated environment, our filmmakers were obviously trying to work out a troubling paradox: that the very technologies we had embraced to make life more convenient, more efficient, more pleasurable were contributing in ways we had only begun to measure to the very destruction of our way of life through air and water pollution, deforestation, the eradication of natural habitats, and the extinction of other species. As these films attest, the science fiction genre had pointedly become a popular and effective vehicle for addressing important cultural concerns, even ones that, in various ways, offered a subversive view of the status quo.

A New Myth

We would also see a kind of recoil in the genre, what some might describe as a conservative turn away from these overtly political and ideologically laden stories, as the genre made its greatest capital by harking back to its mythic origins. In the late 1970s and early 1980s, the science fiction film refigured itself powerfully as an epic vehicle, thanks largely to the efforts of George Lucas and Steven Spielberg. Of course, Kubrick's *2001: A Space Odyssey* had anticipated this trend, with its vision of human and cosmic change, realized through state-of-the-art special-effects techniques and a narrative trajectory that dissolves the immediate moment in the sea of evolutionary history. However, Lucas's *Star Wars* saga, comprised thus far of *Star Wars* (1977), *The Empire Strikes Back* (1980), *Return of the Jedi* (1983) [Fig. 45], and *Star Wars: Episode I – The Phantom Menace* (1999), more fully suggests the nature of this shift in the genre with its heavy reliance on computer-aided effects, its straightforward narrative of heroic endeavors, and its avoidance of immediate cultural issues. In this saga Lucas too set events at a far remove from human history, thanks to *Star Wars*'s opening scroll title – now easily quoted by practically all moviegoers – announcing that what follows occurred "A long time ago, in a galaxy far, far away," while also indicating its indebtedness to the imagery, character types, and, some might argue, the world view shared by the serials of the 1930s and 1940s, which typically opened in the same way. Furthermore, with that scroll opening, recalling the start of so many serial episodes, *Star Wars* also announces something more: that it is, in effect, an homage to a great number of films and film types – the western, war films, Japanese samurai films – all of which have contributed to Lucas's vision here, as well as to the collective cinematic unconscious of his intended audience. It marks, however modestly, the stirrings of a postmodern pastiche influence that has increasingly characterized our science fiction films, and that proves particularly prominent in *The Phantom Menace.*

That remove from the particular suggested by this intertextuality seems especially appropriate for the ensuing narrative, which is a version of what mythographer Joseph Campbell terms the *monomyth* – an archetypal and practically timeless story that relates a hero's call to action, his reluctant acceptance of the call, his penetration into another world wherein he accomplishes great deeds, and his return to his own world as a hero and adult, bringing boons to his people. These films form the most successful body of work, in terms of box-office returns, in the history of the genre, a point underscored and added to when, on the series' twentieth anniversary in 1997, the first three movies were rereleased with added footage and each work, in turn, became the top-grossing film in the United States in the week of its rerelease. We can further measure their importance in the way that the *Star Wars* films inspired a number of successful imitations and parodies, produced a dedicated fan following (now actively discussing on the Internet further additions to the series), and have entered into our collective consciousness, as we might see in the casual discussion about the fate of the Death Star in a film like Kevin Smith's *Clerks* (1994). Equally noteworthy is the way Lucas's series has underscored the importance to the American film industry of product tie-ins and licensing – an importance that few major film projects, especially in the field of science fiction, have since overlooked.

More down-to-Earth in concern, but still epic in scope and equally shy of the sort of political consciousness glimpsed in the previous era's films is Steven Spielberg's production *Close Encounters of the Third Kind* (1977). This film, along with his later and even more successful effort in the genre, *E.T. the Extra-Terrestrial* (1982), brought the fantastic encounter with the alien other into middle America with its story of benevolent space visitors calling ordinary people from throughout the world and the heartland of America to a meeting at Devils Tower, Wyoming. The narrative of that call and the protagonist Roy Neary's desperate efforts to make contact, even at the cost of his family's stability, seems almost a case study in pop culture contrivance in the way it cobbles together a great variety of current fascinations. As Andrew Gordon well sums up the case, *Close Encounters* draws on a variety of popular phenomena, including fundamentalist Christianity, pseudo-religious cults, theories of the gods as visitors from outer space, and belief in the Bermuda Triangle.[48]

Nevertheless, it does so effectively, moves us *in spite of* those almost transparent contrivances, in part because of Spielberg's own skills at cinematic storytelling (amply illustrated in his subsequent films), but also because this film too seems to tap a kind of mythic substrate. Neary may be a little man with a rather mundane job as a power company worker, but he too falls into Campbell's monomythic pattern of the reluctant questor who accomplishes great deeds, and in the process speaks to the common person's unspoken desire for similar ac-

Figure 45. *Return of the Jedi* (1983): The *Star Wars* films offer a new mythology, one compatible with the technological as embodied in the servile robots C3PO and R2D2.

complishment and significance. *Close Encounters* may thus merit special attention not so much for its skillful manipulations as for its ability to reveal the fantastic dimensions of the quotidian, as well as the extent to which a popular audience is ready to accept that very otherness – an otherness almost literally embraced with Spielberg's creation of the cuddly and loving alien of *E.T.*

Postmodern Science Fiction

Another and what may ultimately be the most important effect of the epic constructions of Lucas and Spielberg, then, was their demonstration that the science fiction film could once again be – as it had been throughout the 1950s – a highly appealing and tremendously profitable genre. As a result, a flood of science fiction films appeared in the early 1980s, some trying forthrightly to cash in on the patterns of these major works (see especially a work like Jimmy Murakami's *Battle Beyond the Stars* [1980] and the television series *Battlestar Galactica* [1978]); others, such as the various *Star Trek* films, exploring many of the same concerns for an audience developed through television; and still others opening up new and complex thematic issues. The most important of the latter are those films that begin pursuing what would become, well into the 1990s, the central concern of the science fiction genre – the impact of machine intelligence and robotic automation. In this period – which we might think of, following the theoretical lead of the French critic Jean Baudrillard, as the era of the simulacrum – the robot/cyborg/replicant/android assumes the central role in our films, which set about exploring a dual possibility built into all of our technological imaginings: the ability of our technology to let us, in nearly god-like fashion, craft images of ourselves, and the correspondent possibility that those creations, those emblems of our very power, might well *over*power us and take our place, as was first suggested in the play that introduced the concept of the robot, Karel Čapek's *R.U.R.* (1923), and as the two *Terminator* films (1984, 1991) probably most effectively illustrate. In the many films that explore this dual potential, we both celebrate our technologically driven might and recoil at its possible implications – with each response the mirror image and seemingly inescapable concomitant of the other.

The key film in this development is undoubtedly Ridley Scott's *Blade Runner* (1982), with its story of genetically engineered "replicants," designed to serve as soldiers in place of humans, to work in inhospitable environments, and, in the form of "pleasure models," to satisfy our most basic human desires [Fig. 46]. Set in a decaying urban landscape, by now very familiar to readers of cyberpunk science fiction literature, and drawing on the design and special effects expertise of Douglas Trumbull (well established in science fiction thanks to his work on such films as *2001*, *The Andromeda Strain* [1971], *Silent Running*, *Close Encounters*, and *Star Trek – The Motion Picture* [1979]), it examines the

Figure 46. Through its various "replicants," *Blade Runner* (1982) poses troubling questions about postmodern human identity.

ethics behind the creation of artificial life in the form of replicants who have a programmed life span of only a few years and bear implanted memories designed to keep them from an awareness of their constructed existence. By paralleling those near-human creations to the cynical and alienated bounty hunter (or "blade runner") Rick Deckard, the film poses questions about the level of our own humanity in an increasingly technologized and life-hostile environment.

Indeed, the proliferation of the image of human artifice in films that would follow *Blade Runner* suggests that this figure has become a key cautionary trope for our culture. We might consider, for example, a scene in *Terminator 2: Judgment Day* wherein a "terminator" cyborg from the future lectures a group of humans about the implications of his creation. He begins his story by cutting open his arm to reveal a bloody mechanism underneath, gestures with his newly revealed metal digits to his horrified human audience, and then admonishes them,

"Now listen to me very carefully." The message he offers is one that re-
sounds throughout films of this era – in works such as *Android* (1982),
Killbots (1986), the *RoboCop* series (1987, 1990, 1993, as well as its TV
series spin-off), both *Terminator* films, the Australian *Hardware* (1990),
and many others – reminding us of the difficulties and dangers we face
as we set about forging not only a truly technological culture but also
a thoroughly technologized humanity. It seems that, in crafting ever
more perfect imitations of the self and in placing the technological at
the very center of our world, we increasingly risk, as the philosopher
Robert Romanyshyn has argued, becoming little more than spectators
of our world, "ensconced behind" the window of technology and with
no real place in this world that we continue, ghostlike, to inhabit.[49]

Science Fiction and Gender

In another vein the robotic image has built upon this sense of necessary cultural awakening to raise some specific questions that have become especially crucial to contemporary American society. Particularly, this image of the crafted body has proven extremely useful for
exploring a variety of concerns raised by the women's movement, especially the extent to which gender itself might be seen as a cultural
construct. Early on in *The Stepford Wives* and its sequels, and later in
such works as *Cherry 2000* (1987) [Fig. 47], *Frankenhooker* (1990), *Steel
and Lace* (1990), and *Eve of Destruction* (1991), we find the figure of a
female robot or cyborg used to interrogate our preconceived and culturally sanctioned notions of gender identity, function, and ability. In
this development our science fiction films have certainly paralleled interests found in nongenre features and in a wealth of contemporary literature; but in their emphases on the details of these bodies' physical
construction, on their limited functions, and on a controlling software,
the science fiction films have managed to bring into mainstream consciousness (and even provided that consciousness with a useful set of
metaphors for) many of the most prominent issues raised by feminist
and postmodern theory – particularly concerns with a culture of beau-
ty, with limited, culturally determined opportunities for women, and
with the invisible ideological controls that, they would argue, effectively preprogram feminine aspirations and even a woman's sense of self.
This sense of the gendered self as a cultural construct – a notion liter-
alized much earlier in films like *The Bride of Frankenstein* (1935) and
the British effort *The Perfect Woman* (1949) – has proven one of the

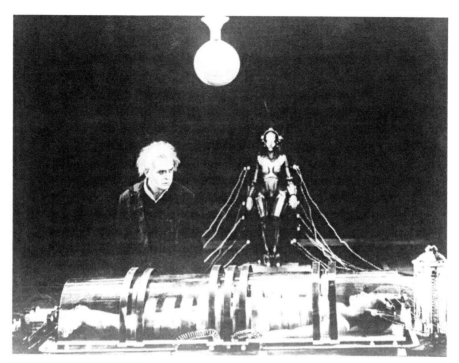

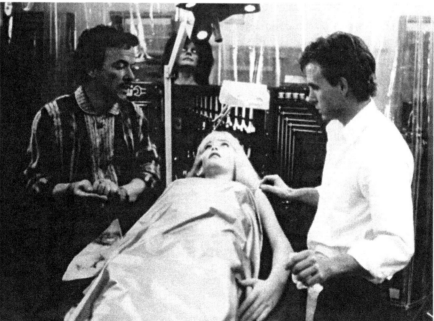

Figure 47. Two versions of the cultural construction of gender: (*top*) The creation of the robot Maria in *Metropolis* (1926); (*bottom*) repairing the perfect robotic mate in *Cherry 2000* (1987).

more important political developments of the contemporary science fiction film.

A further implication of this notion has surfaced in a number of films that explore how science and technology have assisted in that constructive process by appropriating a part of traditional feminine identity: usurping or controlling the very power of procreation. Works like the two *Species* films (1995, 1998), *Gattaca* (1997), and *Mimic* (1997) all update the early science fiction concern with creation found in a work like *Frankenstein,* as they foreground the contemporary issue of genetic engineering and in each case explore how women might be removed from the decision-making processes of conception and birth or find their decisions compromised by a male-controlled genetic technology. The *Species* films are especially illustrative here, for they postulate a full control over not only the process of conception but also the structure of our DNA. In the first of the series, a team of scientists receives a message from an alien culture that includes information on splicing human DNA with that of the alien species. In undertaking this risky and certainly ethically questionable experiment, the lead scientist explains that *he* has decided to make this hybrid creature feminine because she would prove "more docile," easier to control; yet the resulting creature, Sil, proves completely uncontrollable and quite dangerous, as she follows her natural instinct to breed and thus genetically replicate the alien species on Earth. Unable to control her mating and fearing the results of conception, then, the scientists track down and eventually destroy this new feminine species. In the second film a similar creature has been genetically reengineered to retain the powers of her alien species while remaining docile. The ubiquitous team of scientists then uses her to help track down and destroy an astronaut who has been infected with alien DNA and thus poses a similar threat to humanity. Both films seem to be playing out a kind of allegory – one drawn with the broadest of strokes – about male anxieties over control of a new kind of woman, one who promises to propagate others like herself and, in the process, recast human society along nontraditional gender lines.

The *Anime* Influence

Drawing on many of these same concerns and often foregrounding the image of a human artifice is a new tradition in the science fiction film, one that has in its turn inspired several American feature films, while also creating its own dedicated fandom in the United States and elsewhere. The Japanese animated film or *anime,* appearing in the form of the feature film, television series, and direct-to-video release, reflects many of the same concerns found in contemporary American science fiction, such as the recurrent focus on robotics, artificial intelligence, and the consequences of the unchecked development of these technologies. More specific to Japanese culture, the many works in this form (often drawing on the latest advances in computer-assisted animation) illustrate the country's increasing wariness of its many technological achievements and the direction those achievements seem to be signaling for what remains, at its core, a rather traditional culture, as well as an anxiety over how much the traditional Japanese sense of self is rapidly being reshaped, constructed, and controlled by a bewildering variety of external forces. In this respect, they recall the various science fiction monster films of the 1950s and 1960s, works such as the original *Godzilla (Gojira,* 1954), *Rodan* (1956), and a host of others, which also clearly responded to Japanese society's fears of its past and future "fallout." *Anime,* however, typically plays out these issues and anxieties against a peculiar backdrop, one that draws simultaneously on medieval Japanese traditions, on American cyberpunk styles, and on an imagery of ethnic and cultural mixture (of the sort envisioned in *Blade Runner*) that never quite evokes any *specific* human society, but that in various ways hints of the American dream of a multicultural society and suggests the extent to which the American science fiction film has become a key narrative type for much of contemporary culture.

Of the three typical and dominant subgenres of *anime* films – *mecha,* romantic comedy, and horror fantasy[50] – the first, with its emphasis on machine-influenced transformations of society and of the individual, most obviously bulks into the realm of science fiction; and indeed, the successful *Guyver anime* series (1986, 1989, 1991) has inspired two American live-action science fiction features, *The Guyver* (1991) and *Guyver: Dark Hero* (1994). However, even the other two subgenres, with their fantasy orientation, have in various ways overlapped into *mecha* territory and quite often exploit the conventional imagery of science fiction, while all three share a common focus on the sort of postmodern issues of individuality and gender identification that, as already suggested, have become commonplace in the American science fiction cinema. In fact, in her overview of the form, Annalee Newitz suggests that we see the whole field of *anime* as fundamentally "bound up with gender identity."[51] Although that view probably makes for too narrow a construction of the *anime* narrative, it does point to a larger, central

Figure 48. The Japanese *anime* influence: Apocalyptic imagery in *Akira* (1988).

anxiety to which all of these films, in kinship with the American science fiction genre, seem to respond: their concern with the troubled state of the postmodern self, a self that finds its gender, identity, even its very human nature called into question by the new technological environment it inhabits and that seems to be inevitably reshaping our identities.

Within the more specific confines of *mecha anime,* we should note two particular trends that dominate and especially resonate in the context of American science fiction film: first, works such as *Appleseed* (1988), the *Bubblegum Crisis* series (1985), and *Mobile Suit Gundam* (1981) that talk about various encrustations of the technological; and second, films like *Akira* (1988) [Fig. 48] and *Ghost in the Shell* (1995) that take as their focus crucial transformations of society and the individual. In the former, power suits or robotic guises either are assumed by humans or (and this narrative development seems especially telling for cultural attitudes toward the technological) *forcefully* attach themselves to human hosts, in the process allowing those hosts to perform superhuman feats – often to battle and defeat an antihuman or out-of-control robotic technology, but often also at the cost of human control [Fig. 49]. Such films dramatize the problematic relationship of what Newitz terms "two radically different orders of being: human and ma-

Figure 49. The *anime* protagonist (*Akira*, 1988): Half-machine, half-human, literally a product of postmodern culture.

chine,"[52] a concern that crops up repeatedly in American science fiction films of recent vintage, but probably most notably in works like *Terminator 2* and *The Matrix* (1999). In the latter trend, we focus not so much on external alterations as on internal changes, to the individual or to society at large – changes that occur both because of and *despite* our desires, changes that are irresistible, and changes whose ultimate consequences (as we see especially in the case of *Akira*) remain indeterminable. It too is a pattern echoed in such contemporary American films as the remake of *The Fly* (1986) and the recent examination of genetic manipulation, *Gattaca;* yet the popularity of both film groups suggests far more than, as Newitz suggests, that Americans "are . . . being colonized by Japanese pop culture."[53] Rather, it underscores the extent to which our world has become a kind of shared technological culture, one that draws its life from technology, recognizes how much we all participate in the dangers bound up in that technology, and worries over the alterations that technology seems inevitably to impose on both the self and our world.

Special Effects

The Japanese *anime* tradition also points us in a key direction for our parting comments on science fiction film history. That is, it is obviously a form that responds, in the way that our most effective generic texts do, to the latest cultural and technological developments, as well as to the anxieties with which they seem automatically freighted. Moreover, because of its reliance on the latest developments in computer-assisted animation, it suggests the importance to the genre of another history, that of the development of computerized special effects, which have lately become crucial to the form's development. Although trick photography and image manipulation have always been central to cinema's fantastic visions – from Méliès's editing tricks in *A Trip to the Moon* (1902), to the stop-motion animation of *The Lost World* (1925), to the computer-controlled linkage of models and cameras in *Star Wars* (1977), to the creation of convincing digital dinosaurs in *Jurassic Park* (1993) – computer-generated imagery (CGI) is a relatively recent yet also quickly dominant influence on the science fiction film.

The first significant work in this area stems from research done on the graphics capabilities of the latest computers in places like Bell Laboratories. It was followed, particularly in the mid-1970s, by its use in a variety of short, experimental films and, to more popular recognition, in creating television commercials and animating logos.[54] Appropriately, at approximately the same time that our films were starting to focus on the issue of human artifice – with 1982's *Blade Runner*, as we have noted, the milestone work – the science fiction film began its own technical alliance with the sort of artifice that breakthrough developments in computer graphics offered. That same year also saw the premiere of Disney's *Tron* (1982) [Fig. 50], which drew upon a Kray Supercomputer – the sort previously limited to military applications and advanced scientific research – to visualize, in an interestingly reflexive turn, what it might be like for a human to be sucked into the inner workings of a computer and to be rendered the plaything of its godlike artificial intelligence [Fig. 51]. Shortly after, *The Last Starfighter* (1984) employed CGI to create a variety of animated spaceships and to depict

Figure 50. CGI (computer-generated imagery) first surfaces in the genre to suggest the inside of a computer world – *Tron* (1982).

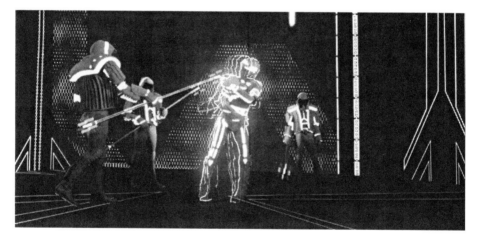

Figure 51. CGI combines with live action to produce a new kind of "animated" figure in *Tron* (1982).

combat in space. Although neither film proved particularly successful at the box office, we should probably find the fault not so much in the computer animation itself but rather, as Mike Lyons has suggested, in the fact that in both cases "the stories weren't strong enough to back up the visuals."[55]

A more effective use of the virtually unlimited visual possibilities available through CGI showed up in the more complexly plotted *The Abyss* (1989), James Cameron's tale of aliens hiding on the ocean floor. This film used the new technique of "morphing," or blending one image into another – pioneered a year earlier in Ron Howard's medieval fantasy *Willow* – and with it won an Academy Award for best visual effects. Shortly after, Cameron and his visual-effects technicians would duplicate that achievement in a film that placed the CGI morphing effect at the very center of its narrative, *Terminator 2* (1991); for the key visual effect of the film proved to be the ability of its liquid metal T-1000 Terminator from the future to morph into and thus mimic anything with which it comes into contact. That technique has since become a standard effect not only in contemporary science fiction cinema (see, e.g., *Stargate*, 1994; *The Fifth Element*, 1997; *Alien Resurrection*, 1997; *Dark City*, 1998; and *The Matrix*), but across the whole spectrum of film and video production.

The potential of CGI has also allowed filmmakers to turn to narrative account one of the great promises of computer engineering, the creation of virtual realities. Already extensively used in architectural design, medical experimentation, military training, and elsewhere, virtual reality harnesses the power of the computer to create a cyberspace, filled with simulacra, into which one can be projected, there to manipulate objects, explore areas, and experience things that might prove too dangerous, difficult, costly, or simply forbidden in reality. Having become a solid fixture of cyberpunk literature, virtual-reality experiences have become popular attractions at science museums and amusement parks, such as Walt Disney World, and have increasingly shown up on television. Both the *Star Trek: The Next Generation* and *Star Trek: Voyager* TV series, for example, feature a "holodeck" for the amusement and distraction of the space travelers; that is, a virtual-reality room or, as Janet Murray describes it, "a universal fantasy machine, open to individual programming: a vision of the computer as a kind of storytelling genie in the lamp"[56] – or perhaps as the ultimate movie experience.

Virtual reality has also figured prominently in such films as *The Lawnmower Man* (1992), *Lawnmower Man 2: Beyond Cyberspace* (1996), *Johnny Mnemonic* (1995), *Virtuosity* (1995), *Dark City*, *The Matrix*, and *The Thirteenth Floor* (1999), among others. While each of these films plays off of the attractions of the very otherness signaled by these electronic environments, of the fantastic difference they represent, each also pulls back from the simulacrum, recognizing a danger in its seductive appeal. Of course, in such narratives we also see film coming face to face with its own potential other, its own possible replacement, since virtual-reality technology holds out the very near possibility of fulfill-

Figure 52. Apocalyptic scenarios of the 1930s and 1950s return for the new millennium in such films as *Starship Troopers* (1997).

ing what André Bazin had termed the informing dream of cinema – the perfect reproduction of reality. It might be fruitful, therefore, to view that narrative recoil not only as the sort of technophobic response we so often encounter in our science fiction films, but also as a kind of industrial response to a potentially competitive medium, to the seemingly limitless powers of reproduction and recreation bound up in the computer and its multimedia applications.

One particularly noteworthy application of the seemingly boundless capacity of CGI effects for "making visible" our almost unimaginable fantasies has moved beyond this long fascination with artifice in a telling way. In fact, it marks a return to a territory first explored during the Depression in such films as *Deluge* (1933) and *S.O.S. Tidal Wave* (1939), and again during the cold-war years in works like *When Worlds Collide* (1951) and *The Day the World Ended*, that of the apocalyptic disaster. In *Independence Day* (1996) an alien civilization suddenly appears, apparently intent on wiping out human civilization and, like interstellar locusts, consuming all of our planet's resources before moving on to another doomed host. *Starship Troopers* (1997) [Fig. 52] builds upon this same impulse with its tale of interplanetary warfare, impelled by asteroids sent to crash into Earth by the insect inhabitants of the distant planet Klendathu. With *Deep Impact* (1998), *Armageddon* (1998), and several similar narratives, we see Earth's inhabitants confronting a seemingly inevitable end (a situation previously envisioned in Abel Gance's science fiction epic *La Fin du monde* [*End of the World,* 1931] and the British film *Meteor* [1979]), one that all of their technological attainments seem practically powerless to avert. Obviously linked to the coming of the millennium (in much the way that the closing years of the nineteenth century similarly saw a proliferation of literary works on futuristic and apocalyptic themes), these films seem intent on suggesting both the limits of our technological attainments and our ultimate dependence on those same attainments. Indeed, in *Deep Impact* the spaceship that, through a suicide mission, manages to save Earth from an Extinction Level Event, as it is termed in the film, is named *Messiah.* Significantly, in all of these films what makes that last-moment technological salvation possible is something far more fundamental, more human than any scientific creation – it is the coming together of a group of individuals, of mismatched and unlikely heroes whose selflessness and imagination manage to overcome or work around the initial, and seemingly final, failures of their technology.

These works seem a most fitting cap, then, for the end of the millennium, for a century of science fiction films, and even for this brief historical overview; for in them we see brought into the foreground both the fundamental tensions and the ultimate stakes in the human relationship to the technological that is a central part of the human story and of our science fiction films. In the best traditions of the fantastic, these disaster films draw upon the very technological foundations of the cinema in order to "make visible" that which could be, even the unimaginable end of both humanity and all of its cinematic imaginings. If the genre has, throughout its history, limned our strained relationship to science and technology, one that, as Robert Romanyshyn explains, at times leaves us feeling as if we were caught in a "dream of distance" from our world and, at others, as if we were engaged in a necessary journey of "understanding" that world,[57] in these more recent works it seems to capture both terms in that relationship and visualize their connection. Of course, that accomplishment, that sort of dynamic vision, is what we might hope to find after a century of effort in a genre, as well as a testament to just how well the fantastic has served the American imagination.

PART THREE

Film Analyses

4

The Science Fiction Film as Fantastic Text

THX 1138

In an essay comparing our utopian projections to the broader category of ideology, Paul Ricoeur observes some fundamental similarities. He begins on a somewhat negative note, suggesting that we consider both utopian thinking and ideology "as deviant attitudes toward social reality," and utopianism especially as a kind of "escapism," concealing "under its traits of futurism the nostalgia for some paradise lost."[1] In so doing he addresses a common criticism of most utopian thinking, echoed as well in the work of Fredric Jameson: the notion that our visions of utopias – or dystopias, for that matter[2] – ultimately risk producing a problematic relationship to our world because of their "eclipse of praxis,"[3] that is, the way such fantastic constructions, much like any culture's dominant ideology, too often distract us from what might be done here and now. Nonetheless, he certainly does not dismiss utopian schemes, but suggests that this "nostalgia" is useful when properly approached, the desire for escape or alternative structures a beneficial "pathology" if it can help us to interrogate the prevailing conditions of our culture. While he lays this knotty relationship of escapism and interrogation at the door of a vague function that he terms the "cultural imagination,"[4] the very irresolution of this issue points to another, deeper difficulty with which Ricoeur and other commentators on the utopian imagination typically struggle. It is, very simply, the difficulty of gauging that imagined world against any "social reality," and ultimately against the real itself – a problem only compounded by the widespread contemporary feeling that reality seems to have disappeared into a variety of cultural constructs.

This problematic relationship to the real also underlies our own project here, that is, our consideration of such schemes – particularly of utopian and dystopian film narratives – as variations on what Todorov terms the fantastic proper; for the fantastic, that middle ground between the marvelous and uncanny, as Rosemary Jackson reminds us, "is predicated on the category of the 'real,'"[5] and more specifically, on disclosing a troubled relationship to and thereby questioning the real. To do so, it deploys a kind of double strategy. As Todorov explains, on the one hand, the fantastic text works to create "an integration of the reader [or viewer] into the world of the characters";[6] that is, it offers signs that lead us to accept that world as coterminous with our own. In fact, it draws much of its power to affect us precisely from our recognition that this world stands for ours, and that, by extension, we inhabit *it*. On the other, it places us in a troubling relationship to that world as well as our own, for it forces a "hesitation," as it compels us to "a kind of reading" wherein, given our normal sense of things, we try to make sense of what appears to be a disturbing, fantastic reality.[7] The seeming instability of the narrative and our own resultant uncertainty combine to upset our usual assumptions about the real and can easily lead us to interrogate the very fabric of our world. On a more pragmatic level, as Jackson offers, the fantastic text, insofar as it "betrays a dissatisfaction with what is,"[8] also opens onto the politics of the genre, onto a kind of cultural unease that is always implicit in the form and that seems most obviously featured in our various utopian/dystopian narratives.

Certainly, that political dimension, with its own attendant hesitations, seems very near the surface in the long literary tradition of utopias and dystopias, a body of texts recognized and studied by literary scholars long before it became associated with the broad stream of science fiction. We can trace this lineage back to Plato's *Republic* and follow it through a range of works, some of which are typically seen as quite outside the bounds of the science fiction genre – such as Sir Thomas More's *Utopia* (1516), Tommaso Campanella's *City of the Sun* (1623), and Francis Bacon's *The New Atlantis* (1626) – and others of which are viewed as central to the form's development of its social dimension – and here we might especially mention Edward Bellamy's *Looking Backward* (1888), H. G. Wells's *When the Sleeper Wakes* (1899), Aldous Huxley's *Brave New World* (1932), and George Orwell's *1984* (1949), among others. In most cases, these texts set about offering a positive model for social alteration. *The Republic,* for instance, written in the wake of the Peloponnesian War, when much of the region around Athens had been devastated, suggested a model for constructing the ideal society (or reconstructing Greek society) – one based, as Lewis Mumford explains, in such things as "a common physical standard of living," a common level of education, and a common set of beliefs.[9] Of course, in other cases they may fashion a negative model of what might be, one intended to sound a warning about our cultural trajectory in hopes of effecting some political or ethical solution. One of the most prominent cases in point is *Brave New World,* which describes a society in which the government controls practically every element of human existence: It engineers births in its state "hatcheries," encourages euthanasia for the old or disaffected, and provides the pleasures of drugs and sex to distract its citizens from their condition. Whether as model or warning, such texts speak of a fundamental impulse, one that quite naturally flows into the mainstream of science fiction, to engineer human society.

In either case, we should also note, such utopian and dystopian works typically reveal two basic principles at their core. As Mumford in his classic study of the utopian form explains, every such text, even those that simply project a positive vision of tomorrow's world, conveys "an implicit criticism of the civilization that served as its background," while also working "to uncover potentialities that the existing institutions either ignored or buried beneath an ancient crust of custom and habit."[10] In that element of criticism, predicated on a dissatisfaction with the world as it is currently constituted and a belief in the possibility of change, we can most clearly see the political dimension of the utopian story; while from that other vantage, of a world of undiscovered or interred potential, we can also glimpse something of that underlying sense of the real itself, which these texts ultimately lay open to interrogation.

Although of relatively short history in comparison to that long literary tradition of utopian/dystopian narratives, this subgenre of the science fiction film has produced a number of significant works that point even more directly to this problematic relationship to the real that seems the most compelling characteristic of the fantastic proper. Among this group we find several of the most noteworthy movies of the genre, including Fritz Lang's *Metropolis* (1926), the H. G. Wells–scripted *Things to Come* (1936), *Logan's Run* (1976), *Brazil* (1986), two versions of Orwell's *1984* (1956, 1984), as well as lesser-known and rarely seen films like *The Mysterious Island* (1929) and *Just Imagine* (1930). In every case their strategy appears similar. On the one hand, these utopian and dystopian tales find their greatest attraction in their power to visualize what *could be*, a fully imagined and convincing world, one they must struggle to make seem real through, for example, elaborate model work, technologies clearly extrapolated from those of today, and attention to the details of everyday life in a vastly altered ur-

ban context. On the other, however, they most often displace us from
the real, even toy with our convention-bound sense of reality as they
typically achieve this vision in a highly stylized fashion. Simply put, the
fantastic texture of these utopian/dystopian films typically seems to
implicate at every turn a troubled relationship to the real. Our ques-
tionings of society thus often become bound up with an unspoken suspicion about reality itself.

We can most easily glimpse this correlation in what are probably
the two most famous films of this type, and the two that have also most
directly influenced American film's utopian/dystopian visions. *Metropolis,* for example, offers a thoroughly worked out critique of futuristic
life, one that reflects the economic and cultural chaos that was post–
World War I Germany and responds to it by pushing the obdurate logic
of early twentieth-century capitalism to its self-destructive extreme.
Here society has divided itself into a working class and an elite, man-
agerial class, the one living underground, inhabiting slums, and tend-
ing the machines that make possible the comfortable life of the other,
privileged class, living aboveground; and when the workers can no
longer abide their repressed condition, they revolt, in the process destroying the machinery that not only supports the upper world but
also maintains their own fragile conditions. The film shades this conception in a starkly expressionist scheme: with heavy shadows, angu-
lar compositions, stylized character motions, a symbolic dominance of
things over people – all elements that detach this cinematic world from
any immediate connection to our own and, for many, undermine much
of its subversive power by translating its vision into an aesthetic fascination. It is precisely that aesthetic fascination that seems to power
its American imitator, *Just Imagine.* In similar fashion, a later work like
the British *Things to Come* extrapolates from the very real international tensions of its day (1936), looming threats of another world war,
and popular antimachine sentiments in British culture[11] to describe a
decades-long conflict that reduces most of civilization to rubble yet
also opens the way for a new world order, one modeled on the technocratic social vision of the film's writer, H. G. Wells. Its vision of this new
order, though, is a starkly monumentalist one, marked at every turn
by an outsized and imposing relationship between that reconstructed
world and the human, a relationship that almost renders the human irrelevant. If slightly less obvious, this pattern no less characterizes a
more recent American effort in this vein like *Logan's Run* with its transparent cultural context drawn from post-Vietnam and post-Watergate

politics, all dressed out in near-psychedelic trappings that immediately evoke the politics of the counterculture. In framing their futuristic visions in these stylized ways, such films always risk the dangers of that "escapism" Ricoeur notes; for a major effect of their stylizations is to reinscribe the fundamental question of reality, the sense of how our notion of the real – which undergirds those ideological constructs on which society depends – is always implicated in these "nostalgic" projections.

One way of accounting for this condition is to think of the utopian/ dystopian film as always a kind of protopostmodern text, albeit one that does not necessarily share the full postmodernist sensibility. Its postulating of a possible trajectory for human history, for example, certainly runs counter to postmodernism's predilection for denying history; yet in its assault on the status quo and the manner in which it couches that assault, this sort of film inevitably implicates the question of the real in a postmodern – as well as a fantastic – manner. In the very way it constructs another world and marks it off from our own, stylistically signaling its otherness, the utopian/dystopian film foregrounds the constructed nature of all film worlds, their cultural status as products of our celluloid "dream factories," as well as that knotty issue of involved critique and nostalgic escape on which Ricoeur focuses. Moreover, because this sort of narrative is typically set in some future, marked – and supposedly enabled – by great technological advances, it additionally assumes a kind of reflexive posture shared by most science fiction films, in terms of what Garrett Stewart terms their persistent "videology," an emphasis on the mechanics of visualization that reveals the "more than ordinarily close collusion between cinematic illusionism and futuristic fantasy."[12] In such a context, the connection between the cinematic utopian/dystopian text and the real can begin to inflect the story itself. The ideological implications of that envisioned world, the one on which our critical commentary typically focuses, can shift valence to become little more than a function of the text's own attitude toward the real.

To bring this relationship into better focus and to offer an example of fantastic science fiction, I want to turn to George Lucas's film *THX 1138* (1971), a dystopian narrative about life in a futuristic society that capitalizes precisely on this shift in valence. In fact, its production history already suggests something of the difficulty of bringing the dream of another world into reality. The film began as a student work entitled

Electronic Labyrinth: THX 1138: 4EB, done during Lucas's first semester of graduate film studies at University of Southern California. It won first prize at the National Student Film Festival and garnered him some attention from the film industry. While working for another USC alumnus, Francis Ford Coppola, Lucas was encouraged to expand this short work, and he set to work on a feature-length script. Coppola, agreeing to produce the film, helped to arrange a finance and release deal with Warner Bros., although one that brought Lucas a very modest working budget of $750,000 and a schedule of just ten weeks. In response to these limitations, Lucas set out "to make a kind of *cinema vérité* film of the future."[13] Instead of shooting in a studio, he determined to do it away from Hollywood on real locations, using twenty-two sites in the San Francisco Bay area, including the Oakland Coliseum, the Marin County Civic Center, and the tunnels of the then under-construction Bay Area Rapid Transit Authority.[14] While the resulting film with its minimal dialogue and unobtrusive camera style certainly achieved that desired realistic look, studio officials found it less than promising, and audiences generally did not respond to it, in part because the film was so solidly anchored in the real rather than the sort of fantastic world typically associated with science fiction cinema.

Forecasting Lucas's own conflict with the studio, the film's plot focuses on a worker in a futuristic society who runs afoul of the authorities. In a world where sexual activity is banned, where drugs are used to control the people, and where everyone looks the same, the worker THX 1138 stops taking his daily medication and impregnates his roommate LUH 3417. As a result of this misconduct he undergoes a reconditioning process and is thrown into prison, but with another inmate he escapes and eludes a pursuing robotic police. Eventually he makes his way out of this enclosed, hermetic world and, alone, reaches the outside, where he stands against the background of a setting sun. It is ultimately a story of the struggle for freedom and of individual triumph, albeit a triumph qualified by the loss of LUH and the unknown nature of that world to which THX finally escapes.

If the plot itself is generally familiar, the film on the whole demonstrates the interrogative potential of such utopian/dystopian narratives. Certainly, it lays bare some of the more disturbing elements of American cultural ideology – particularly an inherent racism, a deadening disjunction between the individual and his or her work, and a capitalist reduction of everything and everyone to bottom-line budgetary numbers. Still, even as the film undertakes this sort of pathological interrogation, it does so in a way that repeatedly opens onto the relation between the utopia/dystopia and the real; for *THX 1138* penetrates beyond the social conditions, as well as the ideology that informs and enables those conditions, to remind us of the extent to which reality itself can become the focus of such fantasies. In fact, the film sketches an environment akin to that which Paul Virilio has described in his account of an ongoing refashioning of the human environment, what he terms the pending "cinematic derealization"[15] of our world, that is, the replacement of the real by a virtual reality. Lucas's film seems intent on cautioning about the sort of reality we buy into – today as well as for the future – and thus about our own problematic human trajectory, our seeming destiny, as Virilio puts it, "to become film."[16] Although any use of the term "real" today typically produces some critical recoil, particularly within that postmodern context that would simply describe the real as a kind of illusion or, more precisely, a cultural construct, a focus on this notion might help us better to assess *THX 1138*'s fantastic vision and, in the process, to reconsider that knotty relationship that underlies all of our cinematic utopian and dystopian visions and on which they inevitably comment.

As I have suggested, on one level *THX 1138* functions in precisely the interrogative way we expect of our utopian/dystopian narratives, for its futuristic vision consistently lays bare a series of representations or ruling ideas that inform contemporary American culture. Here the common worker, as exemplified by the title character THX (Robert Duvall), is a drugged-out drone, reduced to a number, removed from the purpose or product of his labor, and closely monitored and controlled by supervisors who can measure his respiration and heart rate, and even induce "brain lock" to shut down his actions, as if he were simply a machine that could be turned off at will. Racial "others" are presented either as foul-smelling dwarfs who inhabit the "outer shell" of this futuristic world or as black entertainers and holograms, substanceless figures whose primary function seems to be entertaining or serving a dominant white culture. Moreover, this futuristic society judges everyone and every action by bottom-line economic considerations, as we see when THX escapes from prison and is pursued only so far as the government's budgetary constraints allow. Through these figures and situations Lucas's film reveals a variety of class, racial, and economic tensions that characterize life in late-industrial capitalist society, tensions that most of our ideological representations, particularly our film narratives, typically work to dissolve or dismiss.

In the tradition of films like *Metropolis, Things to Come,* and *Logan's Run,* all works that carefully stylize their futuristic worlds and, in the process, set their reality at a safe aesthetic distance from our own, *THX 1138* too reaches for a distinct visual scheme, a highly stylized rendition of this other place. However, instead of the sort of monumental look we find to some degree in most utopian/dystopian films, it turns in another direction, offering a stark simplicity: cubicles and bare walls that frame the individual within severe rectangles, imprisoning the subject but also replicating the film frame itself and thereby rendering the person as doubly a "screened" image. In a further development of this design scheme, seen especially in the futuristic prison-without-walls to which THX is consigned, it emphasizes horizonless, open space that has the effect of reducing dimension, turning the self into a two-dimensional figure. More pervasive, though building to a similar effect, is the monochromatic color scheme. The constant white-on-white, recalling the initial descriptions of the future world in Huxley's *Brave New World*, not only suggests a sterile and lifeless world [Fig. 53], but also diminishes the individual by making the subject blend into the background and again appear two-dimensional. Individuality and individuation simply have no place here. The overall effect of this visual design scheme is to consistently frame subjects in an abstract space, removing them from a conventionally real world and, in the process, reconfiguring them as part of a derealized environment.

In keeping with this effect, *THX 1138* also brings into the foreground the very *role* of representation here and its implications for future life; for from its start this film manifests a kind of self-consciousness, evoking the mechanism of the movies and asking us to consider the effects of that mechanism. We see this impulse in the constant iconography of video screens, computer terminals, and surveillance technology, in the whole mechanics of reproduction on which the genre so often focuses. Of course, that sort of imagery hardly seems out of place here, since such icons typically fill our science fiction narratives. As Garrett Stewart notes, these various "mechanics of apparition," through their omnipresence, have indeed become a kind of generic signature.[17] However, *THX 1138*'s opening pushes the issue by establishing this context even before the narrative starts. Prior to the credits we see a clip from a trailer for the 1939 *Buck Rogers* serial, a preview that further nests itself in a reflexive context as Buck and his companions view images on a monitor that are lifted from the earlier utopian fantasy *Just Imagine* (1930), itself modeled on *Metropolis*. These images represent more than

Figure 53. THX is trapped in the sterile, horizonless prison of the futuristic world envisioned by *THX 1138* (1971).

just an homage or generic context for what follows, as the trailer's voice-over commentary makes clear through several alterations and emphases that let it speak to both the ensuing narrative and our own experience of it. Instead of the expected announcement that this story is about Buck Rogers "in the twenty-fifth century," the narrator places this tale "in the twentieth century," the time frame of Lucas's audience. It further describes Buck as "just an average guy," hardly the case for the serial hero, but precisely suggesting the soon-to-be introduced THX, while also implicating the film's audience. Finally, the trailer ends with a warning that we should not miss the "next exciting episode," entitled "Tragedy on Saturn." Of course, a "tragedy" is precisely what the film then depicts, situating it right here on Earth: a fall of humankind thanks to its technological hubris. This prologue, consequently, points directly toward the following narrative, establishes certain signposts that will prove useful for evaluating its events, and even suggests that we see it within a lineage of popular science fiction – one that often couches commentary about the most pressing cultural concerns in a fantastic and disarming context, at both a temporal and aesthetic distance from our world.

Though the rest of *THX 1138* has a decidedly reflexive thrust, it does not develop this dimension in any sort of nostalgic way, certainly never as forthrightly as in that prologue's homages to the serials and other science fiction ancestors. Rather, as Michael Pye and Lynda Myles note, the key scheme of its futuristic vision "is voyeuristic, full of cameras that pry, screens that show, observers heard casually asking for tighter close-ups."[18] In effect, it sets about establishing the mediated nature of this world by underscoring that "cinematic derealization" of which Paul Virilio speaks, while also demonstrating its effects on the individual. We see that the character THX is constantly watching a futuristic version of television, projected holograms that are comic, sexual, or extremely violent in nature, and whose ghostly materializations reflect on his own existence. The stupor into which he descends as he watches and the way he uses this entertainment to avoid interacting with his companion LUH (Maggie McOmie), even to substitute for her companionship, suggests how the media have become a kind of drug, a way of dropping out of or escaping the real world and an extension of that larger drug culture that this society, much like the one described in Huxley's *Brave New World,* has fostered in order to control its people. As noted above, the fact that the subjects of these programs are invariably black points to a way in which racism is implicated in and reified by the media, even institutionalized in this culture. In a kind of ultimate ideological development, the media have, it seems, simply become the source of all ideas here, constructors of the abstract or cinematized reality that these people, through some untold catastrophe or wrong turn in social development, have come to inhabit and to accept unquestioningly. Constant announcements on the job substitute for human conversation, comparing productivity for different sectors and encouraging laborers to "keep up the good work." An accident announcement smoothes over troubling events, assuring the workers that they have nothing to worry about, even as explosions occur, radiation warning signs light up, and chaos reigns. When a consumer wonders why a certain product is no longer available, a prepared message intones that "consumption is being standardized," but that one should still "Buy now. Buy more now. Buy . . . and be happy." Just as the children in this world are given their knowledge through a painless, intravenous drip plugged into their arms, so the people, through the almost imperceptible "drip" of the media, are being told how to think and act, and having constructed for them, in this "electronic labyrinth," a thoroughly unreal world.[19]

Of course, this vision of the future foregrounds our sense of the real in another register by pointing up our relationship to the movies themselves; for in its emphasis on that voyeuristic perspective and the mediated nature of this world, the film challenges us to be less naïve in the face of a mediated world, to be more wary about the sorts of images we consume, even those marketed to us by the movies. In fact, it suggests how the cinema and the media in general conspire to fashion an ersatz reality and situate us within it as subjects of their powerful and pervasive address; but that attitude seems to spring from a concern about our seemingly mindless consumption of and constant molding by media products, from the sense that we have let the media become our material and moral compass. Hence, the film's ultimate indictment of this derealized world is probably its transformation of the spiritual into the electronic, its substitution of a televised image for God. When our media pretend to offer us God, when the spiritual is effectively realized as a video image, complete with preprogrammed, random responses to our prayers, questions, and confessions, *THX 1138* suggests, we greatly need a new level of self-consciousness about the media and all their offerings. At the same time, the customary response of this god Om – "The blessings of the State, the blessings of the masses" – reminds us that the film's aim is not a simple political one; for such pseudocommunist cant invokes a kind of socialist dream turned nightmare, and it almost ironically clashes with the film's parallel excavation of the ideology of a capitalist society. Along with this sort of rhetoric we repeatedly hear on the sound track the interrogation, "Are you now or have you ever been," a phrase that obviously evokes the activities of the House Un-American Activities Committee amid the red scare of the 1940s and early 1950s, and in the process suggests the archconservative repression of that era. The juxtaposition of such politically loaded rhetoric throughout the narrative hints of a deep distrust of either extreme, and thus Lucas's valuation of the individual and individual freedom – a position reconsidered in a film like *Star Wars* – over conventional political solutions. Seen in this respect, the film takes on the coloring of an *ironic* utopia, in the manner of such works as *Logan's Run* or *Demolition Man* (1993). Moreover, its seemingly conflicted politics begin pointing to something far deeper than any naiveté on Lucas's part at this early stage in his career; they might sug-

gest how reality itself has begun to collapse all distinctions and become victim here.

Still, even that level of self-consciousness which the narrative repeatedly offers, the film suggests, may well prove elusive, thanks to our
own seemingly inevitable complicity in a world of mediation, through
our own tendency "to become film." As Virilio explains, "the development of the new technologies of digital imagery and of synthetic vision," nicely anticipated in this film, has resulted in "the ascendancy
of the 'reality effect' over a reality principle,"[20] that is, a tendency on
the cultural level to buy into or accept the ideology of a mediated reality, to embrace the virtual over the real. Thus our current human trajectory, he suggests, is to follow suit, to become on the individual level
much like what that cinematic "effect" implies. Here, then, is what I see
as the real key to *THX*'s reworking and interrogation of the utopian/
dystopian film: its sketching of the dimensions of this "cinematic" human, of what might or might not be on the human scale.

That sketch begins with the narrative's opening, for at that point we
first see THX as a grainy image on a screen. It is the perspective produced by the video camera in his medicine cabinet, and one that sub-
stantiates the "voyeuristic" description Pye and Myles attach to this
narrative. As we quickly see, this "medicinal" camera is just one of a
series of monitoring devices that are everywhere and that render this
world a kind of Foucaultian panopticon, that is, a realm much like the
nineteenth-century French prison Michel Foucault describes wherein
prisoners were always under surveillance as a way of enforcing social
discipline. At every turn – when he is at work, when he makes love to
LUH, when he is put on trial for "criminal drug evasion," when he is
being "conditioned" prior to imprisonment, even when he is escaping
from this world – THX becomes just one more fuzzy image on a video
monitor or radar screen, constantly under some sort of surveillance.
When he – or LUH – opens the medicine cabinet, an automatic electronic voice interrogates his video image, "What's wrong?" While that query
establishes the basic premise of this film – that there is indeed much
"wrong" with this, and indeed our own, world – the image itself establishes the key terms of that wrongness; for that grainy image, barely
recognizable as the figure we later see, points toward the abstract re-
figuration of the human – as a visual image, a function to be monitored
and manipulated, already a kind of derealized hologram.

Perhaps the key scene in fully developing this seeming fate of humanity is when THX is being reconditioned prior to imprisonment. As

in the case of the medicine-cabinet shots, he is here reconstituted as an image on a video screen, accompanied by several offscreen voices. Of the two voices we hear, one seems in charge, explaining to the other how to use a new mechanism for controlling human subjects, a device that allows for varying views – for example, zooming in and out on the subject, like a movie camera – and for complete physiological manipulation through an electronic "cortical bond." The other, admitting that he has "never had any experience with the Mark 8 board," clumsily handles the situation, as he asks questions, tries out new power and frequency variations on his control deck, and carelessly lets some of the settings go beyond the allowed maximums. We measure these effects largely by the video image of THX – a body distorted into all sorts of positions, contorted in pain, and set in uncontrollable movement. He screams in agony, but of course from their distant, detached position, his audience cannot hear and pays no attention in any case. He is, after all, for them simply a collection of pixels, a video image accompanying and illustrating a set of superimposed numerical readouts that take precedence. It is as if he has become a kind of electronic puppet, an electrically animated figure, a model of those same CGI effects that, thanks in great part to Lucas's later technological innovations, have come to dominate, even become the star attraction of, the contemporary science fiction film. Once translated into an image on a screen, the film suggests, an individual like THX no longer has any human value or substance; he is simply a product of the vision machine that is society.

After these conditioning experiments, THX is put into a futuristic prison that illustrates another dimension of that human trajectory "to become film." Once situated within the new "reality effect," the sort of virtual reality of the cinematized world, a true *fantasy* realm, Virilio argues, "we have lost our points of reference to orient ourselves"; as a result, "the de-realized man is a disoriented man."[21] Fittingly, therefore, imprisonment in such a world radically differs from traditional incarceration. A monochromatic open area with no horizon line and seemingly no walls, the prison offers no point of reference for orientation, no boundaries toward which one might move or try to cross, no restraints of any sort against which to struggle. It is the nearly perfect embodiment of the indeterminate realm of the fantastic, the realm where boundaries are constantly blurred or simply disappear, leaving one, like the reader of a fantasy tale, unsure how to make sense of this experience. The prison becomes little more than abstract space, like the dead white screen of a video monitor, and its inhabitants easily take on the characteristics of this situation, as we see SEN (Donald Pleasence) and others engaged in pointless philosophical debate, caught up in their own pointless abstractions. Underscoring that effect is the muttering of one anonymous prisoner: "deciding where we are . . . talking about leaving . . . trying to determine the future . . . it's ridiculous. What about keeping things livable here, now?" It is a feeble protest against the pull of abstraction, a weak call back to reality, but one that goes barely heard on the densely layered sound track and that never registers on the expressionless faces of the other prisoners. Set down in an abstract, totally fantastic world, conditioned out of their natural human reactions, these people have already become little more than abstract figures, having no more real substance or ability to act autonomously than subjects on a video screen.

Especially telling in this context is that one of the few figures able to see through this disorienting effect and even point a way out is one of those "impostor or something" figures that typically populate the genre. In this case it is an escaped hologram, a figure that explains how it "always wanted to be part of the real world" and so revolted against the electronic, cinematic, and spectacular status to which it had been relegated. As THX and SEN wander around in the all-white, dimensionless prison, apparently walking in circles thanks to their lack of orientation and with no prospects of escape, they encounter this figure coming from the opposite direction. From its contrary position, its rebellion against a cinematic reality, the hologram points the way out – looking directly into the camera, extending a finger toward us, and affirming, "That's the way out." This look of outward regard indicates not only a need to shift to the other side of that viewer–viewed relationship that characterizes this panopticon society, but also our own responsibility for such imprisonment (another version of fantastic "hesitation"), for being trapped in a derealized world. The ease with which this trio then escapes through an unlocked door suggests our very real ability to deal with this situation and echoes Lucas's view of our contemporary situation, that "If you want something bad enough, you can do it. We are living in cages with the doors open."[22]

When THX and his hologram guide attempt to hide from the authorities in what resembles a morgue, the hologram offers another observation on this world that helps explain why so many do "hesitate" and do not simply walk out of those cages or escape from their programming. After inspecting several of the bodies they find, it asks THX, "Did you know all the insides are gone from these people?" Since the hologram is an outsider, it seems able to see things that THX and the others cannot: not only the potential for escape, but also the paralyzing condition of its human counterparts. What it recognizes is not simply a hidden horrific activity – the harvesting of organs, the ultimate reduction of the human to a commodity – but another sort of reduction that is already widespread here. Through the forced use of drugs, the infusion of selected knowledge, and implanted cortical controls, all the inhabitants of this world are in the process of becoming all surface without any "insides," all image without any substantial sense of self or reality of their own – in effect, holograms with nothing beyond the surface, without even that will "to be part of the real."

Escaping from a world of abstraction, returning to the real, consequently, is not as simple as walking out an open door. SEN, for example, once separated from THX, loses his will and with it his direction. On the very brink of freedom, he becomes afraid and returns to a train that will take him back to his prison life. The hologram who has initially pointed a way out fares no better, for when pursued by the robotic police, it enters a car only to find that, because it is a creature of an abstract, electronic realm, it lacks the requisite practical knowledge of the real world – it has no idea how to drive and immediately crashes. In contrast, THX easily makes off in a car, disposes of several pursuing robotic policemen, and overcomes one of the shell dwellers who attacks him. Through physical force and personal willpower, through a determined physical confrontation with the real, he eludes both the various electronic monitors tracking his escape and the police, only to be warned, as he reaches a ventilation shaft leading to the Earth's surface, away from the artificial world and back to the real, "You have nowhere to go." With that warning, he pauses momentarily, as if embodying the very spirit of the fantastic text, suggesting again the "hesitation" between different interpretations of events that Todorov sets as its abiding and defining characteristic [Fig. 54].[23] Although THX's continued movement and his emergence on the surface, on a bright red landscape silhouetted against a large sun, seemingly resolves that hesitation, even this conclusion carries a weight of irresolution. Hardly an unalloyed affirmation, the film's final image of THX, a small figure posed against a fiery sun in the process of setting, suggests a precarious success at best and recalls another warning of his robot pursuers, that "you cannot survive outside the shell." Still, he stands in a first confrontation with the real, or simply with the natural world, and a single bird that flies past at least holds out a hope for life here, outside a constructed world that has also sought to reconstruct the human along its own derealized lines.

This escape from the cinematic may seem a rather strange vision for someone like George Lucas, who has proven himself the master of merchandising his own cinematic dreams, and whose best known and most successful fantasy of the future is set "A long time ago, in a galaxy far, far away." *THX 1138*'s cultural commentary, couched in warnings about our own embeddedness in a cinematic reality, simply does not square so easily with *Star Wars* action figures, sheets, costumes, napkins, wallpaper, nor with that film's lavish efforts at fashioning a variety of minutely detailed and convincing alien environments – at least not unless we see it within a properly fantastic context. Albert LaValley certainly senses some of this bothersome element in the earlier film, as he argues that, for too much of the narrative, *THX 1138*'s elaborate visuals take center stage and "subvert the drama of individual awakening, rendering it innocuous. We enjoy looking at the odd new underground world so much that we lose interest in Robert Duvall's plight."[24] Yet I would suggest that the visual design, as well as any tendency to become lost in it, to become caught up in a cinematic fascination, is very much the point here, just as the fact of a universe believably teeming with great varieties of life is the point in *Star Wars*. There is, very simply, a seductive lure to these designs of another world, a power that, as Jean Baudrillard has argued, emphasizes the potent appeal of the surface, "the charms and traps of appearances," that too often insinuate themselves in place of the "meaning" of discourse.[25] What Lucas tries to do in his earlier film is to effect a reversal of this surface effect by exploring "what's wrong" with our cinematic reality, whereas in *Star Wars,* a work we might see more in the marvelous vein, he has sought to use those "charms and traps" to construct an effective countermyth.

Of course, in the postmodern context "reality" itself always remains a troubling term, something that we usually feel compelled to qualify or put in quotation marks; for in an environment "unhinged by simulation," as Baudrillard, the apostle of the disappearance of the real, puts it, reality typically seems little more than a series of constructs[26] – or as Virilio more neatly puts it, the "reality principle" gives way to the "reality effect." In such a context, utopias and dystopias, themselves simply elaborate simulations, can seem almost redundant categories. Peter Ruppert in his study of the utopian influence points in this direction as he offers, "what remains of utopia once we accept the inevit-

Figure 54. THX hesitates in the midst of his long, difficult climb to freedom in *THX 1138.*

ability of . . . change?"[27] But a film like *THX 1138* offers some answer to that question. As its fantastic vision shows, what always remains is the desire to find a standard or yardstick by which we might measure out human desire and aspiration, something outside the scope of what Virilio terms "an entirely cinematic vision of the world."[28] Prodded by that "hesitation" central to the fantastic proper, we confront conflicting pressures. In need of some measure, a way of gauging our desires for another place – a locale that, we should remember, always turns out to be "no place"[29] – yet haunted by the vanishing nature of such measures, the seeming disappearance of the real, we are left to consider, as the key to change, the very fabric of our futuristic worlds. In the face of such a difficult context, utopian/dystopian films like *THX 1138* or even more recent works such as *The Truman Show, Dark City* (both 1998), or *The Matrix* (1999) can point to a constructed, mediated, ghostly, even cinematic world, something *substituted* for the real.[30] Moreover, even as they acknowledge and lay bare that derealized world, they also begin to suggest an alternative to a destiny that promises to derealize us as well. In such fantastic worlds – and since we seem to have so much trouble today talking about the real, perhaps *only* there – a *human* reality can begin to reappear.

It is a reality that Lucas's film measures out for us in a variety of other ways, as we can see by taking a final look at it through the glass of several of those central themes of the genre. As I have suggested earlier, throughout the science fiction film we can find, perhaps surprisingly, an emphasis on feelings, emotions, and passion as a counterweight to the form's iconic enthronement of a reason–technology–science triad. The implication is that this emphasis, what I have termed the "kiss and tell" motif, helps to weigh our humanness against the scale of a thoroughly technologized environment, one whose very system of values seems to derive from the world of science. It is a system made most explicit in *THX 1138* through the various ways in which society has effectively quantified the individual: identified as a letter–number designation, measured in terms of organ-donor potential, understood as a series of numerical readouts on a superimposed grid, evaluated in terms of the cost of capture and imprisonment; yet that quantification speaks only to a greater reduction of the human to a piece of the larger social machine, or what I have here termed the "vision machine" that is this future society. In compensation, the film offers an awakening of the sexual and the emotional dimensions of THX's life. As LUH prods him to withdraw from his mandatory drugs (he is eventually charged by the state with "criminal drug evasion"), he enters into an intimate relationship with her. The repeated images of the isolated person, framed within frames, give way to extreme close-ups of THX and LUH in embrace, touching each other and exploring their bodies. The flattening white-on-white color scheme is disrupted by the play of varied flesh tones. It is precisely in these "touch-and-tell" scenes that the individual eventually emerges – an individual who finally finds meaning in his relationship not to "the masses," but to another.

THX 1138's indictment of this emotionally deadening environment, one that has sought to sunder the self from the real, finds further development in that "stop trying to rationalize" motif described in the introductory chapter (§ "Genre Determinations"). As we have already noted, helping to create the "reality effect" of this world is a pervasive media environment, one that offers constant announcements, intrudes an interrogative voice into the home, and lures the individual into a kind of public discourse. In what clearly seems a variation on Orwellian "doublespeak," a public voice deflects consumer complaints with the reassurance that "consumption is being standardized" for greater satisfaction. The robotic police, whom we several times see beating individuals with clubs and shocking them with cattle prods, assure THX that they "only want to help" him. The medicine cabinet in THX and LUH's apartment not only asks "what's wrong" every time it is opened, but also apparently produces a printout elsewhere, a report on their responses. In addition, as we have already noted, this culture has created an ersatz god, Om, little more than a broadcast image to which the people are encouraged to confess their disaffections and thus their "sins" against the masses. The overall effect is of a public voice, a dominating discourse whose function is to explain away all problems, to dissolve them – like the suddenly audible voice of ideology itself – in a calming message, to constantly assure the drugged populace that there is indeed nothing wrong here. More than that, this public voice seems designed to evoke a complicit voice from the people, a discourse through which they are encouraged to assist in rendering everything – even every human tic or urge – as part of society's sensible regime; yet that "sense," that cultural rationale, is also precisely the problem, part of the generating principle behind the very dissatisfying reality effect that *is* this dystopian world.

What *THX 1138* offers us, then, is a fantastic vision clearly focused on the very problematic relationship we have both to our own world and to those we might conjure up as alternatives. Here, just as Orwell and others have prophesied, we find reason mobilized to produce a new and ultimately deadening reality, even as human feelings are essentially proscribed because of their potential challenge to that regime. Still, in holding open the possibility for a way out, for the promise of life beyond "the shell," the film also emphasizes the fluid, uncertain nature of this fantastic reality, what Rosemary Jackson, in an effort to suggest a certain indeterminacy, simply calls "the unnatural."[31] It reminds us that the utopian/dystopian narrative, like the various ideologies that subtly shape our thinking, is finally all about the imaginary ways in which we experience our world. At the same time, it suggests our own ability to contest the power of that experience, to speculate, in the precise sense of the fantastic, on what might or might not be, now or in the future.

5

The Science Fiction Film as Marvelous Text

Close Encounters of the Third Kind

Help! I'm lost. – *Close Encounters*

As Rosemary Jackson emphasizes, the fantastic text seems to have, as its underlying purpose, a desire to put "the real under scrutiny."[1] In offering its alternative version of everyday experience or calling into question the rules that would seem to govern that everyday world, it transports us to a new territory – at least "no longer in Kansas," as Dorothy tells Toto – or perhaps more precisely into a kind of liminal position wherein we must start figuring out the rules anew. Essentially, it *fantasizes us.* That effect, I would suggest, becomes especially evident in and significant for the marvelous dimension of fantasy, which focuses on forces from outside the human realm, forces that, in other contexts, we have traditionally associated with the supernatural, that unexpectedly come into play and compel us to reconceptualize our world by seeing it as part of some larger and more complex realm. As conventional explanations prove unavailing, the effect of that otherness or outside intervention typically proves disorienting – both to characters and to the audience – as we see in the above comment by a character in Steven Spielberg's first science fiction effort, *Close Encounters of the Third Kind* (1977). Faced with a power outage, power company employee Roy Neary (Richard Dreyfuss) has set about his assigned task of finding the problem, fixing it, and restoring power and thus light to his world – of bringing it back to normalcy. However, not only can he not find the problem, he cannot even find himself – that is, where he is at present, his coordinates on a map. In this case another kind of supernatural force has intervened: the science fiction version of the supernatural, the alien other, which has almost immediately and incomprehensibly unhinged his reality and left him crying out in the darkness for help, for reorientation, for a better map of what now seems a far more mystifying reality. It is on this effect that I want to focus primarily as we turn our attention to marvelous instances of the science fiction film.

As was suggested in Chapter 1, we might see any science fiction films that examine the impact of forces outside the human realm, that depict the conventional encounter with alien beings or other worlds, for example, as corresponding to the marvelous branch of the fantastic. This category would thus include near-apocalyptic narratives like *War of the Worlds* (1953), as well as ones with an almost theological dimension like *Contact* (1997). The former, adapted from H. G. Wells's famous novel, effectively shatters the boundaries of the human world with its Martian invaders who devastate Earth and nearly wipe out humanity. Its cataclysmic images, along with vague clues as to what the Martian invaders look like, effectively point up how vulnerable we are to forces and beings completely beyond our conception. The latter film, taken from Carl Sagan's novel of the same title, explores the contemporary fascination with the possibility of powerful alien beings in a far different way, not as a story of invasion and destruction but as one of scientific curiosity and even invitation. Moreover, it pairs its story of an astronomer's search for signs of some intelligent life in the universe with the larger question of humanity's spiritual yearnings, using both types of search to point up our desire to find meaning in our existence. Despite their external differences, then, texts like *War of the Worlds* and *Contact* effectively draw on that marvelous impulse, as they set about expanding the scope of our knowledge, especially the knowledge of our own nature.

To focus this discussion more precisely, I want to concentrate on Spielberg's *Close Encounters,* a film that, along with George Lucas's *Star Wars* of the same year, helped bring the science fiction genre back to the high level of popularity it had enjoyed in the 1950s. It is, of course, a relatively early work from a figure whom we now closely associate with fantasy, thanks to his subsequent direction of films like *Raiders of the Lost Ark* (1981), *E. T, the Extraterrestrial* (1982), and *Jurassic Park* (1993), as well as to a series of fantasy efforts produced through his company Amblin Entertainment, particularly the three *Back to the Future* films (1985, 1989, 1990). *Close Encounters* began as a series of conversations between Spielberg and producers Michael and Julia Phillips about the impact of UFOs on public consciousness, conversations that Spielberg eventually fashioned into a script about mysterious visitations and sudden compulsions, shared by people around the world, to visualize a mountain in America and journey to it, as if on a pilgrimage to some newfound holy place – an attitude quite in keeping with what we might see as a marvelous dimension of the science fiction film. Although Spielberg would stock his story with a host of easily recognized conventions of the science fiction genre – mysterious activations of machinery, official denials of alien existence, alien contact with a select few humans, unnatural behavior by those few – that story did mark a rather different turn in American attitudes toward the alien or other. Here, in contrast to the many stories of alien invasion and disaster that through the early cold-war period dominated the genre – a body of work that had once led Susan Sontag to characterize science fiction as representing the "Imagination of Disaster"[2] – and different too from the epic treatment of other cultures we find in its contemporary, *Star Wars,* we find a story of belief, acceptance, and quasi-religious affirmation that humans are not alone in the universe, not really "lost," as the film's Roy Neary initially fears.

For Columbia Pictures, doing such a story on the large and costly scale Spielberg envisioned was a gamble. In fact, its $19 million budget marked it as the most expensive Columbia production to date. At this point too, science fiction was not a particularly marketable proposition: Only the double box-office punch of *Star Wars* and *Close Encounters* really changed that market. Moreover, entrusting such a project to a director with only three feature films to his credit, albeit one of them the great box-office success *Jaws* (1975), was also risky business. As fellow filmmaker John Milius predicted at the time, "It will either be the best Columbia film, or it will be the last Columbia film."[3] While neither best nor last, *Close Encounters,* like *Star Wars,* did generate enormous revenue – it grossed $300 million worldwide – and won numerous awards,[4] results that suggest it served Columbia well and that its marvelous vision struck a most responsive chord in its audience.

Before looking at this film in more detail, we should acknowledge that, at first glance, the science fiction genre must seem a most unlikely site for the development of marvelous themes; for as Jackson, following Todorov's lead, reminds us, the marvelous text typically will "invest otherness with supernatural qualities,"[5] with the sort of paranormal, transcendent, or even religious dimensions that the reason–science–technology triad would seem intent on banishing or simply replacing with its own human-centered regime. In his effort to explain the appeal of science fiction, however, Damon Knight would strike a similar chord, as he explains that "our undiminished wonder at the mystery which surrounds us is what makes us human," and that science fiction's inherent "sense of wonder" specifically allows us to "approach that mystery."[6] Certainly, most science fiction invests science itself with that sense of wonder – as we muse over what strange things our science might someday bring to pass – or links science to it through the task of explaining away the seemingly inexplicable or supernatural. We should not be surprised, then, to note that the marvelous is precisely where Todorov makes room for science fiction narratives in his fantastic schema. He describes a distinct subgroup of this category that he terms the "instrumental marvelous," stories that circumscribe their events in a rational vantage, even as they describe the operation of "laws which contemporary science does not acknowledge."[7] Of course, not all science fiction films operate in this realm, not all draw their central premise from the positing of a newly discovered set of "laws." For example, we might consider a number of works that simply extrapolate from the known and abide by the scientific laws that govern our world, particularly works focusing on space exploration such as *Destination Moon* (1950), *Countdown* (1968), and *Marooned* (1969). Consequently, I believe that simply taking on face value Todorov's placement, positioning all or even most science fiction narratives in this category, would help very little in clarifying our sense of the genre. By viewing the subset of alien-invasion/encounter films as versions of the marvelous tale, though, we can begin to ask important and differentiating questions about them. The alien-encounter films are ultimately about a causality that transcends the human, that pulls us out of the everyday, that requires us to move beyond and to interrogate our normal experience of the real, every bit as much as if they were testaments about a spiritual experience. While this subgroup usually does not implicate the sort of spiritual or supernatural powers that we so easily find in many horror narratives – in films such as *Nosferatu* (1922), *The Exorcist* (1973), and *The Omen* (1976), for example – their specific focus on "the other" challenges our sense of the real and the everyday in much the same fashion as do texts that we would more readily identify as marvelous.

Of course, a number of these other-themed films actually do move in just such a conventionally marvelous direction, do at least implicate some sort of transcendent order and thus offer a convenient jumping-off point for this discussion. Since the extraterrestrial encounter and its consequent contravening of known "laws" and cultural traditions provide a mechanism for posing the question of a kind of ultimate otherness, resonances of the supernatural should not seem completely out of place; in fact, such references often surface as metaphors in these works. Among the science fiction films that do make an almost literal "leap of faith," we might consider a most obvious example, the British film *The Man Who Could Work Miracles* (1936). Based on an H. G. Wells story, it begins as a gentle fantasy about an English shop clerk upon whom a trio of gods bestows nearly unlimited power. From this premise it develops a science fiction trajectory as the clerk then uses that power in an effort to create a utopian society, but, as in many similar narratives, he also winds up nearly destroying Earth. More recently, we have seen variations on this motif in a number of American films that push the marvelous impulse to its logical extreme, blurring the boundaries between the world of science and technology, the traditional ground of science fiction, and the spiritual world. Most obvious in this category are the *Star Wars* films with their positing of "the Force" as a kind of spiritual underpinning for all existence and demonstration of its power over even the greatest technological accomplishments of the Empire, as we see in the Force-guided destruction of the Death Star at the end of the first film. Perhaps more to the point, however, are such works as *2010* (1984), the sequel to Stanley Kubrick's *2001: A Space Odyssey* (1968), which transforms the earlier film's mysterious monoliths into runic messages from God; *Star Trek V: The Final Frontier* (1989), wherein the starship *Enterprise* is hijacked in an effort to reach the planet where God supposedly resides; and *Contact* (1997), which describes how transmissions from outer space revive a spiritual dimension in an atheistic scientist. These and similar films, because of their very exaggeration of the marvelous impulse, make the satisfactions of that branch of the fantastic all the more apparent; for these marvelous texts achieve, as Todorov explains, an almost "impossible union," as they allow audiences to "believe without really believing,"[8] to have the pleasures of hope, of the possibility of the future, and of otherness while still anchored within a skeptical present – or in these instances, in the world of modern science.

That sense of the mysterious and, perhaps more accurately, even the mystical, of a world almost eager for some intervention by supernatural forces, easily resonates in *Close Encounters of the Third Kind* and suggests its marvelous character. In the conventional fashion of so many other works about alien encounters – films that ascribe either life-affirming (*The Day the Earth Stood Still,* 1951) or apocalyptic (*Independence Day,* 1996) possibilities to those encounters – it offers us a world that is perceptibly like our own, certainly one steeped in recognizable popular culture icons of the era, and yet also undeniably different, a world at least where it no longer seems possible to deny the presence of mysteries in that culture or to explain them away as mis-observed or misunderstood natural phenomena. It is, in fact, a world that seems designed to justify faith in a most fundamental sense, as be-lief in an order beyond easy demonstration, beyond common reason, or here, simply beyond the human. This quasi-religious ground for the narrative was quickly recognized by critics, as is apparent in Stanley Kauffmann's review that describes *Close Encounters* as "not so much a film as an event in the history of faith."[9] Yet for those same reasons, and particularly for the way it cobbles together and capitalizes on var-ious popular forms of the spiritual experience and mixes them with obvious generic conventions, the film was also scorned. Andrew Gor-don offers the best summary of this view in an early article on the film, wherein he describes it as "a purified, Disneyized version of religion" and as a commercially adroit exploitation of 1970s pop mysticism and religious euphoria. It cashes in on several recent and closely related phenomena: the revival of "born again," fundamentalist religion; the popularity of various gurus and cult leaders in what has been called "the spiritual supermarket" of contemporary America; Erich Von Dani-ken's series of books and films on gods from outer space; the presum-ably inexplicable disappearances in the Bermuda Triangle; and, finally, the persistent UFO cultists.[10]

For our purposes, of course, we need not embrace either of these points of view. We do not have to determine whether the film affords a genuine postmodern version of religious mysticism or simply capital-izes, in a rather obvious way, on what we can clearly recognize as the contemporary appetite for new versions of such an experience, unbur-dened by the baggage of traditional religion. It is enough to recognize that *Close Encounters* follows in the long tradition of marvelous narra-tives that from the outset and in many different ways seem to present otherness within a context of "supernatural qualities."

The primary representation of that otherness, the alien figure, is the obvious focal point for any inquiry into the marvelous. To suggest the larger, cultural dimensions of this representation, we might turn to Ed-ward Said's classic treatment of the other in Western culture. Drawing on the West's depiction of the oriental and of orientalia, he argues that all such representations of the other proceed not from "an inert fact of nature," but rather from what he terms a particular "style of thought," one in which we manage "to produce" the other that we desire to see.[11] If we look at the depiction of the alien or extraterrestrial, a very stark conception of otherness, as a construction that we culturally fashion and a reflection of that fashioning mind, then, we can begin to understand better how the marvelous narrative works for us, how it places the producing subject (or re-places that "lost" self) in a secure position. The alien-encounter narrative can, of course, take many forms, each predicated on a different sense of the other. The invasion narrative, often reflecting a conservative ideology – a suspicion and even fear of the other – suggests one line of development. Exemplified by films like *The War of the Worlds,* the various versions of *Invasion of the Body Snatchers* (1956, 1978, 1993), and *Starship Troopers* (1997), with their aliens variously depicted as squidlike, vegetable, and insect, respectively, this line conventionally visualizes the other as pointedly nonhuman, often as something from which we naturally recoil. In stark contrast, we might think of the many benevolent-alien films and those that would paint the universe in the colors of a liberal politics, as simply another sort of multicultural society – especially works like *Star Wars*, *The Last Starfighter* (1984), and *Batteries Not Included* (1987). In either case, we should emphasize what that other represents, not simply as a correspondence to something in the real world but as a powerful "style of thought." It is evidence of a way of generically constructing all that is outside of the self, which ultimately reflects much about the producing self.

One of *Close Encounters*'s chief accomplishments is the way in which it mines both of those generic veins described above, as if it were trying to be all things to all science fiction viewers. The sense of mystery established at the opening of the film, with the discovery of the famous lost squadron of torpedo bombers incongruously set down in the Sonora Desert in the middle of a duststorm, is clearly linked to a sense of possible menace – the danger of the unknown and the inexplicable. In fact, testifying to Spielberg's thorough knowledge of the genre, the setting, sound effects, and general construction of the scene echo a similar discovery scene at the start of another famous "invasion" film, this one about giant mutant ants, *Them!* (1954). As the narrative advances, Spielberg employs a variety of tricks, reminiscent especially of the horror film and worked out in his previous movies, like *Duel* (1971) and *Jaws,* to further that eerie tone and manipulate our sense of the other. Electrical appliances that turn on and off, as if moved by some unseen power, mechanical toys that suddenly start up by themselves, blinding lights from various mysterious or unknown sources, strange noises, jump cuts for shock effect – these are the sorts of effect that we encounter at every turn in *Close Encounters.* When combined with the justifiable terror of the mother, Jillian Guiler (Melinda

Dillon), whose four-year-old son Barry (Carey Guffey) is apparently kid-
napped by the aliens, as well as the antics of the protagonist Roy Neary,
who seems practically possessed by alien forces, these effects build up
a consistently disturbing and even threatening context. They lead us
to construct a particular view of the aliens, one clearly informed by the
long tradition of alien-invasion films. We expect that, when the aliens
finally appear, they will represent a powerful physical threat and radically jeopardize our human hegemony. Their *unseen* presence, in short,
speaks to our fears of the unknown, of the other, and, perhaps more
disconcertingly, to a sense of our own frailty as a species.

Neverthelesss, as the narrative unfolds, these conventionally menacing signposts are increasingly matched by other incidents of a different tenor, and finally an alien appearance, that indicate that all of those
mysterious manifestations around which Spielberg has constructed his
fantastic frissons have just been signs of a cosmic – and certainly a
directorial – playfulness. In this context we might consider Neary's en-
countering others who not only believe in the aliens but find their light-
show-like manifestations not so much threatening as entertaining, or
the masses in India who react to signs of alien presence as if they
marked an extraordinary religious moment. Little Barry Guiler's innocent delight (as Andrew Gordon suggests, we could see the name as indicating a certain *guilelessness* the adults lack)[12] at the aliens' appearance also points the way here, suggesting that receptivity rather than
fear might be a more appropriate response. Most important, though,
is the very appearance of the aliens in the film's final sequence. In preparation for this appearance, the narrative gradually transfers the real
sense of otherness from the aliens to the government and its forces –
the police, army, scientists – all of whom are working, at times quite
violently, to "protect" the people by covering up the visitors' presence
[Fig. 55]; and that transference frees up our expectations, opens other
possibilities for the aliens' appearance. When their great mother ship
lands on Devils Tower [Fig. 56], it debarks a number of small, childlike
figures who seem strangely illuminated as they freely mingle with the
humans gathered there. Not the "Devil's" minions, not even insectlike,
and hardly a threat, they are creatures of innocence, of playfulness, of
wonder – figures who bring a new light of understanding to humanity,
who represent a quite different "style of thought" than that at which
the narrative initially hinted.

Along with this shift in the presentation of the other, *Close Encounters* also develops a shifting perception of self, as the aliens, in the usual manner of that "impostor or something" motif, serve to reflect an

Figure 55. The official effort to track and make "sense" out of the UFO visitors in *Close Encounters of the Third Kind* (1977).

"other" or different sense of our own nature – one that, the narrative suggests, has typically gone repressed or simply never been recognized. The particular challenge that the other brings out in this film – and perhaps even more pointedly in Spielberg's later film *E.T.* – can be glimpsed in the childlike nature of Roy Neary. Early in the film we see him playing with toy trains; it is, we suppose, his hobby, although it also suggests a similarity between the father and his children, a similarity that has largely been overlooked or forgotten. He is, as various other details begin to suggest, simply an open and playful person, a most fitting choice by the aliens to receive their message. His character is far more receptive, more childlike than most; unlike so many others in his society, he has never quite lost contact with his own childlike innocence and sense of wonder. At the same time, we should note the curious manner in which the film treats Neary's children. They are depicted not, as we might expect, simply as additional models of some innocent state to which we need to return, but almost like little savages

Figure 56. A "marvelous" intervention into the rational world, as an alien ship arrives at the scientific installation atop Devils Tower in *Close Encounters of the Third Kind.*

– loud, ill-mannered, and having scant respect for their parents. Himself a child of modern suburban America, Spielberg recognizes the often disturbing effects that our culture can have on its young with its self-absorbed parents, reliance on television as teacher and babysitter, and generally chaotic home life. Indeed, he would later be involved in a project that underscored and capitalized on the potentially horrific nature of American suburbia in *Poltergeist* (1982), a film he both wrote and produced. Through the comparison of father and children here he seems to be tentatively mapping that cultural territory, suggesting how, even as we misplace the innocence in ourselves, we are also warping it in our children, in those who should naturally possess it, as we cut them off from any real sense of adulthood or responsibility. However, as an alternative, *Close Encounters* does hold out a key potential, a possibility for a combination of growth and renewal that might result from the alien/other experience and thus from the new sense of reality it brings. The film suggests that Neary and, by extension, the rest of humankind, might grow to a new maturity, one in which he will be able to maintain a sense of that child within, or at least of that childlike wonder and naiveté that are ultimately necessary for opening up to and understanding the human place in the universe.

More than just, as Andrew Gordon suggests, a limning of "the beatitude of the crazy or of the childish innocent,"[13] then, *Close Encounters* draws from this child imagery an important sense of what the encounter with the other (both alien and "other" self) might entail. It forces us to reconsider our own nature, particularly the ways in which we have drawn unnecessary and debilitating limits around it. Here, for example, we see how the government has itself become a kind of protective parent: determining what we should know; trying to insulate us from any disturbing and thus potentially dangerous revelations by explaining away UFOs and other mysterious encounters as sightings of military aircraft; staging elaborate dramas, such as a deadly anthrax outbreak, to frighten off people from the Devils Tower site; even gassing civilians to get them "out of the way" of its "expert" efforts at dealing with the extraterrestrials – in sum, doing all it can to keep the people in a preternaturally childish state. It is that *abnormal* childishness, though, that finally seems so dangerous and even incapacitating here, and a fundamental target of *Close Encounters*'s marvelous vision; for it clearly traps people in a most unnatural condition, so that they become like Roy's wife, Bonnie (Teri Garr), who simply "cannot cope" with life's pressures, or like his kids, who seem incapable of ever moving into responsible adulthood. What is finally needed, the film offers, is a kind of growth and development *through* the innocent and open vision of the child. Thus Spielberg suggests in an interview that we might think of the aliens as having "come all this way perhaps to observe growing up in the twentieth century."[14]

Neary illustrates this process through the radical transformation he undergoes in the course of his encounters with aliens. His initial behavior, wherein he too seems interested simply in play, shuts out others, including his own family, and seems quite literally "lost," gradually gives way to a sense of serious purpose. Singled out, marked with the stigmata – burns from his first "close encounter" with the alien ship – that both indicate his special state and lend another religious note to this experience, he grows aware of others around him who have shared his experience and becomes involved with them – especially with Jillian, the mother who has lost her child to the aliens. That awareness and involvement enable him to move beyond the limits of his suburban subdivision, to take directed action, as we see when he is able to cut across country, to navigate by dead reckoning – as if guided by Spielberg's own version of "the Force" – in order to avoid government barricades and reach Devils Tower. He in effect grows up in the course of

Figure 57. Roy Neary is greeted by the childlike alien visitors of *Close Encounters of the Third Kind.*

this story, a result rendered dramatically when Neary, described by Andrew Gordon as far too much like a "Cub Scout,"[15] receives the same outfit as all of the carefully chosen government representatives – all tall, square-jawed, and muscular – and is permitted to march into the main alien spacecraft with this scientifically selected group for a journey into the unknown and into the future. It is a journey that represents humanity's own growth into something like cosmic adulthood, and one that begins, appropriately enough, with these aliens who look very much like children [Fig. 57], who seem possessed of the same sort of wonder at our species as we earlier see registered on the face of little Barry Guiler and, eventually, on the faces of many of the scientists gathered at the Devils Tower site. Only from such an innocent and open attitude, a truly *marvelous* perspective, as opposed to the closed model of government response, the film suggests, can the necessary growth of the species begin.

What that growth represents in this case is far more than just some sort of individual development or personal maturation, however. Although certainly steeped in the classical Hollywood narrative of individual striving, Spielberg ultimately has a broader cultural intent here. Seen in the marvelous context outlined above, this narrative of growth signals the far larger need of the species to find itself in the vastness of the universe. *Close Encounters* develops this aspect of its marvelous story on the one hand through its repeated dislocations. When Roy is initially sent out to deal with a sudden and inexplicable power outage, he quickly finds that he is facing not one "grid" that has gone out, but *all* the grids in the area. With all grids equally blacked out, there is no longer any point of reference for him, and it is little wonder that he quickly finds himself "lost," much as does the character THX when in the white, dimensionless prison of *THX 1138* (1971). *Close Encounters* further develops this sense of disorientation, shows it to be a common modern condition, and even extends it to the audience through a series of jump cuts that shift us about to a variety of Earth locations – the Sonora Desert in Mexico, the Gobi Desert in China, a plain in India, various locales in the United States, including atop Devils Tower – all helping to develop a larger sense of mystery and dislocation here. At these and various other sites, though, as well as in the brains of selected humans throughout the world, there are also traces of location, hints not only of an alien presence but also of a rendezvous point, a place of answers, where we might come together and no longer feel "lost." Hence, much of the narrative focuses on that mysterious pilgrimage of different peoples, for reasons they cannot comprehend, to the strange natural formation of Devils Tower. Andrew Gordon offers an interesting reading of this site choice. He describes the "ambiguously named" Devils Tower as one of a number of similarly ambiguous effects in the film – elements that function essentially *as effects,* like the visceral thrills of an amusement park ride.[16] This reading speaks directly to a weakness that has often been charged to Spielberg's films, and particularly to the Indiana Jones films (1981, 1984, 1989), which have, in fact, been turned into attractions at both Disneyland and Walt Disney World. Although such visceral thrills are indeed central to most of his films and one key to their popular appeal, we might note in those effects evidence of a deeper design at work, in *Close Encounters* just as in many of Spielberg's other films: a subtle sense of how much we are

indeed afraid of the unknown, how we invest it with a sense of foreboding or menace, and, consequently, of how we recoil from rather
than approach with the proper sense of wonder those phenomena that
might lead us to a better understanding of our world.

This concerted, worldwide movement of peoples to a single place,
a *meaningful* location, responds to a comment we hear several times
from Neary: "This means something." Troubled by that vague moun-
tainous image in his head and determined to work out its significance,
he repeatedly tries to visualize it: in mashed potatoes on his dinner
plate, with mud shoveled into a child's swimming pool, through model-
ing clay atop his train table. It is an effort to wrest meaning out of this
vision from above, and one whose success also points toward the usual climax for the marvelous tale, the attainment of a kind of reorientation within a larger, typically supernatural scheme. As the novelist
Walker Percy has put it, this sort of attainment marks a shift in humans
from feeling as if we are "lost in the cosmos"[17] to a sense of our place
in that scheme to which we have been suddenly awakened.

This sense of the impact of the other, its effect on that widespread
"lost" condition, is perhaps most dramatically represented when the
team of experts studying the recent upsurge in mysterious events inter-
cepts and tries to interpret an alien message. Represented as a series
of numbers, this message seems to stump the team of experts until
an assistant, fittingly a translator for this international group, suggests
that the numbers might indicate lines of latitude and longitude, coordinates on Earth. The subsequent search for a map that would allow
them to check this simple hypothesis produces nothing, only the suggestion that a large globe might be useful. The scene in which they
obtain that globe, by breaking into an office, forcefully ripping it from
its mounts, and then rolling it around seems most telling. It literalizes
what has happened, with the world violently displaced from its usually stable position, liberated from the conventional perspective that has
circumscribed it. Breaking free from that old perspective, countering
that "lost" feeling, it seems, is a difficult task, requiring force, an imaginative leap, even a willingness to break the rules; but the result is a better map – of the sort Neary sought earlier in the film – a new sense of
our place in the universe.

This marvelous pattern we have traced should also begin to suggest
another dimension of the narrative, as it powerfully resonates with one
more of those key science fiction themes discussed earlier, what I have
termed the "stop trying to rationalize" motif of the genre. *Close Encoun-*

ters's take on this theme, its own effort at calling into question a single-minded rational world view, is interestingly lodged largely in a sympathetic scientist figure, the Frenchman Claude Lacombe. In a clever bit of casting, Spielberg casts as Lacombe his fellow director François Truffaut, a figure well known for his sympathetic perspective toward children (as is evidenced by such films as *The 400 Blows* [1959], *The Wild Child* [1969], and *Small Change* [1976]). Here, he is a figure pointedly open to the naïve or innocent perspective, such as that of Neary and little Barry, and thus quite unlike the many scientists who populate this genre's films of the 1950s, those whose expertise, like that of the people who helped construct the atomic bomb, is unquestionably on the side of the military. Michael Pye and Lynda Myles point up this difference as they note how he "resists all military schemes to harm the handful of human beings called by chance to meet the aliens. Yet he is never seen as a scientist. When someone has to translate those figures beamed from space into a location on Earth, the answer is found by the scientist's interpreter. . . . The scientist is more shaman than laboratory worker. He is full of wonder, not calculation."[18] In this respect, he plays a key role in establishing the marvelous atmosphere of the film, as his point of view, set in parallel to that of Neary, motivates much of the sense of wonder here. We follow Lacombe around the world, as he checks on a variety of mysteries, such as the reappearance of Flight 19's planes in Mexico, the inexplicable appearance of a missing ship in the Gobi Desert, and the spontaneous gathering of great crowds in northern India, all chanting and pointing to the sky. He becomes, in every one of these instances, a measure of what that strictly rational perspective we typically associate with the scientist cannot compass, while at the same time he also reminds us of the true role of the scientist or researcher. We might more precisely think of Lacombe, then, as a scientist in the fundamental sense of the term, as someone who, moved by a sense of wonder, is dedicated to *knowing* through whatever methods will avail.

At the same time, and in a way that pointedly speaks to a growing distrust of the establishment in this era – and, we might remember, at a time before Spielberg himself had become firmly entrenched as part of the filmmaking establishment – Lacombe is set in opposition to the government. As we have noted, the government seems to have decided that its task is twofold: investigating these mysteries and trying to defend the citizenry against them, as if anything that seemed to fall outside of the rational regime as it is currently established – UFOs, mys-

Figure 58. The "light show" conclusion to *Close Encounters of the Third Kind.*

terious appearances and disappearances, strange physical or psychic phenomena – would pose a threat to its own power. The government, consequently, becomes a force of rationalization, of cover-ups, of hiding the truth behind a seemingly reasonable facade. While Lacombe sets about trying to find a new way of understanding – an adaptation of the Keidaly hand signals, for example – the government tries to cut off that understanding; while he reaches for what is effectively a new language, even something outside of what we would typically think of as the rational scheme – here it is variously the play of musical tones or shifting patterns of light – the government resorts to bureaucratic jargon and lies, to the old language of obfuscation. "Trying to rationalize" or "talking sense," talking in the old way, in a way that supports the status quo, finally gives way to talking imaginatively, to opening up whole new lines of communication that might lift humanity to another level of development. In this context, it seems only fitting that the narrative ends not with any sort of rational formulation of this experience but rather with a completely nonverbal experience – the movement inside the giant alien ship that resembles a mandala, with what many critics of the time dismissed as simply a psychedelic "light show" [Fig. 58].

Almost in spite of the critics, Spielberg would eventually extend that spectacular visual conclusion in his reworked version of the film, *Close Encounters of the Third Kind: The Special Edition*, released in 1980. Given $2 million by Columbia to rework the film, he added thirteen minutes of additional footage, while also trimming a number of original scenes. As Spielberg explains, in addition to interpolating material he had been unable to shoot or use earlier for various reasons, he wanted to demonstrate that "film is not necessarily a dry-cement process. I have the luxury of retouching the painting."[19] Foremost among the additions he made is an extended ending wherein Neary enters the alien mother ship and marvels at the literally marvelous visions therein – essentially an even more elaborately developed "light show," created by special-effects expert Robert Swathe. Though Spielberg has asserted that this "Special Edition" is the only authentic version of the film, we should note that Columbia's parent company, Sony Pictures, through its Film Restoration department, would create yet another version of the film in 1999, one that digitally remastered the sound track and combined footage from both the original release version and the "Special Edition," but which also eliminated that end scene inside the mother ship.

Nevertheless, that ending – in either form – seems noteworthy for its emphasis on a vision that transcends all language, even the supposedly universal Keidaly signals. In it we might see a rendering of Todorov's own effort at not becoming too essentialist in his description of the categories of fantasy. As he reminds us, when we talk about the fantastic experience, we should be careful to "insist as much upon the perception" of the fantastic object or event "as upon the object" that carries the fantastic charge.[20] We are thus always implicated in a pattern of what he terms "themes of vision" and "themes of discourse."[21] With its "light show" conclusion, therefore, *Close Encounters* presents us, in the best tradition of fantasy, with a challenge to how we usually see the world and how we fit those perceptions into our normative categories, how we account for this new vision of things. As we have previously noted, in the lineup of carefully selected space travelers, all similarly attired, all of similarly exemplary physical stature, and all wearing sunglasses to protect their eyes against this light show, Neary stands out, an almost comic misfit; yet his inclusion ensures a far from uniform, conformist, and "shaded" perception of this new reality. Moreover, it reassures us that now no account can emerge that will represent only the government line, the powerfully authoritative discourse that has previously dominated and shaped thinking about such "close encounters." Our world, indeed, our sense of the universe, will now have to formulate a new explanatory discourse, perhaps one that begins from scratch employing a new and truly universal language.

Notwithstanding, as we began by noting, this nexus of perceptions and discourse hardly constitutes what we would conventionally think of as the supernatural, the key defining element of the marvelous narrative. I chose *Close Encounters* as an illustrative text, though, precisely for the ways in which it foregrounds this issue, turns it into the very subject of its narrative. However we might normally define it, "the supernatural," as Todorov offers, "always appears in an experience of limits, in 'superlative' states,"[22] in effect, in all of those various instances when we push beyond the limits of the known; and such states are precisely what *Close Encounters,* far more than a relatively recent and similarly popular film like *Independence Day,* finally explores. While it certainly demonstrates Spielberg's genius for tapping into the popular consciousness, for drawing on the established conventions of the genre, and for using those elements to "play" his audience in some very fundamental ways, it also does much more. *Close Encounters* takes us to and beyond certain perceptual and epistemological "limits," moves us into unfamiliar "states," and in the process challenges our customary sense of both the real and the supernatural. Here, human purpose, higher, determining powers, transcendent potential – all dimensions of the supernatural as conventionally conceived – effectively find their space-y correspondence; and in this experience of limits, which they translate for us, we can begin to see the nature of the satisfactions that attach to such marvelous tales. *Close Encounters,* with its conventionally transcendent experience, lets us encounter a world yanked free from its traditional moorings, as do a variety of subsequent Spielberg films: *E.T. the Extra-Terrestrial* with its own childlike alien vision, *Jurassic Park* with its demonstration of how our science might assert control over the evolution of life on Earth, or even *Amistad* (1997) with its history of the United States that finally draws into the foreground the repressed issues of slavery. All of these films compel us to abandon a particular way of seeing our world and an established set of boundaries, and in compensation offer an alternative, acceptable, in some cases even comfortable vision of where we might fit in a new scheme of things. *Close Encounters* especially suggests that, despite the rapid and dizzying changes we have experienced in the past century, as well as those to which an increasingly technologized world promises to expose us, if we can but go armed with this vision we might, like Roy Neary, no longer feel quite so "lost."

6

The Science Fiction Film
as Uncanny Text
RoboCop

What is experienced as uncanny is an objectification of the subject's anxieties, read into shapes external to himself. – Rosemary Jackson[1]

Since the early 1980s, the figure of the robot, android, replicant, or cyborg has contributed what is probably the single most dominant image to the American science fiction film [Fig. 59]. Particularly, the appearance of the film *Blade Runner* (1982) marked a rising fascination in the cinema – and certainly in American culture – with the possibilities of a human artifice, a fascination traced out in short order in such films as *Android* (1982), the two *Terminator* films (1984, 1991), *D.A.R.Y.L.* (1985), *Making Mr. Right* (1987), the three *RoboCop* films (1987, 1990, 1993), *Cherry 2000* (1987), and *Eve of Destruction* (1991), among many others. These films speak immediately of a growing cultural concern with what might be described as an industry of human synthesis, one involving the creation and transplanting of artificial organs, the development of mechanical prostheses, the manipulation of human genetics, the widespread availability of cosmetic surgery, the introduction of industrial robots into the workplace, and especially the development of artificial intelligence. They chronicle – and in complex ways respond to – the start of nothing less than a cultural revolution, one in which we would begin the process of remaking, reshaping, perhaps even perfecting the self, while at the same time germinating the technology that could eventuate in these same technological creations finally replacing the self. Such developments would naturally produce both an intense fascination – a fascination that feeds upon the genre's fundamental impulse to visualize what "could be" – and a kind of recoil, a hesitation, even a fear at the potential implications of "playing god" in this way. It is the humanly reflexive focus of these films, their "objectification" of our anxieties about these developments, as Rosemary Jackson puts it, that marks this branch of the science fiction film as a singularly *uncanny* site, a field of texts that deploy their own generic mechanisms to interrogate our human reality, to explore what Todorov broadly terms "themes of the self."

Among those themes of the self Todorov lists are a variety of concerns that, we should readily recognize, are implicated in practically any narrative about robotics or what we can more broadly term human artifice. Those concerns include instances of what he terms a "special causality," an instigation or purpose that clearly lies outside of our common sense of the real or the everyday; the appearance of multiple personalities or of a doppelgänger figure; and the seeming collapse of the normal distinctions between subject and object. These, along with a few other motifs, constitute what Todorov describes as "the basic network of . . . themes" that typically characterize uncanny texts.[2] This sense of a "network" of possible themes is an important point to establish at the outset of this chapter because it helps to account for the very variety in the narratives that we might cluster under that uncanny heading, while also suggesting a unifying element that holds them, net-like, in common cause. It allows us to think from the start, as I believe a proper understanding of genre mechanisms requires, both differentially and essentially; for even as Todorov identifies this variety of themes that surfaces throughout our uncanny stories, he also finds in them a consistent thread or root, that is, a uniform sign of the fragile limit between mind and matter, the subject and the world outside, that reflects on what increasingly seems a frail *human* reality. It might be possible to think of them all, he says, as "themes of vision," as concerned with the problematic ways in which, at the instigation of the fantastic, we come to perceive our world and thereby situate ourselves in it.[3]

Set in the context of the science fiction film, this sense of the uncanny narrative should help us better understand the self's relationship to that reason–science–technology triad on which the genre focuses. For example, that sense of special causality, as Todorov terms it, immediately evokes the strange and extreme influences of our technology on the individual, as it sets about making us into something other than the self – a *Terminal Man* (1974), a *Circuitry Man* (1989), a *Lawnmower Man* (1992), or perhaps *Stepford Wives* (1975), as the titles of some similar American science fiction films proclaim. By the same token, those themes of the double focus attention on a range of results from these influences, as we technologically fashion or project our own duplicates or simulacra – genetic clones, mechanical robots, even technological projections of the psyche, such as we find in that classic text *Forbidden*

Figure 59. The robot Maria of Fritz Lang's *Metropolis* (1926) provides a recognizable model for the technologized Murphy of *RoboCop* (1987).

Planet (1956). In addition, the collapse of subject–object distinctions – that which occurs, for example, when the self becomes some*thing* – points up the most disturbing implications of those results, the consequent qualitative shift in our sense of the self or of others; hence *Blade Runner*'s effective evocation of racist attitudes through its narrative about replicants and their desire, like the rest of humanity, simply *to live*. This network of concerns, in turn, foregrounds the rational world view behind these technological creations, the vantage from which we have set about effectively constructing – and reconstructing – the human, in fact, seeing the human as little more than one more construct within a world of artifice.

As our key text for exploring the science fiction film as this sort of uncanny text, we shall turn to Paul Verhoeven's *RoboCop* (1987), a narrative about the creation of a super crime-fighting cyborg from the body of a policeman shot down in the line of duty. It is a film that has had a major impact on both the larger genre of science fiction and the subgenre of robot or human artifice films, as is evidenced by its two sequels, various imitators, both live-action and animated television series, action figures, and host of other consumer spin-offs. Equally important, it is a work that neatly suggests the broad range of implications to be found in the uncanny narrative, its expected "network" of themes. Using it as an example, we shall be able to trace out those motifs of special causality, of doubling, and of a subject–object collapse that Todorov describes, and in the process illustrate how one might profitably employ this uncanny category as a vantage for analyzing similar films.

For all of its impact, however, *RoboCop* is also a film that almost did not get made, as the script lingered in the American film industry, having been rejected by a great number of directors before finally being offered to Verhoeven, who had just come to the United States. After directing a series of successful films in his native Netherlands, he had run afoul of a highly politicized government film committee and was finding it increasingly difficult to obtain funding for his projects. Shortly after arriving in America in 1986, he accepted the *RoboCop* project, even though, as he readily admits, he initially "thought it was too silly to do,"[4] and in light of his past work, it certainly seemed a most unlikely fit for him. As Verhoeven explains, in his Dutch films "everything was based on reality," but with *RoboCop*, as well as such subsequent science fiction efforts as *Total Recall* (1990), *Starship Troopers* (1998), and *Hollow Man* (2000), he had to move into the realm of "non-reality. There is nothing real here – it's all fantasy," a fantasy that, he fortunately recognized, offered resonances of a classic tale about human artifice, Mary Shelley's *Frankenstein*.[5] Of course, that dichotomous explanation Verhoeven offers is a bit disarming and disingenuous, for despite the disclaimer, *RoboCop* as it was realized contains much that is real; at any rate, much that the studio saw as so real that it posed a threat to the project's prospects – particularly a far too real violent content.[6] The director's initial impulse was to exaggerate the action and violent content that the script called for, to try for, as Verhoeven puts it, a "comicbook, over-the-top violence," in fact, something "so completely over-the-top that it was just *funny*." However, the initial cut did not strike quite the intended tone with either studio executives or the Motion Picture Association of America ratings board; and after repeated editing in efforts to remove the X rating it at first received, the film seemed to become "more real and more violent."[7] However, that very combination of fantastic and realistic impulses, as well as the way in which one can easily shade into the other, even prompt the interrogation of the other, speaks tellingly about the uncanny nature of this film.

As has already been noted, the uncanny narrative is, in effect, about the workings of the human mind and its impact on our sense of the real. In the typical uncanny story, the fantastic projections of the mind – dreams, reveries, hallucinations – essentially become reality for an individual, as we see most clearly in a horror film like Alfred Hitchcock's *Psycho* (1960), wherein Norman Bates effectively *becomes* his murderous mother. This situation is at the heart of a number of Verhoeven films. *The Fourth Man* (1983), for example, plays with that fragile boundary between mind and matter with its tale of a writer who begins having disturbing visions about his new lover, visions that suggest she might be planning to kill him, as she may also have done to her three previous husbands; but whether he is simply hallucinating or having psychic premonitions about his impending murder, we never learn. With *Total Recall* Verhoeven translated that uncanny situation into an elaborate, other-world science fiction context. Its protagonist apparently aids a group of rebels in defeating a repressive government on Mars and transforms the very atmosphere of the planet into one that can support life; but at the moment of triumph, he realizes that he might simply be dreaming all of these events, that he might be "recalling" a scenario that has been implanted in his brain. At the same time, in the uncanny text the distorting or distorted mind of the protagonist typically plays against our own sense of the real; for it presupposes a "natural" world beyond those strange effects.

That resulting tension is especially significant, however, for as Rosemary Jackson offers, the fantastic element thus tends "to hollow out the 'real' world, making it strange," in effect, "subverting" our sense of both reality and self,[8] calling what we would think of as natural into question and thereby posing a challenge to the cultural norm. In this context we might recall Darko Suvin's description of science fiction as a "literature of cognitive estrangement,"[9] a form intent on defamiliarizing reality. What Jackson tries to do is to anchor that defamiliarization in a pointedly social context, thereby suggesting that the fantastic text interrogates our world, our reality, precisely in hopes of altering its seemingly monolithic nature. Although *RoboCop* does not provide us with the sort of generative unconscious that drives films like *The Fourth Man* and *Total Recall* or, to some extent, a classic science fiction movie like *Forbidden Planet,* it does set the human mind at the very center of its narrative and uses that focus, as have so many films that tell a story about human artifice, as a way of examining both our individual and social reality. In this regard, *RoboCop* can serve as an especially useful model for gauging how the science fiction film comes to take on the sort of social relevance that many of its detractors simply refuse to recognize.

One way in which it does so, of course, is through its development of that theme of "special causality," a motif that here entwines the workings of economics, scientific development, and pure chance to suggest the variety of forces that operate upon the psyche, that shape the self, that throughout this tale of a cyborg's creation seem to redefine human nature itself. Embodying that economic imperative is the multinational conglomerate Omni Consumer Products or OCP, a company that functions as the unseen and seemingly irresistible causal principle, as it sets about redesigning the human environment – replacing Old Detroit with the gleaming modern planned community of Delta City, complete, as we eventually learn, even to an element of planned crime and corruption. However, before it can do so, OCP finds that it must distract and pacify the urban population by bombarding people with commercials and public relations ploys, and especially by eliminating or controlling the current criminal elements. In effect, it sets about creating a kind of roboticized populace, one that will allow it to carry out its plans for their future, that will assist in its own subjugation. Hence, the "RoboCop" of the title and the central figure of this narrative signify a similar sort of roboticization, a cultural one such as we find more elaborately worked out in a film like *THX 1138*. Although not already accomplished as Lucas envisions, that roboticization, this narrative suggests, is certainly well under way, driven by a variety of social forces, but especially by the economic system under which this culture functions.

The creation of the specific RoboCop or cyborg crime-fighter underscores how our sense of self might become complicit with and fundamentally subject to those forces, and particularly to a world of industrial design and corporate planning. To create this amalgam of man and machine, the industrial giant OCP must first obtain a "human chassis" for its project. As company vice-president Bob Morton (Miguel Ferrer) coldly but cryptically explains the plan, in order to prepare for the RoboCop cyborg program, "We've restructured the police department and placed prime candidates according to risk factors." This obfuscating jargon thinly veils OCP's commodification of the self, its transferring of certain officers – risk takers or "poor schmucks," as they are variously styled here – to dangerous precincts where, the program directors expect, they will be either killed or so disabled that they will provide the company with the biological base for its new "urban pacification" prototype. When officer Alex Murphy (Peter Weller) is predictably shot to pieces, then, he becomes simply a piece of useful property, more valuable to the company's bottom line in his near-death condition than alive. As one OCP executive explains, "He signed a release form when he joined the force. He's legally dead. We can do pretty much what we want" with him. The result of this corporate planning of the self, combined with the individual's signing over of rights – or "release" – is a new sort of being, part man, part machine, and one whose mind essentially becomes a projection of OCP's dictates. From this Faustian bargain comes RoboCop, a being that, as Morton succinctly puts it, "doesn't have a name; he's got a program. He's *product*" [Fig. 60]. It is in that very description that the irony of the company's name begins to show through. Omni Consumer Products suggests the modern corporate world and its bottom-line concern not just with creating products for the consuming public, all sorts of products, but with transforming the consumer *into* product and ultimately with *consuming* the very public it purports to serve.

This perversion of economic forces springs from another sort of fantastic causality here – yet one with which every science fiction viewer is already familiar. A key question driving most science fiction is not what we *should* do with our scientific knowledge, but rather, given a particular power, what we *can* do with it. In the face of scientific possibility, ethical questions such as those about free will or the soul are usually elided, a point made over and over in the many *Frankenstein* films. In this case, OCP, in order to carry out its larger goal of transforming Old Detroit into the futuristic Delta City, has set its various technological branches to work solving the problems involved in that transformation, foremost among them the pacification of unruly elements of society. The twin programs it has created are the cyborg RoboCop and ED 209, a completely mechanical "enforcement 'droid." When the latter suffers a major malfunction, or "technical glitch," as executive officer Dick Jones terms it, resulting in the slaughter of a minor company executive, it opens the door for the RoboCop program, while also pointing up the dangers in enthroning that reason–science–technology triad, in giving it life-or-death powers over humanity. Produced by another sort of Faustian compact, the combined efforts of medical science and the computer industry, RoboCop is a human torso onto which powerful mechanical prostheses have been grafted and into which memory chips and a controlling software program have been implanted. When the doctors announce that they have managed to save one of Murphy's human arms, Bob Morton orders them to amputate it anyway, suggesting the extent to which the desire to produce a more powerful cyborg takes precedence over any human considerations. With "off-the-shelf" availability and performance the key issues – for here lies the path to company profitability – the scientific world has simply determined to do "pretty much what we want."

Still, the RoboCop program, in its development of that "impostor or something" motif that comments on the irrepressible powers of the human mind, proves no more predictable or controllable than the totally mechanical ED 209 system. Though RoboCop represents an entirely new sort of being, as we see when OCP engineers have a kind of birthday party for his completion and going "on line," he is a being that is supposed to be moved not by his own desires, not by what we traditionally label free will, but rather by his industrially programmed brain. That is, at the core of this creation is a program with a series of key directives, apparently modeled on Isaac Asimov's famous Three Laws of Robotics: "One, a robot may not injure a human being, or, through inaction, allow a human being to come to harm. Two, . . . a robot must obey the orders given it by human beings except where such orders would conflict with the First Law. And three, a robot must protect its own existence as long as such protection does not conflict with the First or Second Laws."[10] Asimov designed these laws, in consultation with John W. Campbell Jr., to suggest how humans could employ the great power afforded by robotics while also maintaining control over their creations, rendering them, in effect, fail-safe. However, in the case of *RoboCop* those controlling directives serve a more satiric function, suggesting how the corporation and especially its chief executive officers might use such programming to place themselves and their determinations beyond the reach of the "law" as they have reconstituted it, even beyond RoboCop's seemingly irresistible power. Nevertheless, the film also quickly suggests the frailty of such technological causality, when RoboCop's programming begins to fail as he experiences spontaneous flashbacks – that is, as he begins dreaming and, in those dreams, recalling his past life: his home, family, the criminals who murdered him, and ultimately even his human identity. An engineer's explanation that "the system was never designed to experience detailed somatic response" simply reminds us how much our scientific planning fails to account for, how much of the human still falls outside of

Figure 60. RoboCop, the perfect technological crime-fighter, goes into action.

its purview, how much can never be programmed or explained. Of course, it is a problem with which the scientific world is quite familiar. In an interview, Verhoeven has focused attention on the Heisenberg uncertainty principle, the law of physics that schematizes an inevitable indeterminacy or uncertainty in all scientific calculation, and thus the necessity of "different realities" or different interpretations of reality.[11] It is a law that indicates, if not the play of chance or randomness, at least the unpredictable nature of this world, in spite of the best efforts of our science at rendering it a rational, predictable, and thus thoroughly controllable system.

These various sorts of causality, as we have already noted, lead directly into *RoboCop*'s most important uncanny element, its development of the double or doppelgänger theme. As Rosemary Jackson explains, the fantastic image of the double typically suggests the "dispersal and fragmentation" of character and of mind itself, and thus a most fundamental threat to our common notion that we are "unified, rational selves,"[12] our usual sense of the individual as a whole and unique subject [Fig. 61]. In its image of the cyborg policeman, *RoboCop* offers an obvious objectification of this threat, not only insofar as it instigates a variety of other doublings that constellate around the cyborg, but also as it implicates the "law," the reign of normalcy to which everyone is supposedly bound, even the "real" as consensus would have it. Through the cyborg, of course, not only Murphy but the human itself is doubled, presented as some*thing* that is easily dismembered, fragmented, and prone to a variety of de/reconstructions. Moreover, by identifying that figure – and indeed, the very regime of duplication – as part of the world of law enforcement, as a kind of em-body-ment of the rules of society, the film lays bare a fundamental cultural bias: how the law itself functions as an index of the real, the right, and the true, of reality as it is ideologically established and subtly affirmed in the everyday workings of life.

The key mechanism for that revelation, of course, is the system of doublings that this film offers, as characters, events, and things all find another side projected for comparison. Officer Murphy, as the narrative early on establishes, in an effort to amuse his son adopts characteristics of the television hero T. J. Lazer, a doubling that foreshadows his transformation into another sort of mechanized and mediated hero, RoboCop. Dick Jones (Ronny Cox), the corrupt chief executive of OCP, has his doubles in both the criminal mastermind with whom he works, Clarence Boddecker (Kurtwood Smith), and in the up-and-coming junior executive Bob Morton, his chief rival at OCP. Murphy also has another sort of double in his partner Anne Lewis (Nancy Allen), who subsequently becomes RoboCop's partner, and, when she is shot up by Boddecker's gang, just as Murphy was, potentially another RoboCop: As she lies badly wounded near the film's end, he reassures her that OCP will fix her up just like him, since "they fix everything." In the pattern of repeated events, we might think of the scene that anticipates Murphy's fate, as a young executive who happens to be standing nearby, another "poor schmuck," is volunteered for the ED 209 demonstration and subsequently shot to pieces. Similarly, the initial hunt for Boddecker's gang at the abandoned factory reverses itself in the film's

Figure 61. The double or doppelgänger theme visualized as RoboCop apprehends his own "killer."

culminating shootout, as the gang hunts down RoboCop in the same place. The hostage drama in which a deposed city councilman holds the mayor and his staff under threat of violence prefigures the climactic confrontation in which Dick Jones holds the OCP president hostage. Of course, a most fundamental sort of doubling is the generative force for the entire narrative, as Old Detroit is about to be transformed – like Murphy into RoboCop – into the gleaming planned metropolis, Delta City. As we eventually learn, the chief agent of this transformation, OCP, not only runs the privatized police force of Old Detroit but is also, through Dick Jones, in charge of organized crime in the area. Moreover, in a nod to the pervasive influence of the military–industrial complex, OCP proves to be not only the largest corporation in this futuristic United States, but also, as Jones proudly asserts, "We practically *are* the military." Through this complex pattern of doublings we begin to see a world of multiple possibilities and people of multiple personalities, both equally unstable and hard to sort out. Striking at any sense of a fixed or knowable reality, as well as a stable and knowable self, these doublings carry out much of the subversive work of this fantasy narrative.

One further element of these doublings deserves more detailed examination for the way it speaks to one of the most common themes in American science fiction. At the center of this pattern, of course, is the Murphy/RoboCop double, an amalgam of human and machine in which is inscribed that fundamental science fiction motif we earlier termed "kiss and tell." As the opening chapter detailed, this motif emphasizes the importance of feelings or emotions in understanding, expressing, and maintaining our sense of humanity, especially in light of an ascendant rational regime; even in the most highly technologized environment, this motif suggests, our feelings or emotions remain the "telling" marks of human nature, a stable foundation on which we can rely. We find variations on this theme across the entire register of science fiction, as in *E.T. the Extra-Terrestrial* (1982), for example, when the extra-terrestrial reminds his human friend that, although he must leave, he will remain *in his heart.* Similarly, the Terminator of *Terminator 2: Judgment Day* (1991) indicates that he has come to understand humans when he tells his young master, "Now I know why you cry"; and Luke Skywalker of *Star Wars* (1977) learns that he must "feel the force" and rely on it rather than on his computer if he wishes to destroy the Empire's Death Star. In *RoboCop* we early on learn about Murphy's feelings for his family, feelings underscored by RoboCop's recurring dreams of them and especially of Murphy's wife saying, "I love you." Those dreams, in fact, are crucial here, for they remind us that, whereas OCP can order an arm amputated or implant memory chips and controlling software, there are some things over which it can exercise no control – things it can only dismiss from consideration or impotently label "glitches," yet also things that persist and drive our actions. Even as Murphy is renamed, reprogrammed by science, and reconstructed with an indestructible titanium shell and mechanical prostheses, even as he is to all appearances transformed into the perfect mechanical double and fail-safe extension of OCP's power, a powerful human impulse remains that produces those "somatic responses," that recalls the emotional bonds of his family. Love persists, even if only as a dream. Thus, as RoboCop tries to come to grips with his strangely double self, he fixates on his family, inquires about them, and confesses to his partner Anne, "I can *feel* them, but I can't remember them."

Nevertheless, feeling is what, finally, signals the real victory over a cultural doubling and the personal fragmentation that *RoboCop* de-

Figure 62. Officer Lewis helps restore Murphy's identity as she asks him for his name, in *RoboCop.*

scribes. Certainly, Murphy's loss of life is linked with his loss of loved ones, as we see in the images of his wife, child, and home that apparently come flooding into his memory at the point of death. Reconstituted as a "product," driven by software, he seems devoid of any emotion, as we see in his cold, seemingly programmed response to the woman he saves from a rape attempt by two thugs. With the sudden onset of dreams, a return of human feelings – even sundered from real memory, which OCP has tried to erase, as if it were simply dealing with a machine – the narrative shifts to independent action and offers an accompanying sense of triumph.

At this point, instead of merely responding in a behavioral, mechanistic manner to calls on the police radio, RoboCop sets about learning of his own history by plugging into police computer files and acting on his own. When frustrated in those efforts by Dick Jones's attempts to destroy him, RoboCop is saved by Anne, who becomes a kind of replacement or double for his wife [Fig. 62], as she lovingly protects and cares for him. Particularly, we should note the scene at the old factory where she shelters him. As Anne offers assistance, RoboCop removes his helmet and visor – prominently marked with the OCP trademark – and reveals his human face for the first time. Noting that his "targeting system is a little messed up," he asks Anne to "aim for me," in effect, to help him regain a human direction or purpose. The resulting scene is a sexually overdetermined one, as she embraces his body, holds his arm and hand, even strokes the arm, directs his raised gun/phallus, and tells him "that should be about right," as he blasts away at the jars of baby food that OCP had been feeding him. Brought back to life, he has very quickly reached a new maturity and, through his lingering ability to feel, cast off the restrictive grid associated with his helmet and visor that has conditioned and limited how he sees and functions in this world (just as he will later manage to get around the restrictive program that protects OCP executives). With that new "aim," RoboCop seems ready to live in this world not as a robot or machine, or baby, but as a feeling human being, perhaps even a sexual being – Murphy once again.

This development – or redevelopment – of a human aspect already points toward a final uncanny dimension of the film, its depiction of what Todorov describes as the "collapse of the limits between matter and mind."[13] Certainly, one of the great fears this narrative explores is just such a collapse, a breakdown of various conventional boundaries, but especially that between human and machine. That sort of fear seems a rather natural reflection of American cultural anxieties of the 1980s, facing as it was the new challenges posed by thinking machines, biomedical engineering, mechanical prostheses, and readily available cosmetic surgery – by the great variety of technological developments that promise to reengineer the human or perhaps even render us obsolete. The figure of RoboCop may simply seem a somewhat exaggerated tracing or foreboding of the trajectory we might all one day follow; yet it is a tracing that we also see played out in a variety of more subtle ways throughout the narrative, such as the way that the commercials interspersed in the story market the latest in mechanical hearts, the way that Murphy's home is turned over to a robotic realtor, or the way that OCP has set in motion its various projects for replacing all human officers with law-enforcement machines. Driven in large part by the world of commerce that has itself blurred the boundaries between business and government, a cultural transformation and even replacement of the human already seems well under way here.

Undergirding these effects is a more pervasive and finally more per-
nicious boundary blurring that we see sketched out as well in Verhoeven's other science fiction films. *Total Recall*, for example, intersperses
news programs and commercials throughout the narrative, and *Starship Troopers* frames its entire story with news broadcasts and propa-
ganda films. Similarly, in *RoboCop* various news broadcasts and commercials are used to provide important narrative information and to
establish the satiric tone that dominates the film. However, even beyond these interpolated media events, we find evidence of a world
that has become totally reliant on the media and its packaging and representation of reality. For example, when Dick Jones makes his pitch
for the ED 209 program, he does so by deploying a wall of televisions
offering a montage of commercial images, all depicting OCP's most successful technological programs. Repeatedly, even as chaos breaks out
in Old Detroit, we see citizens seemingly mesmerized by a comedy program on television. In addition, Murphy, as we have already noted,
models his fast draw on his son's television hero, T. J. Lazer. What is
being crafted in all of these instances is a pervasive video culture, an
environment characterized by what the French theorist Paul Virilio has
described as a "cinematic derealization"[14] of our world, as all that we
commonly think of as real blurs into its video/cinematic representations. It is this effect, this more fundamental "collapse of limits," that
makes possible the problematic sense of reality that we find in all of
Verhoeven's science fiction films, the troubling and indeed widespread
sense that, as he puts it, "there are different realities possible at the
same moment."[15] With its constant references to a cinematic environment, to the whole "apparatus of deception"[16] that obscures our basic
sense of reality and enables a confusion between human and machine,
RoboCop suggests how we have increasingly come to inhabit a fantastic world and unwittingly give ourselves over to its uncanny regime.

In light of this emphasis on "cinematic derealization," we might reconsider the opening promise the film makes with its selection from
the television news show *Mediabreak*. The first words we hear in the
film are that show's catch phrase: "You give us three minutes and we'll
give you the world." More than just a satiric comment on modern culture's short attention span and the media's own proclivity for the
"newsbite" over any sort of substantive coverage, that phrase seems
to indicate another sort of Faustian bargain at work here, a promise to
deliver up all the world in exchange for very little, just three minutes
of our time – in effect, for our treating the world so slightingly. It is a

variation, as well, on the promise OCP holds out, as it offers to provide the citizens of Old Detroit with a veritable new city if they will simply acquiesce to its methods, pay no mind to its abuses of their freedoms, or even its symbiotic systematizing of crime and law enforcement. What *RoboCop* thereby suggests is the extent to which, through an on-going habit of compromise, we have all assisted in the trivialization of our world and the cheapening of life itself.

Nothwithstanding, the film also seems to hold out an element of hope against that pattern through both its satiric strikes at the apparatus of deception and its resolution that restores at least some of those boundaries. *RoboCop* is, finally, a darkly satiric fantasy, much in the tradition of the work of Jonathan Swift and as intent as Swift's work in prodding us into change. In this context, we might consider the way RoboCop/Murphy turns the tables on Dick Jones. In front of the president of OCP, using the same wall of video monitors Jones had previously employed for his ED 209 presentation, this mechanical mediation of humanity (RoboCop) replays a confession he has recorded, thereby turning the media against Jones. In the process, RoboCop turns his fail-safe programming against him as well, when the company president fires Jones and thus eliminates him from the sanctuary of "Directive 4," which protects all OCP executives from RoboCop; and with Jones removed, we gather, a number of those other "limits" or boundaries may well be restored. At least the link between organized crime and big business seems broken, and a world that has, at every turn, denied individuality – through its corporate yes-men, its lowest-common-denominator television programming, and especially the assertion that RoboCop "doesn't have a name; he's got a program. He's *product*" – seems to make room for the subjectivity of Murphy. Thus, in the film's final lines OCP's president acknowledges the human identity at the core of his company's technological marvel, remarking, "Nice shooting, son. What's your name?" and receiving the simple reply, "Murphy." As Verhoeven explains these concluding comments, they seem to suggest RoboCop's "acceptance of what he has become, of having less and having more. He has taken control of what they have done to him, becoming Murphy again, but in a new way."[17] While that affirmation of identity may appear a small thing, especially in light of the pervasive and powerful technological and cultural forces arrayed against it, conspiring to excise human consciousness and to manipulate that of the consuming public, it remains a victory over those forces, indicates they are indeed vulnerable to resistance, and suggests something of the subversive potential that Jackson sees as fundamental to all fantasy texts.

Before embracing this sort of subversive vision wholeheartedly, though, we might once more recall Verhoeven's explanation of how his movies frequently suggest that "different realities [are] possible at the same moment."[18] As a further gloss on his film's conclusion, then, let us consider a rather similar film about a security robot fashioned by the military–industrial complex, the Australian science fiction film *Hardware* (1990). As a government-fashioned "defense" robot runs amok, we hear on the sound track at film's end a kind of anthem song for this self-destructing world, one that repeats the lines, "This is what you want? This is what you get." It is a message that resonates especially for the ending of *RoboCop*, and one that speaks to a number of similar uncanny science fiction texts. Such films, in the best fantasy tradition, often seem to pose both a question and a warning: a question about our desires for the self and a warning about the consequences of following through on those desires, particularly of tracing the trajectory that the reason–science–technology triad seems to be staking out for remaking and effectively transforming the self. Though *RoboCop* leaves us on a seemingly triumphant note – with a cyborg Murphy returning to a sense of self, to a kind of self-consciousness, marked especially by his removal of his dehumanizing helmet, his momentary freedom from the secret "Directive 4," and his naming of himself – that triumph, in the best tradition of Swiftian satire, must still ring a bit hollow, seem a rather weak sort of subversion, even given Verhoeven's commentary. After all, Murphy remains a strange hybrid, more machine than human, a Frankenstein's monster for a new age, and still bound by that series of prime directives programmed into his very makeup.

Perhaps a more precise reading would suggest that this resolution is the best we could hope for in such circumstances, the best that a postmodern, thoroughly technologized culture such as ours will allow. Such a resolution remains troubling, however, much like the ending to Verhoeven's *Starship Troopers* in which we are reassured that, despite humanity's many losses in its war against the insects of the planet Klendathu, we shall "keep on fighting," continue unquestioningly along a violent, dehumanizing path that has already reduced us to little more than insects ourselves. If this is all that we want, *RoboCop* similarly suggests, this is probably all that we shall ever get – a poor, dehumanizing compromise, a happy acceptance of our own "objectification" by a world of corporate planning and violent behavior. In examining a number of recent science fiction films, Barry Grant points up precisely the genre's general ability to pose such challenges, noting that, "like the horror film, the science fiction genre has the potential for a progressive resistance to dominant ideology."[19] However, he argues that most commonly the form does not live up to that potential, that it "consistently offers . . . not an exploration but an exaggeration and exploitation of the ideological problems" that are most pressing.[20] On the one hand, then, a film like *RoboCop* might well be read simply as an "exploitation" of ideological issues, such as the place of the individual in a corporate-controlled world; but on the other, and like many other of those in this "uncanny" vein, it also seems a nice measure of the genre's potential, precisely because of the way in which it confronts us with the sort of weak compromises to which we are prone.

This confrontation, moreover, springs precisely from the very uncanny character of the film; for through its strange, borderline figure, caught between human and machine, between mind and matter, it foregrounds our humanness and locates it in a consciousness that contributes to the construction of the world we inhabit – one that, in fact, has been targeted by that world precisely because of its unwitting participation in its construction. *RoboCop* argues that this sort of science fiction film finds its focus in a most fundamental human problem: the place of consciousness in a culture devoted to the machine. In a world that has increasingly elevated the mechanical, especially the mechanical brain, to a place of prominence, and that, in the process, has increasingly replaced thought, consideration, and the human weighing of values with a mechanic computing of choices, with the prediction of profits and losses, with bottom-line thinking, this focus finally seems something more than an exploitation of the dominant ideology. In fact, this concern with the persistence of consciousness and its *active* and *persistent* work in constructing this world seems to probe beneath the surface of our ideology to a more personal, human level, to release, as it were, the anxieties that simply cannot be alleviated or contained by so many of our films' revisions or restructurings of society.

7

Crossing Genre Boundaries / Bound by Fantasy

The Fly (1986)

Throughout this overview of the science fiction film we have been using a pointedly discriminatory approach in order to sort out what for many seems a rather amorphous and unwieldy genre. That is, we have turned to contemporary discussions of fantasy and employed those discrete distinctions made by Todorov between the marvelous, fantastic, and uncanny varieties of fantasy in order to help distinguish some of the primary narrative types of science fiction film and to account for some of the genre's appeal. However, the fact remains that all of these films occupy some fairly problematic generic ground, a point often evident in critical commentary on them. In his early but still useful history of the horror film, Carlos Clarens, like a number of others, simply treated science fiction as part of the cinematic territory. Working from an affective approach to genre, that is, considering it in terms of how it primarily affected viewers, he saw science fiction as just another variation of a form usually aimed at producing a sense of shock, fear, or surprise in its audience. Similarly focusing on effects, Bruce Kawin too has described how hard it is for most of us to draw reliable boundaries between horror and science fiction, even as he suggests that trying to do so can serve us "in the interest of working toward a definition" of either genre.[1] Although for the most part the present study has sidestepped that issue of crossed boundaries in favor of a unified and more tightly focused examination of science fiction – that is, in favor of a limited but critically *useful* vantage – we also need to acknowledge and explore the extent to which the science fiction film does connect with other formulas, to which it follows the dictum offered by Rick Altman, that "Hollywood's stock-in-trade is the romantic combination of genres, not the classical practice of generic purity."[2] To begin that exploration, this chapter focuses on a film that very pointedly seems to straddle, with its *many* legs, the horror and science fiction forms: David Cronenberg's 1986 version of Kurt Neumann's 1958 film *The Fly*.

Before turning to this most recent rendering of *The Fly*, we first need to establish the context within which the film works, a context much like the half-human, half-fly subject of the film – that of generic crossbreeds. As an aid we might consider what is probably the key text for all such discussions, the oft-filmed story of *Frankenstein,* which, in its many variations, but particularly the most famous film version of this story, James Whale's 1931 adaptation, situates the work of science within a context pointedly designed to create a horrific recoil in the audience. Sourced in a literary type – the Gothic horror tale – that seems quite secure in its own generic lineage, the 1931 *Frankenstein* is obviously the product of a new era and new attitude. Produced at the height of what we term the Machine Age, this film couches its account of nineteenth-century grave robbing and stitched-together bodies in decidedly twentieth-century technological terms. The charnel-house atmosphere, brooding, Romantic characters, and even the image of a rather horrific "new Adam" of Mary Shelley's novel all dissolve into a spectacle of electrically driven, machine-produced life, after the fashion that we find in such less generically problematic science fiction films of the same era as *Six Hours to Live* (1932), *The Man They Could Not Hang* (1939), and *Man Made Monster* (1941). The typical horror trajectory, that which, as Kawin observes, travels "into the unconscious and through the implications of evil and of dream,"[3] and which is prominent enough throughout the novel, in this film version shifts into a focus on how our science and technology play upon those unconscious impulses and evil dreams of horror, how they draw out or seduce from us – just as they do the scientist Henry Frankenstein (named Victor in the novel) – those desires for power and creation.

One quite specific effect of that shift, as Caroline Picart argues, is to alter radically the narrative's cultural commentary, as the film "severely delimits Mary Shelley's disturbing critique of the Romantic politics of gender."[4] Yet as Frank McConnell notes, a further and far more fundamental effect, as well as one that points up the work's kinship to most of our science fiction films, arises from the self-referential dimension bound up in its technological emphasis; for with that emphasis, *Frankenstein* reflexively evokes the specter of another kind of creative dream machinery fueled by seductive power, that is, the technology of film. As McConnell suggests, the creation of the monster as it is visualized here prods viewers into the "realization that the monster is made possible by precisely the techniques and technologies which also allow us to believe in the humanity of the other characters in the story,"[5] that is, by the mechanism of the cinema itself, which has crafted all of these figures and which derives much of its narrative power from the construction of character types; yet even without that sort of reflexive frisson and thematics, without the specter of a life conjured up from a machine, *Frankenstein* seems very much a tale concerned with the conscious as much as the unconscious, with science as much as with evil, with our waking fixations as much as with our troubling dreams. In effect, it seems to prompt its own sort of fantastic "hesitation," not simply in terms of the source of its challenge to understanding but in terms of the very frame we might try to place around the tale as we try to understand its generic thrust, and that, I would suggest, is a key to its appeal: the way in which it breaks down easy categories, easy distinctions between the nineteenth century and the present-day, easy frames of reference that might let us hold its reality at a safe remove and prevent it from challenging or *infecting* our own.

Nevertheless, *Frankenstein* is hardly unique in this regard, as practically every moviegoer, reflecting upon his or her experiences, will quickly recognize. Whale's subsequent effort, *The Bride of Frankenstein* (1935), as well as the more recent *Frankenstein Unbound* (1990), clearly follows in this same conflicted vein. In addition, the ongoing debates over how one might classify and interpret such works as *The Thing from Another World* (1951), *Invasion of the Body Snatchers* (1956), and *Alien* (1979) largely spring from the same sort of dual codes that typically operate in such texts, codes that, for example, can by turns warn us against "curiosity," as Kawin believes horror films always do,[6] and yet also insist on the necessity of that same curiosity, as when in its conclusion *The Thing . . .* enjoins us to "Watch the skies; keep watching." If *Frankenstein* seems in its ending to shut down all curiosity, with its scientist-protagonist freed from his monstrous obsessions, the monster itself apparently destroyed, and a normal life with his new bride established, it is only after the film has effectively argued for that same curiosity by linking it with science and modernity, and contrasting it with a pointedly outmoded and regressive approach to human knowledge, with a nineteenth-century rather than a twentieth-century sort of attitude.

Frankenstein's specific science fiction thematics also tend to pull the narrative in varying directions, all the while combining to interrogate our own reality. It offers its own version of the "kiss and tell" motif we have earlier described, with Dr. Frankenstein's fiancée and later bride trying to come between him and his monster, seeking to bring him back to normalcy and heterosexual intimacy through her pleadings of love. The conclusion, with husband and wife safely ensconced in their marriage bed and everyone drinking a toast to a "new heir" to the house of Frankenstein, underscores the powerful work of the emotions or feelings in reaffirming our basic humanity – not to mention a culturally confirmed normalcy. Put quite simply, it suggests that *we are,* after all, finally that which we create through our love for each other; and yet its specific inflection of the "imposter or something" motif, its emphasis on the scarred, stitched, and bolted together monster that has effectively taken Frankenstein's name, historically become his double, troubles that issue of human creation. After all, the monster too is the scientist's "offspring," the child of desire to which he – unnaturally – gives birth with sparks and poppings of machinery, with a mechanical rather than biological labor, and it is a creation that pointedly horrifies at first glance. Rather than the sort of shock of recognition at our own humanness that often accompanies this motif in the science fiction genre, that motif here clouds the issue of our humanity. It confronts us with the unnatural notion and *product* of a male-only procreation, as well as the frightening prospect that humanity itself could be little more than a constructed thing – if not something so pointedly stitched together from stolen and scavenged parts, still a construct of sorts with no real essence or identity.

This sort of conflicted, liminal character, we might surmise, may well have been one of the attractions David Cronenberg found in the narrative of *The Fly.* It is a story that had already established a successful hold on fantasy audiences through the production of a string of successful science fiction–horror crossbreeds in an earlier era: *The Fly* (1958), *The Return of the Fly* (1959), and *The Curse of the Fly* (1965). Cronenberg himself is a figure who throughout his career seems to have gravitated to such "mutant" narratives, that is, to ones that call into question any firm boundaries between science fiction and horror, or, as we have already noted, between Canadian and American sensibilities. Moreover, those narratives are typically ones that literalize that "cross-over" effect in their central imagery, as in the case of his earlier *Rabid* (1978), in which a plastic surgeon's tissue transplant takes on a blood-sucking life of its own, or *Videodrome* (1982), wherein violent video transmissions produce in the protagonist hallucinations that he has a videocassette player in his stomach. In *The Fly* that effect takes its most obvious form in a story about scientific experimentation with teleportation that produces a mutant fly–human. Thus, in his overview

Figure 63. Ronnie and Seth recoil at the sight of the first matter-transport experiment in *The Fly* (1986).

of the filmmaker's career, Chris Rodley argues that "horror was not the genre" Cronenberg was trying to work in; but rather, he has consistently tried "to market films which are part horror, part science-fiction, part psychological thrillers and, therefore, something else."[7] And Bart Testa theorizes that much of the difficulty audiences and critics have with the "extremities" of Cronenberg's films arises from the manner in which they slip away from easy classification, as they offer the sort of semantics that invite a reading from the vantage of traditional horror films, yet consistently couch those elements within the syntax of postmodern science fiction narratives.[8] Lending credence to these explanations is Cronenberg's own commentary, that "My films are *sui generis*. It would be nice if they could form their own genre."[9] What that genre comprises, what that "something else" is, might best be seen by examining *The Fly* in the context we have established in our prior discussion, that is, in light of the fantastic and its variant strains.

Obviously, the film sends mixed signals that suggest we read it by turns as horror film and as science fiction tale. The scientist Seth Brundle's (Jeff Goldblum) veiled comments on his failed experiments in teleportation point toward something horrific, and his early effort to teleport a baboon, which produces only a bloody, throbbing mass that he describes as the baboon "turned inside out," materializes that shocking potential [Fig. 63] and prepares us for Seth's own later gruesome transformation into an insect. Another pointed sign shows up when the reporter Ronnie (Geena Davis) enters her apartment and, hearing strange noises, slowly moves toward the bathroom and yanks back the shower curtain to reveal her publisher and former boyfriend, Stathis (John Getz), who has let himself in and is simply cleaning up. It is a sly echo – thanks particularly to its role reversals – of the famous shower scene in *Psycho* (1960), here employed as a suspense-building mechanism and signpost to suggest the sort of shocks this film might yet have in store for us. Moreover, the grisly stages in Seth's transformation into the new creature, Brundlefly, recall the familiar pattern of monstrous metamorphoses found in many of our most famous horror films: *Dr. Jekyll and Mr. Hyde* in its many versions (e.g., 1931, 1941), *The Wolf Man* (1941), even *The Exorcist* (1973). Nevertheless, Ronnie's warning upon seeing the physical signs of Seth's transformation – "Be afraid! Be very afraid!" – hardly conveys the dominant atmosphere of *The Fly*. While an effective tagline, useful for advertising the film and suggesting some of its lure, it marks a fear that never quite controls the narrative, in part because Cronenberg treats the visceral element of the story – its constant concern with "the flesh" in all its mutations – not as a point of dread but as one of near-scientific curiosity, even necessary investigation. Moreover, that horrific sense is repeatedly balanced by what we might think of as a generic counterweight.

After all, *The Fly* is a story about knowledge, about a scientist, and about that fundamental bond between the scientist and his pursuit of knowledge. As a context, it offers us a number of the semantic and syntactic elements we have come to expect in contemporary science fiction narratives: the computer, a lab, strange equipment, talk of project funding, a series of experiments, the recording of results. Above all, it focuses on a familiar type, the scientist who initially seems something of a nerd. Seth Brundle is unable to drink, he seems obsessed with the project he has been working on for the last six years, and a look in his closet reveals that all of his clothes are exactly the same (so that he doesn't "have to expend any thought" on what to wear). Seth, we learn, was a boy genius who was "an inch away from the Nobel Prize for Physics" at age twenty and is now, as he simply asserts, "working on something that will change the world and human life as we know it." Yet he clearly lacks the requisite knowledge for that scientific breakthrough. As he admits, he is at heart "really a systems analyst man," one who knows "too little about the flesh," about organic life and its complexities, to work out his grand scheme of *human* teleportation

Figure 64. Seth tries to program what he knows about "the flesh" into his computer in *The Fly*.

[Fig. 64]. In the fashion of many such narratives and in keeping with the "stop trying to rationalize" motif previously discussed, he is the scientist who must learn precisely what his science has, up to now, not allowed him to know, undergo an education in being human through his newfound interest in the reporter Ronnie.

Of course, the irony here, as well as the film's cautionary point, is that this very education – or "curiosity," as Kawin would describe it – eventually pulls him further away from, even beyond, his humanity. In seeking to learn about "the flesh," he eventually loses his own flesh, literally shedding his skin as he metamorphoses into Brundlefly, and finally suffering a life-denying transformation when, in a teleportation gone wrong, the computer "fuses" him with one of his "telepods." Although Seth eventually becomes something quite gruesome – part fly, part machine, part human – it is an end that registers as much on the tragic as on the horrific scale, as we recognize that this sheltered scientist did indeed need to learn about "the flesh," particularly since it is precisely those weaknesses the flesh is heir to – drunkenness, desire, ambition – and not simply the science here, not simply his commitment to reason, that have brought him to this pass.

What I am suggesting, of course, is that neither the horror nor science fiction genre quite adequately holds or describes *The Fly;* and this bulking beyond generic boundaries seems quite in keeping with Cronenberg's own description of the film. Curiously, he likens it to metaphysical poetry, to a literature "in which normally unharmonious elements are violently yoked together."[10] By shifting focus, pulling back out to the larger category of fantasy, and seeing it as a work that straddles the full range of fantasy, though, we might begin to find the sense in that violent yoking, see the film in a more revealing light, one that shows its boundary crossings as fundamental to its key concerns.

As I have suggested, *The Fly* is, on the one hand, a narrative about human impulses, about the various lures to which "the flesh" seems inevitably drawn. In Seth, Cronenberg offers us a figure apparently drawn from his own experience with science and scientists in his days as an Honours Science student at the University of Toronto. As he explains, he consistently found the academic presentation of science to be "very dry and alien," and the scientist "a classic version of what scientists are supposed to be – detached, distracted, and passionless."[11] Yet Seth, perhaps because his career and, we might suppose, his personal life have gone nowhere, seems ready for a change. Once he begins to move beyond the scientific realm, once he opens the door of his ordered and systematic world to scrutiny, to that of the reporter Ronnie and her videotaping of his every action, and once he tries to embrace that neglected and denied physical element, Seth effectively steps into what we might well describe as an *uncanny* realm. His own thoughts become the key source of disruption, the power of his own mind the chief danger. That pattern is particularly played out through his jealousy of Ronnie's continued contact with Stathis, whose name evokes both his higher "status" and his representation of the "status quo" here. It further surfaces in Seth's determination to experiment on himself [Fig. 65], and his ignoring the signs that something has gone wrong, insisting instead that he has simply undergone "a purifying process." Seth's own scheme to "change the world and human life" invests itself monstrously in him. Seen in this context, the narrative becomes a highly ironic one and a caution against all such hubristic assumptions.

On the other hand, we might also read *The Fly* as a narrative about a kind of invasion, a *marvelous* encounter with an alien other that calls into question our sense of the self as a secure and unified entity, and of our world as a stable place. Through the accidental encounter with the other, with a simple housefly that becomes trapped in his telepor-

Figure 65. *The Fly*'s Seth Brundle experiments on himself with his womblike matter transporter.

tation pod, and his integration with it at the "molecular-genetic level," Seth finds that he is "becoming something that never existed before," the Brundlefly. That force from outside the self thus instigates not a "purifying process," as Seth repeatedly insists, but a kind of infection. It results in a gradual transformation and loss of identity with which he tries to effect some compromise – by forcing a fusion with Ronnie – but too late. However, we should see that invasion as actually beginning much earlier, in Seth's initial encounter with another sort of alien society, that embodied in the cocktail party at the film's opening. Here foundation representatives, members of the press, and the scientific elite come together and schmooze each other for information, money, and publicity. This strange society treats scientists as celebrities, as figures who transcend normal human nature – and who thus might aid us in our own desires for such transcendence, for moving beyond the status quo. Seth, however, as we quickly recognize, is himself something of an alien in this context, an outsider, inexperienced at this game of celebrity and/or unready for the way it is played. As a result, he too easily gets drunk, perhaps on the potential for such status; he quickly falls into a relationship with Ronnie, who soon becomes his own worshipful fan; and he rushes precipitously into his experiments, all too eager to demonstrate to her his rightful place in this other world. The fly – "in the ointment," if you will – simply renders that encounter with the alien other in a more easily recognizable form and drives home its darker consequences. In her discussion of another sort of alien, that of the *Alien* films, Barbara Creed notes this same pattern, suggesting that we see the alien in the context of the *abject,* that is, as a projection of all that we normally exclude or repress in order to sustain our everyday lives, even to maintain our psychic identity. The encounter with the alien other, then, always menaces the norm, including our normal sense of self, as "boundaries, designed to keep the abject at bay, threaten to disintegrate, collapse."[12] Seen from this vantage, the film becomes a story about our need to stay within the bounds of "the flesh," but also to learn about it, to know it and thus properly deal with its drives [Fig. 66]. It is about the boundaries with which we live, as well as our need to understand those boundaries.

Pulled in these two directions, drawn in two distinct yet ultimately complementary generic jurisdictions, *The Fly* also deploys two thematic systems that Todorov links to these categories, what he terms "themes of vision" and "themes of discourse," in effect, how we see the world and how we account for it. Under the former heading we might especially consider as a salient example Ronnie's intrusion of a video camera into Seth's life. It will, she explains, simply provide a visual record of all of his experiments – as if the presence of such a mechanism certified objectivity and truth. Seth's discomfort with the camera and Ronnie's reminder to "talk to the tape; get in the habit" underscore the main trajectory of that theme of vision here. It suggests how easily we might come to objectify the self, to render it as a thing of study. Fittingly, instead of providing a sure record of Seth's experiments, the camera

Figure 66. In one of the first signs that Seth's experiment has gone awry, he becomes sexually predatory in *The Fly.*

fails to register that nearly invisible fly's presence, which ultimately turns these events in a tragic direction; and instead of allowing for a better knowledge of "the flesh," it points toward the objectifying and ultimately dehumanizing – or flylike – vantage that Seth increasingly comes to adopt toward both himself and others. Thus, as he begins to deteriorate and human parts – fingernails, bits of skin, an ear – begin to drop away, Seth gathers them together in a small box which he describes as the "Brundle Museum of Natural History." Not horrified by his manifest disintegration, Seth shows the box to Ronnie and laughs at his display, immune to its horrific implications as a result of the very distance he has achieved from himself, from the flesh, as a result of his quite literal dis-integration from his former humanity.

At the same time that it investigates this sort of visual distance and detachment, *The Fly* also develops a focus on discourse, on what Todorov describes as "the structuring agent of man's relation with other men."[13] This theme takes a variety of forms here. Ronnie, we might recall, appears at the cocktail party because she is trying to dig up an interesting story for *Particle* magazine; and Seth, in an effort to present himself as a potential focus of that story – and thus of her attentions – renders himself as an object of discourse, telling her all about his latest project. Furthermore, he goads her to pursue his story, noting that, though the others there might similarly claim to have story potential, they "would be lying," and that he has "a strong urge to talk about what I'm doing." With their association thus initially defined as a meeting of discursive impulses, of the writer and the writerly subject, their subsequent relationship seems to follow suit, to be marked by a series of efforts at binding up one or the other within a realm of discourse, ranging from the attempt to record Seth's experimentation with a video camera and, in the process, to "tell it what you're thinking," to Ronnie's desire to turn Seth's story into an exclusive book project, and to Seth's compulsive talking after his transformation and his constant arguing that Ronnie should undergo the teleportation process and thereby "be destroyed and re-created" just like him, that is, be rewritten. On the one hand, we might read this pattern as suggesting a necessary opening up of Seth, a reaching for a new "structure" of relationships with others in place of his self-imposed isolation, a situation in which, he admits, "I've never given me a chance to be me." Yet on the other, it points to a danger in that opening up, in such a fundamental alteration, even destruction of the self, as discourse runs amok with Seth's compulsive, rapid-fire talk, his verbal abuse of Ronnie, and his violent insistence that, despite her fears, she continue to "chronicle the life and times of Brundlefly" [Fig. 67].

Seen in the context of these themes of discourse, *The Fly* records a shift from a passive relationship to the world and others to a dynamic, open, and potentially life-transforming relationship – precisely the sort of story that, Kawin would suggest, the science fiction film with its emphasis on "openness" typically offers. However, we also see that relationship go wrong, the transformation become distorted and deformed, and that very openness produce, much like Ronnie's nightmare of giving birth to a giant larva, something from which we recoil. That dreamt thing, which we might put in this same context, as a discourse of the unconscious, points us back to the frightening nature of that which has been created, of a self always seen as an object, a distant thing defined not by nature but by a formal "structuring" pattern that rules human interaction here. Through its development of this discursive motif, then, the film allows us to consider the contingent nature of human relationships, to contemplate how difficult and indeed risky it is in this era to open up the self to others, to move beyond the safe bounds with which we circumscribe our lives as well as our thinking,[14] indeed, to fantasize.

Figure 67. Infused with a fly's genes, Seth becomes compulsive and violent in *The Fly.*

This emphasis on the contingent, even risky nature of our relation-ships might seem far removed from the typical concerns of the science fiction genre. It is certainly the stuff of many horror films, and partic-ularly the focus of the contemporary "slasher" type, begun with Alfred Hitchcock's *Psycho;* yet it is also a logical extension of *The Fly*'s larger concern with knowledge, and particularly with the sort of knowledge that, as Seth asserts, could "change the world and human life as we know it." Before we set about such changes – changes that may very well be inevitable – the narrative implies that we should first undertake another sort of exploration into that terra incognita of the self and of the self's relations with others. As Leonard Heldreth in his overview of Cronenberg's work reminds, "Brundle's fault is not that he goes too far, but that he lacks understanding of himself."[15] What *The Fly* does, then, very much in the fashion of such other films of this era as *Blade Runner* (1982) and *RoboCop* (1987), is to establish a continuum of nec-essary knowledge, suggesting that our efforts at changing the world must send us back to a reconsideration of the self, that changes on one level require changes on the other as well, that knowledge is not limit-ed to one sort – and if we might push the point, to one conventionally

conceived genre. In its underscoring of that which lies outside the mechanical instrumentality of the technology on which we have come to
focus and rely so heavily, in its opening up of the field of inquiry, *The
Fly* simply works one more variation on that "stop trying to rationalize"
everything motif previously cited as central to the science fiction form.
It is in this light that we might see Harvey Roy Greenberg's assertion
that all of Cronenberg's work represents "a subversive inquiry into the
impact of late Twentieth century techno-culture upon psyche and so-
ma, identity and the social contract."[16]

What I am already suggesting, then, is that the very meeting ground
that this film surveys for us – that between science and technology, on
the one hand, and the body with its fleshy imperative, on the other –
opens directly onto the larger generic problem it illustrates; for *The Fly,*
while a film about hybrids and hybrid possibilities, is also a film that
is a hybrid itself, and one that suggests the potential for such hybrid
forms as the science fiction–horror movie [Fig. 68]. In focusing on the
sort of hybrid creature that seems featured in all of Cronenberg's work,
Robert Haas notes a warning that these creations seem to sound. As
he offers, "the integration between human and animal and machine,
between science and nature, between the mind and the body is, in fact,
disastrous in every Cronenberg film."[17] Yet that image lingers and does
not *simply* horrify. In fact, it serves as a very effective way of binding
up for our consideration a variety of contemporary problems: the
sense of a widening schism between mind and body, the seeming an-
tipathy between human and machine, even the often violent relationship between male and female in today's culture. We might see that hybrid image, then, in light of the larger formal issue here, that of genres;
for that terrible figure of failed "integration" stands in almost ironic
contrast to Cronenberg's successful integration of formulas – it is a
"disastrous" image with very positive results for the filmmaker.

What we see demonstrated in *The Fly* – and, one might argue, in the
rest of Cronenberg's work – is not so much a cinema of fantastic hesitation or irresolution, then, as a cinema of effective tension: of narratives
that seem to be pulling against themselves, characters that seem to be,
often quite destructively, at odds with their own natures, cultures that
are pulling apart or violently turning themselves inside out. In fact, the
very cultural context of this film's production speaks directly of such
a tension, and opens onto yet another sort of cross-breeding at work
here: David Cronenberg is a Canadian filmmaker, and his movies, at
least in recent years, have come to be seen as prominent emblems of

Figure 68. Crossing genre boundaries in *The Fly:* The scientific overreacher mutates into the monster of horror.

a vital Canadian film industry, particularly since most Canadian films never find exhibition beyond the major cities of Canada. For Cronenberg, after a career built on low-budget cult films and failed deals to direct such major studio productions as *Total Recall* (1990), *Top Gun* (1986), and *Witness* (1985), *The Fly* represented a breakthrough effort into mainstream, American-style cinema, a chance to show he could do an American fantasy film. Here he found backing with a big-time Hollywood studio, Twentieth Century–Fox, was paired with an American producer, Stuart Cornfeld, and received a relatively lavish budget (by Cronenberg standards) of $10 million with which to work. The result was a film that played well with American audiences – indeed, that presents itself as an American film – yet also one that was shot in Canada with Cronenberg's "usual crew" of Canadians.[18] In fact, we should note a significant irony here: Whereas the original American version of *The Fly* was set in Canada, Cronenberg's updating has an American setting, but with Toronto standing in for New York. Bart Testa suggests that this double cultural pull bears special significance for understanding both *The Fly* and Cronenberg's work more generally. Much of the misunderstanding of or even reaction against Cronenberg's films, he theorizes, comes from efforts to read them in very traditional generic contexts and especially against the grain of his Canadian-ness. If, Testa argues, Cronenberg's "imagistic extremity violates the conventional decorum of the science fiction film," especially as it has been constructed within the American cinema, it may be because "behind the Canadian Cronenberg is not just a cinema genre, but a discourse on technology springing from the Canadian ethos" toward the technological.[19] The implication is that, even in trying to make an "American" science fiction film, Cronenberg is still telling a fundamentally Canadian story and, in the process of making the film, illustrating precisely the sort of tension on which *The Fly* focuses.

However, the kind of question that most seems to intrigue Cronenberg is *how* one deals with such situations, with such tensions or afflictions, with both the insistent desires and the ultimate limits of "the flesh," the body – perhaps even the desires of the filmmaker to "make it" in Hollywood. That he would be drawn to the borders of genre in addressing them should seem quite natural, at least in part because the postmodern context seems to find conventional narratives of every sort, and certainly conventional generic formulas, rather inadequate for taking the measure of such a world. The horror–science fiction film, though, seems to fit the bill quite well, to offer a better means of gauging this highly technologized yet still fundamentally flesh-bound world, precisely since it seems to allow the filmmaker to range across the entire spectrum of fantastic narrative possibility, to interrogate the conventional reality of our world and that of the self at the same time. At least it seems to have allowed Cronenberg to better accomplish what, for him, is the filmmaker's key task: "A complete film-maker should be able to appeal to all facets of human existence, the sensual as well as the cerebral. If you do get this mixture together properly, you have a perfect example of healing the Cartesian schism. You have something that appeals to the intellect and to the viscera. If you mix them together you get a whole movie."[20]

What this discussion points to, though, is a continuing problem of categorization, and one that our use of the categories of fantasy will hardly eliminate. As Altman reminds us, "generic purity" is something we can expect seldom if ever to encounter, particularly since what he terms "fully formed" genres usually "work *against* the economic interests of the studio that spawned" them and its fundamental concern with product differentiation.[21] Instead, he suggests that, especially when we focus on the American film industry, we might think of genres in terms of periodic cycles that successfully combine two or more generic patterns – and are expressly marketed in terms of that combination – for Hollywood usually "labours to identify its pictures with multiple genres, in order to benefit from the increased interest that this strategy inspires in diverse demographic groups."[22] While this approach suggests how difficult, perhaps even impossible, it is to pin down and adequately account for a particular genre's workings, it might also underscore the value of the vantage taken here; for as our discussion of *The Fly* has illustrated, the use of a broad category such as fantasy might well allow us not only to embrace generic combinations, but even to expect a certain element of narrative blending. Moreover, we might begin to account for the elements of that association, and better understand how they appeal and draw our interests in rather different directions. As Cronenberg in *The Fly* and elsewhere effectively reminds us, a filmmaker often must ignore what audiences might conventionally assume to be rigid boundaries if he or she wants to "get a whole movie." That injunction holds for audiences as well, who must also be ready to see across those borders if they want to "get" the film. A fantasy view of science fiction, and especially of the postmodern American science fiction film, might assist us in that task.

8

Conclusion: A Note on Boundaries

Throughout this study of the science fiction film we have repeatedly taken up questions of borders and boundaries, in part because all questions of identity, including those relating to film genres, immediately seem to call for an outline, a point of separation between one thing and another. Boundaries have traditionally made for easier discussion. At the same time, we should recognize that this issue is especially pertinent to any discussion of science fiction because its very subject matter – the reason–science–technology triad to which I have often referred in this book – typically focuses our attention on borders: the borders of our knowledge, those of our experience, those that separate us from what we often, from the vantage of today's thoroughly technologized society, might disparage as "nature." Thus, in his discussion of the Western scientific tradition, Robert Romanyshyn describes our science and technology as tools that have created another sort of border by reconfiguring the human as "a spectator self ensconced behind its window" on the world.[1] Certainly, moreover, the films we commonly place within the science fiction classification repeatedly visualize this boundary situation. Most obviously, the robot stands as a border figure between the human and the machine; the rocket, spaceship, or flying saucer is a tool for traversing the boundaries of space; the scientist, such as *The Fly*'s (1986) Seth Brundle, holds the key to other knowledge, perhaps even other states of being. If the larger field of fantasy might be described as about the tracing of limits, then, science fiction might well be termed, with some precision, as a genre of borders, particularly as one that speculates on our ability to cross conventional borders [Fig. 69].

Nevertheless, I want to emphasize this notion of borders or boundaries here not simply as a final thematic statement about science fiction, but to point up several other margins at which this study has constantly played and that bear some parting acknowledgment. One of those follows from the very nature of the series in which this book is an entry. As part of the Genres in American Cinema series, this volume has focused on the varieties of science fiction film and particularly American-produced entries in this form. As the fantasy perspective employed here and especially the chapter on *The Fly* suggest, this work inevitably chafes slightly at its generic confines. We have repeatedly noted, for example, how a certain blurring of boundaries characterizes most studies of science fiction film; and indeed, our science fiction and horror films *do* share many of the same conventions, *do* deploy many comparable characters, *do* work through a number of similar themes. In my own course on film genres, I have often also included the musical as near kin to both of these forms, particularly as it suddenly reveals some hidden knowledge, like "the hills are alive with the sound of music," or as its characters transcend normal human behavior, like *Top Hat*'s (1935) Fred Astaire, who notes how he will often and inexplicably "suddenly find myself dancing." Such links should serve to remind us not so much that genres in the Hollywood context often combine or borrow from each other, but rather that the genres we so readily identify and think of as discrete forms may well draw on much larger structures whose markings are simply not so easy to discern.

Also following series guidelines, I have confined major commentary to American entries in the genre, although from time to time some of the form's key foreign examples – notably such works as *Aelita* (USSR, 1924), *Metropolis* (Germany, 1926), and *Things to Come* (England, 1936) – have figured in the discussion, and a film like *The Fly* with its Canadian connections complicates such nationalist boundaries. As our historical overview notes, the literary form of science fiction owes much of its development to such major European writers as Jules Verne and H. G. Wells, and some of the earliest French films follow in this tradition. However, the genre, particularly since the 1940s, has largely been dominated by American productions, and with the current emphasis on special-effects-laden, big-budget efforts, demanding the sort of resources seldom available outside of the American film industry, it figures to remain so, thanks to the frequent box-office successes of such films.[2] The hope is that the commentary on these dominant productions will serve usefully for thinking about the science fiction work of other national cinemas as well. As I have tried to suggest elsewhere, despite its preeminent success within the Hollywood big-budget, special-effects-laden context, the science fiction film finally knows no cultural borders.[3]

Figure 69. A nightmarish image of genre boundary crossing in the cult classic *Robot Monster* (1953).

Critical Consensus

The second issue of boundaries is perhaps more complex and follows from a trend in recent film criticism that haunts this volume's effort at offering a systematic yet flexible approach to the study of the science fiction film. This issue, as Nick Browne neatly summarizes, is bound up in a current tendency to view film genres as "specific assemblages of local coherencies – discrete, heterotropic instances of a complex cultural politics."[4] That is, we have increasingly shifted our focus away from trying to explain generic "coherencies," from thinking of genre as a kind of essential story composed of constant, if somewhat interchangeable elements, as well as various new additions. That movement derives in part from critical concurrence, the sense that we have simply mined this vein far too long, but also in part because postmodern criticism has become highly suspicious of any sort of essentializing tendency. Instead, now we more often talk of a genre as if it were a constantly shifting field of elements, responding to varying cultural pressures or perhaps to underlying economic factors, and thus having little in the way of a fundamental identity. This attitude tends to focus attention on the specific generic artifact at the expense of the larger generic field, and finds value in that artifact precisely insofar as it provides us with a trace or fingerprint of those "complex cultural politics" that, at this moment, have helped to shape it. Such a view has well served the evolving field of cultural studies and provided film studies an easy link to its concerns. More particularly, it has brought into sharper focus a little-explored function of our formulaic films, their status as what Browne terms "repetitive, contested sites of stagings" for various versions of our life.[5] The specific generic text becomes, in effect, a place where we can find the traces of those many cultural influences that together construct our identities and indeed our world.

Still, that approach to genre has its inherent limitations and establishes its own sort of borders with which this study has tried to work some compromise; for insofar as we rack focus specifically on a "cultural politics," we always run the risk of transforming the elements of genre to little more than a blurry background and seeing them not as part of that complex but simply as a convenient context or as unexplained "assemblages." Thus the common iconographic elements of science fiction – robots, spaceships, futuristic cities, time and matter transporters – could come to seem just a different sort of livery in which we dress up the most recent cultural issues, and as having little significant or consistent evocative potential in themselves, save insofar as that audiences, for the moment, find them exciting or curious (as if the "cinema of attractions" had never developed beyond its primitive state). In following up, perhaps even overemphasizing, the notion that generic narratives are constantly evolving structures, marvelous and developing sets of inventions, we have sidestepped any sort of discussion that suggests there is a character or concern that is fundamental to one genre and not necessarily to another. One result of this aversion to the essential is that we fail to recognize anything as particularly special or meaningful about a genre's patterns, nothing that finally merits distinguishing one form from another – or merits the writing of a book on, say, science fiction. Nonetheless, certain genres at particular points in our history have seemed especially adept at or useful for addressing, codifying, and imaginatively working out our cultural anxieties. As a most obvious example, we might consider the western, which has certainly treated the conflict between civilization and wilderness, between acculturating and asocial forces, far more effectively than the musical or melodrama has ever managed to do. Alternatively, we might just as evidently think of the science fiction film, which has arguably provided the most evocative context for working out our culture's conflicted attitudes toward the technological and those changes it heralds; yet some fear that admitting to any level of generic constancy might gainsay the demonstrably dynamic patterns observed in our formulaic films, or obscure their political thrust and coercion.

Dynamics of Genre

In the face of these difficulties, which might well seem of little consequence to most students of genre films, I have tried to stake out a *useful* ground for genre thinking, one that finally straddles some borders, for example, by admitting the dynamic while still holding onto something essential, and by describing narrative and thematic patterns that open onto the ideological. As we have seen, the American science fiction film displays a certain level of coherence, even as it also seems pulled at various times and by a variety of cultural forces in very different directions. That coherence at least superficially derives from what we have traditionally viewed as the "marks" of genre – the semantic and syntactic conventions that typify all formulaic discourse. What I have also suggested here is that other marks of coherence pertain as well. These include the structural marks shared by all of those narratives that do the work of fantasy, a form that, as Rosemary Jackson offers, "traces a space within a society's cognitive frame. It introduces multiple, contradictory 'truths'; it becomes polysemic."[6] As we have seen, fantasy does so by deploying its uncanny, marvelous, and fantastic patterns; that is, it actuates certain conventional ways of interrogating our world, often by describing alternative realities. Those patterns that force us to look inward, compel us to consider wholly exterior influences on our world, or simply confront us with mystery, with what might or might not be, can provide a convenient overlay for the science fiction genre, allowing us to group its narratives, more readily to gauge its changes and the dynamic interplay between those groupings, and to see more clearly specific themes that attach to this genre more commonly than to another.

Nevertheless, like so many other approaches – or theories, if you will – this way of looking at our science fiction films remains just an

Figure 70. Within that land without borders that is science fiction narrative: *2001: A Space Odyssey* (1968).

overlay, one tool that might be used along with a variety of others to help us ask questions about the genre. Insofar as it helps students to organize this field for their thinking, insofar as it draws them closer to the films and their implications for the American cultural landscape, insofar as it aids them in framing some of those questions about the genre, it should prove useful. If we see it, though, as simply an organizational scheme, a way of accounting for everything from *Alphaville* (1965) to *Zombies of the Stratosphere* (1952), it will prove of only minimal benefit. In effect, my aim too has been to offer another sort of border or outline for thinking about this genre, but one I encourage readers and viewers to feel free to cross, to transgress as their studies dictate.

The real appeal of this study, though, is the same for the writer as it is for the science fiction film audience. It comes not from trying to frame an approach to genre, but from exploring what for many seems to be the most important contemporary film genre. As Scott Bukatman offers, "there is simply no overstating the importance of science fiction to the present cultural moment, a moment that sees itself *as* science fiction."[7] For the science fiction film today typically seems to provide us not so much with the sort of "escape" the critics of the movies once ascribed to all genre productions, but rather with a mirror of and access to our increasingly complex cultural landscape. Brooks Landon describes this effect most tellingly when he suggests that the province of contemporary science fiction is not so much "what the future *might* hold, but the inevitable hold of the present over the future – what the future could not fail to be."[8] What he suggests, as viewers of such cinematic masterworks as *Blade Runner* (1982), *RoboCop* (1987), and *Terminator 2: Judgment Day* (1991) well know, is that we are already and always within that science fiction context, that land without borders, that world which bears all the trappings of a genre [Fig. 70]. An attempt to understand that genre better, or even to frame specific questions about its workings, can only help us to live in that world and perhaps to push a bit more effectively at its own boundaries.

Notes

PART I. APPROACHES

1. Introduction: The World of the Science Fiction Film

1. Cited in Edward James's *Science Fiction in the Twentieth Century* (Oxford: Oxford University Press, 1994), p. 50. Campbell is, of course, one of the most important figures in the shaping of modern science fiction literature.

2. David Hartwell, *Age of Wonders: Exploring the World of Science Fiction* (New York: McGraw–Hill, 1984), pp. 4, 10, 20.

3. James, *Science Fiction,* pp. 1, 2.

4. Darko Suvin, *Metamorphoses of Science Fiction: On the Poetics and History of a Literary Genre* (New Haven: Yale University Press, 1979), pp. 10, 4.

5. Ibid., p. 12.

6. As examples of that tendency to conflate horror and science fiction, we might note a number of early yet still valuable histories, most notably Carlos Clarens's seminal study, *An Illustrated History of the Horror Film* (New York: Capricorn, 1967) and John Baxter's *Science Fiction in the Cinema* (New York: Paperback Library, 1970).

7. Most commentaries on the nature of film genres describe and give a name to this problem. Edward Buscombe, for example, terms it the "philosophical problem of universals" in his "The Idea of Genre in the American Cinema," in Barry Keith Grant, ed., *Film Genre Reader II* (Austin: University of Texas Press, 1995), pp. 11–25, at p. 13.

8. For an example of this approach I might suggest my own treatment of perhaps the most amorphous American film genre, the film noir, in *Voices in the Dark: The Narrative Strategies of Film Noir* (Urbana: University of Illinois Press, 1989). Here I initially accept, for purposes of establishing a field of investigation, all those films that prior commentators have included in the noir category. From that inclusive starting point I was better able to identify and then describe the variety of narrative strategies involved in that genre.

9. Bruce F. Kawin, "Children of the Light," in Grant, ed., *Film Genre Reader II,* pp. 308–29, at pp. 319, 321.

10. Ibid., p. 313.

11. Ibid., p. 319.

12. John G. Cawelti, "The Question of Popular Genres," *Journal of Popular Film and Television 13,* no. 2 (1985): 55–61, at p. 56.

13. Tzvetan Todorov, *The Fantastic: A Structural Approach to a Literary Genre,*
    trans. Richard Howard (Ithaca: Cornell University Press, 1975), p. 14.
14. Ibid., pp. 35, 56.
15. Ibid., p. 8.
16. James, *Science Fiction,* p.13.
17. We might note that, as he set about describing the field of the horror film,
    Bruce Kawin also delineated three dominant narrative types. These types
    – tales of the supernatural, tales of the monstrous, and tales of psychosis
    – might arguably be described in terms of Todorov's fantastic categories
    as well, thereby further suggesting the natural links between these two
    forms. See Kawin, "Children of the Light," p. 326.
18. Todorov, *Fantastic,* p. 56.
19. Ibid., p. 120.
20. Ibid., p. 139.
21. His approach can be seen in Buscombe, "Idea of Genre."
22. Rick Altman, "A Semantic/Syntactic Approach to Film Genre," Grant, ed.,
    Film Genre Reader II, pp. 26–40, at p. 30.
23. Susan Sontag, "The Imagination of Disaster," *Against Interpretation and Oth-
    er Essays* (New York: Dell, 1966), pp. 212–28, at p. 223. Specifically, Sontag
    suggests that all of the genre's technological trappings essentially stand
    in for "the universal rule of reason."
24. Rosemary Jackson, *Fantasy: The Literature of Subversion* (London: Methu-
    en, 1981), p. 53.
25. Rosemary Jackson makes a similar point: She argues that all fantastic texts
    find their true appeal not so much in the sort of "escapism or . . . simple
    pleasure principle" (ibid., p. 2) that many critics emphasize and also use
    to dismiss the form from serious consideration, but rather in the way they
    "trace the unsaid and the unseen of culture" (p. 4), thereby exposing and
    subverting its limiting forces.
26. Ibid., p. 4.
27. Garrett Stewart, "The 'Videology' of Science Fiction," in George E. Slusser
    and Eric S. Rabkin, eds., *Shadows of the Magic Lamp: Fantasy and Science
    Fiction in Film* (Carbondale: Southern Illinois University Press, 1985), pp.
    159–207, at p. 159.
28. Albert J. La Valley, "Traditions of Trickery: The Role of Special Effects in
    the Science Fiction Film," in Slusser and Rabkin, eds., *Shadows of the Mag-
    ic Lamp,* pp. 141–58, at p. 141.
29. Ibid., p. 149.
30. Todorov, *Fantastic,* p. 115.
31. La Valley, "Traditions of Trickery," pp. 157–8. This tendency to see the sci-
    ence fiction film as too often detached from real-world consequences
    shows up in Susan Sontag's oft-cited discussion of the genre, "The Imag-
    ination of Disaster," wherein she argues that the genre is characterized
    by "an inadequate response" to the problems of the day (p. 227). Judith
    Hess Wright launches a far more fundamental assault on the genre, as she
    charges that genre films in general, and science fiction films particularly,
    inherently serve the status quo and are simply incapable, by their very
    conservative and nostalgic nature, of advancing a truly challenging or sub-

versive vision. See her "Genre Films and the Status Quo," in Grant, ed., *Film Genre Reader II,* pp. 41–9.

32. Robert D. Romanyshyn, *Technology as Symptom and Dream* (London: Routledge, 1989), p. 117.
33. Jean Baudrillard, *The Ecstasy of Communication*, trans. Bernard and Caroline Schutze (New York: Semiotext(e), 1987), p. 15.
34. Jackson, *Fantasy,* p. 13.
35. See Will Wright's *Sixguns and Society: A Structural Study of the Western* (Berkeley: University of California Press, 1975).

2. Science Fiction Film: The Critical Context

1. William Johnson, "Journey into Science Fiction," in Johnson, ed., *Focus on the Science Fiction Film* (Englewood Cliffs, N.J.: Prentice–Hall, 1972), pp. 1–12, at p. 1.
2. Tim Bywater and Thomas Sobchack, *Introduction to Film Criticism: Major Critical Approaches to Narrative Film* (New York: Longman, 1989), p. 27.
3. John Baxter, *Science Fiction in the Cinema* (New York: Paperback Library, 1970), pp. 7, 11.
4. Ibid., p. 207.
5. Denis Gifford, *Science Fiction Film* (London: Studio Vista, 1971), p. 151.
6. Harry Geduld, "Return to Méliès: Reflections on the Science Fiction Film," in Johnson, ed., *Focus on the Science Fiction Film*, pp. 142–7, at p. 142.
7. Susan Sontag, "Against Interpretation," *Against Interpretation and Other Essays* (New York: Dell, 1966), pp. 13–23, at pp. 17, 19.
8. Ibid., p. 21.
9. Susan Sontag, "The Imagination of Disaster," *Against Interpretation and Other Essays*, pp. 212–28, at p. 216.
10. Ibid., pp. 215, 218.
11. Ibid., p. 225.
12. Ibid., pp. 227, 228.
13. Ibid., p. 227, and "Against Interpretation," p. 23.
14. Terry Eagleton, *Literary Theory: An Introduction* (Minneapolis: University of Minnesota Press, 1983), p. 14.
15. Vivian Sobchack, *Screening Space: The American Science Fiction Film*, 2d ed. (New York: Ungar, 1987), p. 302.
16. Michael Stern, "Making Culture into Nature," in Annette Kuhn, ed., *Alien Zone: Cultural Theory and Contemporary Science Fiction Cinema* (London: Verso, 1990), pp. 66–72, at p. 72.
17. Michael Ryan and Douglas Kellner, "Technophobia," in Kuhn, ed., *Alien Zone*, pp. 58–65, at p. 62.
18. Ibid., p. 65.
19. Ibid., p. 60.
20. Judith Hess Wright, "Genre Films and the Status Quo," in Barry Keith Grant, ed., *Film Genre Reader II* (Austin: University of Texas Press, 1995), pp. 41–9. at pp. 41, 47–8.
21. Bywater and Sobchack, *Introduction to Film Criticism,* p. 185.

22. Margaret Tarratt, "Monsters from the Id," in Grant, ed., *Film Genre Reader II*, pp. 330–49, at p. 331.
23. Ibid., p. 338.
24. Ibid.
25. For a detailed account of the impact of Lacanian psychology on narrative studies, see the collection by Robert Con Davis, ed., *Lacan and Narration: The Psychoanalytic Difference in Narrative Theory* (Baltimore: Johns Hopkins University Press, 1983), especially the editor's introduction.
26. Bywater and Sobchack, *Introduction to Film Criticism*, p. 187.
27. Constance Penley, "Time Travel, Primal Scene and the Critical Dystopia," in Kuhn, ed., *Alien Zone*, pp. 116–27, at p. 120.
28. Ibid., p. 125.
29. Vivian Sobchack, "The Virginity of Astronauts: Sex and the Science Fiction Film," in Kuhn, ed., *Alien Zone*, pp. 103–15, at p. 104.
30. Ibid., p. 114.
31. Patrick Lucanio, *Them or Us: Archetypal Interpretations of Fifties Alien Invasion Films* (Bloomington: Indiana University Press, 1987), pp. 6, 83, 54.
32. Ibid., p. 131.
33. Ibid., p. 127.
34. See especially the interview with Haraway conducted by Constance Penley and Andrew Ross, "Cyborgs at Large: Interview with Donna Haraway," in Penley and Ross, eds., *Technoculture* (Minneapolis: University of Minnesota Press, 1991), pp. 1–20, at p. 3.
35. Donna Haraway, "The Actors Are Cyborg, Nature Is Coyote, and the Geography Is Elsewhere: Postscript to 'Cyborgs at Large,'" *Technoculture*, pp. 21–6, at p. 21.
36. Mary Ann Doane, "Technophilia: Technology, Representation, and the Feminine," in Mary Jacobus, Evelyn Fox Keller, and Sally Shuttleworth, eds., *Body/Politics: Women and the Discourse of Science* (London: Routledge, 1990), pp. 163–76, at p. 163.
37. Ibid., p. 174.
38. Ibid., p. 170.
39. Barbara Creed, "*Alien* and the Monstrous-Feminine," in Kuhn, ed., *Alien Zone*, pp. 128–41, at p. 129.
40. Ibid., p. 140.
41. Ibid., p. 129.
42. Claudia Springer, *Electronic Eros: Bodies and Desire in the Postindustrial Age* (Austin: University of Texas Press, 1996), p. 9.
43. Ibid., p. 8.
44. Ibid., p. 10.
45. Ibid., pp. 10, 100.
46. For background on the debate about the "objectivity" of science studies, see the collection *Science Wars* (Durham, N.C.: Duke University Press, 1996), especially the introduction by its editor, Andrew Ross, pp. 1–15.
47. Jean-François Lyotard, *The Postmodern Condition: A Report on Knowledge*, trans. Geoff Bennington and Brian Massumi (Minneapolis: University of Minnesota Press, 1984), p. xxiv.
48. The reader might begin to gauge the variety of postmodern readings of the

genre in Jameson's "Progress vs. Utopia; or, Can We Imagine the Future?" in *Science-Fiction Studies 9,* no. 2 (1982): 147–58; Landon's "Bet On It: Cyber/video/punk/performance," in Larry McCaffery, ed., *Storming the Reality Studio* (Durham, N.C.: Duke University Press, 1991), pp. 239–44; Telotte's *Replications: A Robotic History of the Science Fiction Film* (Urbana: University of Illinois Press, 1995); and Annette Kuhn's collection *Alien Zone.*

49. Scott Bukatman, "Who Programs You? The Science Fiction of the Spectacle," in Kuhn, ed., *Alien Zone,* pp. 196–213, at p. 204.
50. Scott Bukatman, *Terminal Identity: The Virtual Subject in Postmodern Science Fiction* (Durham, N.C.: Duke University Press, 1993), p. 9.
51. Ibid., pp. 217, 220.
52. Ibid., p. 329.
53. Giuliana Bruno, "Ramble City: Postmodernism and *Blade Runner,*" in Kuhn, ed., *Alien Zone,* pp. 183–95, at p. 184.
54. Ibid., p. 185.
55. Ibid., p. 193.
56. Per Schelde, *Androids, Humanoids, and Other Science Fiction Monsters: Science and Soul in Science Fiction Film* (New York: New York University Press, 1993), p. 3.
57. Ibid., pp. 8–9.
58. Ibid., p. 242.
59. Ibid., p. 82.

PART II. HISTORICAL OVERVIEW

3. A Trajectory of the American Science Fiction Film

1. David Hartwell, *Age of Wonders: Exploring the World of Science Fiction* (New York: McGraw–Hill, 1984), p. 42.
2. H. Bruce Franklin, *Future Perfect: American Science Fiction of the Nineteenth Century,* rev. ed. (New York: Oxford University Press, 1978), p. vii.
3. Ibid., p. viii. In *Future Perfect* Franklin offers a detailed discussion of both major and minor contributors to the American science fiction tradition, as well as samples from their works.
4. Edward James, *Science Fiction in the Twentieth Century* (Oxford: Oxford University Press, 1994), p. 13.
5. Harold Beaver, "Introduction," in Beaver, ed., *The Science Fiction of Edgar Allan Poe* (New York: Penguin, 1976), pp. vii–xxi, at p. xiii.
6. James, *Science Fiction,* p. 28.
7. Franklin, *Future Perfect,* p. 269. For background on the popularity of American utopian fiction, also see James D. Hart, *The Popular Book: A History of America's Literary Taste* (Berkeley: University of California Press, 1963).
8. James, *Science Fiction,* p. 43.
9. Franklin, *Future Perfect,* pp. viii–ix.
10. Howard P. Segal, "The Technological Utopians," in Joseph J. Corn, ed., *Imagining Tomorrow: History, Technology, and the American Future* (Cambridge, Mass.: MIT Press, 1986), pp. 119–36, at p. 122. I am indebted to this essay for much of the background on turn-of-the-century American utopi-

an thought. For a discussion of different types of utopian narrative, consult Peter Ruppert's *Reader in a Strange Land: The Activity of Reading Literary Utopias* (Athens: University of Georgia Press, 1986).

11. For a detailed discussion of the naming of the science fiction genre, see James, *Science Fiction*, pp. 7–11, as well as Hartwell, *Age of Wonders*, pp. 118–19. Although the term "science-fiction" was first used in England in 1851, this label did not catch on, largely, we might suppose, because there was no significant body of work for it to designate. We might also note that the designation "pseudo-scientific stories" continued to be used by a major reference work like the *Readers' Guide to Periodical Literature* until 1961.

12. Quoted in Paul A. Carter's *The Creation of Tomorrow: Fifty Years of Magazine Science Fiction* (New York: Columbia University Press, 1977), p. 9.

13. Ibid., p. 65.

14. James, *Science Fiction*, p. 57.

15. Ibid., p. 58.

16. Although I emphasize some major differences between the pulps and the early science fiction comics, I should acknowledge one area of near-kinship. A pulp fanzine, *Science Fiction*, first printed a two-page strip of Superman, a figure that was picked up in 1938 by the new *Action Comics*. An even closer line of kinship shows up in the case of *Marvel Mystery Comics*, which published a number of the more popular figures, such as Captain America, the Human Torch, and the Submariner; and this comic was itself an offshoot of a pulp science fiction magazine, *Marvel Science Stories*.

17. For a brief background on these and other science fiction illustrators, see the essay "Science Fiction Art" in Brian Ash's *The Visual Encyclopedia of Science Fiction* (New York: Harmony Books, 1977), pp. 286–92.

18. James, *Science Fiction*, p. 54.

19. Scott Bukatman, *Terminal Identity: The Virtual Subject in Postmodern Science Fiction* (Durham, N.C.: Duke University Press, 1993), p. 6.

20. Veronica Hollinger, "Cybernetic Deconstructions: Cyberpunk and Postmodernism," in Larry McCaffery, ed., *Storming the Reality Studio* (Durham, N.C.: Duke University Press, 1991), pp. 203–18, at p. 204.

21. William Gibson, *Neuromancer* (New York: Ace Books, 1984), p. 5.

22. Larry McCaffery, "Introduction: The Desert of the Real," in McCaffery, ed., *Storming the Reality Studio*, pp. 1–16, at pp. 1, 14.

23. Richard Kadrey and Larry McCaffery, "Cyberpunk 101," *Storming the Reality Studio*, pp. 17–29, at p. 17.

24. Brian McHale, "POSTcyberMODERNpunkISM," *Storming the Reality Studio*, pp. 308–23, at p. 320.

25. Garrett Stewart, "The 'Videology' of Science Fiction," in George E. Slusser and Eric S. Rabkin, eds., *Shadows of the Magic Lamp: Fantasy and Science Fiction in Film* (Carbondale: Southern Illinois University Press, 1985), pp. 159–207, at p. 159.

26. Ibid., p. 161.

27. Terry Ramsaye, *A Million and One Nights: A History of the Motion Picture* (New York: Simon & Schuster, 1926; rpt., New York: Touchstone, 1986), pp. 154–5.

28. Ibid., p. 159.

29. For a discussion of the nature and appeal of early film, consult Gunning's

influential essay "The Cinema of Attraction: Early Film, Its Spectator and the Avant Garde," *Wide Angle 8,* nos. 3/4 (1986): 63–70. As he has explained, early cinema should be considered in terms of its fascination with novelty and its repeated emphasis on the act of display, elements for which a burgeoning science fiction cinema was quite well suited.

30. Albert J. La Valley, "Traditions of Trickery: The Role of Special Effects in the Science Fiction Film," in Slusser and Rabkin, eds., *Shadows of the Magic Lamp,* pp. 141–58, at p. 146.
31. Raymond Durgnat, *The Crazy Mirror* (New York: Dutton, 1970), p. 71.
32. Richard Guy Wilson, Dianne H. Pilgrim, and Dickran Tashjian, *The Machine Age in America: 1918–1941* (New York: Abrams, 1986), p. 23.
33. One of my own studies examines early science fiction film in the context of the Machine Age and especially in light of the specific set of cultural values that accompanied the era's fascination with machine technology. J. P. Telotte, *A Distant Technology: Science Fiction Film and the Machine Age* (Middletown, Conn.: Wesleyan University Press, and Hanover, N.H.: University Press of New England, 1999).
34. Joseph J. Corn, "Introduction," in Corn, ed., *Imagining Tomorrow: History, Technology, and the American Future* (Cambridge, Mass.: MIT Press, 1986), pp. 1–9, at p. 8.
35. Cecelia Tichi, *Shifting Gears: Technology, Literature, Culture in Modernist America* (Chapel Hill: University of North Carolina Press, 1987), p. 240.
36. Ibid., p. 42.
37. We should note how pervasive this emphasis on using technology to cheat death was in this period. In addition to the obvious example of *Frankenstein* (1931) and its numerous sequels, the notion of a rejuvenating power shows up in *Just Imagine, Six Hours to Live, The Phantom Empire* (1935), and *The Man They Could Not Hang* (1939), among other films. This motif's recurrence in a fledgling science fiction cinema certainly suggests the sort of great, if naïve hopes that this era attached to the developments of science and technology.
38. See Alan G. Barbour's *Cliffhanger* (Secaucus, N.J.: Citadel Press, 1977) for an overview of the form.
39. John Baxter, *Science Fiction in the Cinema* (New York: Paperback Library, 1970), p. 75.
40. Tichi, *Shifting Gears,* p. 16.
41. In my historical treatment of the robot image in film, I offer a more detailed discussion of serial storytelling, particularly focusing on its rather mechanical approach to narrative. See J. P. Telotte, *Replications: A Robotic History of the Science Fiction Film* (Urbana: University of Illinois Press, 1995), pp. 91–110.
42. Baxter, *Science Fiction in the Cinema,* p. 101.
43. James, *Science Fiction,* p. 13.
44. Peter Biskind, *Seeing Is Believing: How Hollywood Taught Us to Stop Worrying and Love the Fifties* (New York: Pantheon, 1983), pp. 159, 158.
45. For a useful listing and categorization of films of the Atomic Age, see the annotated filmography "The Atomic Age: Facts and Films from 1945–1965" by Bryan Fruth et al. in *Journal of Popular Film and Television 23,* no. 4 (1996): 154–60.

46. Rosemary Jackson, *Fantasy: The Literature of Subversion* (London: Methuen, 1981), p. 13.

47. For much of my discussion of *2001* I am indebted to what remains one of the best commentaries on the film, Mary McDermott and W. R. Robinson's "*2001* and the Literary Sensibility," in *The Georgia Review 26* (1972): 21–37. Clearly impelled by a sense of the film's importance to both the science fiction genre and to film narrative, the authors suggest that it might be "the most affirmative work of art in Western visual culture" (23), and their analysis supports that assertion by placing it in another sort of evolutionary context, that of Western culture's increasing movement from verbal to visual narrative.

48. Andrew Gordon, "*Close Encounters*: The Gospel According to Steven Spielberg," *Literature/Film Quarterly 8*, no. 3 (1980): 156–64, at p. 156.

49. Robert D. Romanyshyn, *Technology as Symptom and Dream* (London: Routledge, 1989), p. 114.

50. For a detailed discussion of these three genres, as well as of their similar focus on postmodern problems of "gender identity," see Annalee Newitz, "Magical Girls and Atomic Bomb Sperm: Japanese Animation in America," *Film Quarterly 49*, no. 1 (1995): 2–15.

51. Ibid., p. 4.

52. Ibid., p. 9.

53. Ibid., p. 12.

54. Mike Lyons traces out the development of CGI effects, with a particular emphasis on their applications to screen fantasy, in his "Cyber-Cinema," *Cinefantastique 28*, no. 8 (1997): 40–3, 62.

55. Ibid., p. 41.

56. Janet H. Murray, *Hamlet on the Holodeck: The Future of Narrative in Cyberspace* (Cambridge, Mass.: MIT Press, 1997), p. 15.

57. Romanyshyn, *Technology as Symptom and Dream*, p. 67.

PART III. FILM ANALYSES

4. The Science Fiction Film as Fantastic Text

1. Paul Ricoeur, "Ideology and Utopia as Cultural Imagination," in Donald M. Borchert and David Stewart, eds., *Being Human in a Technological Age* (Athens: Ohio University Press, 1979), pp. 107–25, at pp. 107, 122.

2. In treating the utopian and dystopian narratives simply as variations on a similar impulse, I follow a tradition in such commentary best summed up by Peter Ruppert, who notes that "just as every utopia contains within it, explicitly or implicitly, an anti-utopia that it tries to transform, so every anti-utopia implies a utopian alternative, the construction of which is left up to the reader." See Ruppert, *Reader in a Strange Land: The Activity of Reading Literary Utopias* (Athens: University of Georgia Press, 1986), p. 116.

3. Ricoeur, "Ideology and Utopia," p. 121.

4. Ibid., p. 107.

5. Rosemary Jackson, *Fantasy: The Literature of Subversion* (London: Methuen, 1981), p. 26.

6. Tzvetan Todorov, *The Fantastic: A Structural Approach to a Literary Genre*, trans. Richard Howard (Ithaca: Cornell University Press, 1975), p. 31.
7. Ibid., p. 32.
8. Jackson, *Fantasy*, p. 18.
9. Lewis Mumford, *The Story of Utopias* (New York: Viking, 1962), p. 37.
10. Ibid., p. 2.
11. For a discussion of these cultural tensions, and particularly of the conflict between a technocratic and an antitechnology spirit in England during this period, see J. P. Telotte, *A Distant Technology: Science Fiction Film and the Machine Age* (Middletown, Conn.: Wesleyan University Press, and Hanover, N.H.: University Press of New England, 1999), pp. 139–61.
12. Garrett Stewart, "The 'Videology' of Science Fiction," in George E. Slusser and Eric S. Rabkin, eds., *Shadows of the Magic Lamp: Fantasy and Science Fiction in Film* (Carbondale: Southern Illinois University Press, 1985), pp. 159–207, at p. 159.
13. Sally Kline, ed., *George Lucas: Interviews* (Jackson: University of Mississippi Press, 1999), p. 10.
14. Much of the background on the filming of *THX 1138* is taken from ibid., pp. 8–10.
15. Paul Virilio, *War and Cinema: The Logistics of Perception*, trans. Patrick Camiller (London: Verso, 1989), p. 79.
16. Paul Virilio, "The Last Vehicle," in Dietmar Kamper and Christoph Wulf, eds., *Looking Back on the End of the World* (New York: Semiotext(e), 1989), pp. 106–19, at p. 115.
17. Stewart, "'Videology' of Science Fiction," p. 161.
18. Michael Pye and Lynda Myles, *The Movie Brats: How the Film Generation Took Over Hollywood* (New York: Holt, Rinehart, 1979), p. 117.
19. That sense of the labyrinthine seems central to the film's original conception, as is suggested by the source for the feature movie, George Lucas's award-winning short student film entitled *Electronic Labyrinth: THX 1138: 4EB* (Pye and Myles, *Movie Brats*, p. 115).
20. Paul Virilio, *The Vision Machine*, trans. Julie Rose (Bloomington: Indiana University Press, 1994), p. 60.
21. Louise Wilson, "Cyberwar, God and Television: Interview with Paul Virilio," *CTheory* (www.ctheory.com/a-cyberwar_god.html).
22. Pye and Myles, *Movie Brats*, p. 118.
23. As Rosemary Jackson explains, this sort of "inscription of fantasy on the level of narrative *structure*" is not only one of the form's defining features, but it also functions "as a displacement of fantasy's central *thematic* issue: an uncertainty as to the nature of the 'real'" (Jackson, *Fantasy*, p. 48).
24. Albert J. La Valley, "Traditions of Trickery: The Role of Special Effects in the Science Fiction Film," in Slusser and Rabkin, eds., *Shadows of the Magic Lamp*, pp. 141–58, at p. 156.
25. Mark Poster, ed., *Jean Baudrillard: Selected Writings* (Stanford, Calif.: Stanford University Press, 1988), p. 149.
26. Ibid., p. 174.
27. Ruppert, *Reader in a Strange Land*, p. 119.
28. Virilio, *War and Cinema*, p. 66.

29. "No place," we should recall, is the literal translation of the word "utopia."
30. In this notion we might see a key distinction between the thinking of Baudrillard and that of Virilio; for while the former consistently talks of *simulation,* the latter emphasizes the distinct difference that *substitution* represents. As Virilio offers, "we are entering a world where there won't be one but two realities . . . the actual, and the virtual. Thus there is no simulation, but substitution. Reality has become symmetrical. The splitting of reality in two parts is a considerable event which goes far beyond simulation," and one in which he sees potentially dangerous consequences (see Wilson, "Cyberwar, God and Television").
31. Jackson, *Fantasy,* p. 25.

5. The Science Fiction Film as Marvelous Text

1. Rosemary Jackson, *Fantasy: The Literature of Subversion* (London: Methuen, 1981), p. 19.
2. Susan Sontag, "The Imagination of Disaster," *Against Interpretation and Other Essays* (New York: Dell, 1966), pp. 212–28. Sontag's article has proven one of the most influential on science fiction film criticism, particularly for its symptomatic reading of the genre, as indicative of a (dominantly American) mindset that is highly skeptical, even afraid of the products of our science and technology. See Chapter 2 for a summary of this essay.
3. Quoted in Michael Pye and Lynda Myles, *The Movie Brats: How the Film Generation Took Over Hollywood* (New York: Holt, Rinehart, 1979), p. 241.
4. *Close Encounters* was nominated for the following Academy Awards: Art Direction, Cinematography, Director, Editing, Screenplay, Sound, Supporting Actress, and Visual Effects; it won in the area of Cinematography. Among many other awards, it was named Best Picture of the year by the New York Film Critics Circle.
5. Jackson, *Fantasy,* p. 24.
6. Damon Knight, *In Search of Wonder: Essays on Modern Science Fiction,* rev. ed. (Chicago: Advent, 1967), p. 4.
7. Tzvetan Todorov, *The Fantastic: A Structural Approach to a Literary Genre,* trans. Richard Howard (Ithaca: Cornell University Press, 1975), p. 56.
8. Ibid., p. 83.
9. Stanley Kauffmann, "Epiphany," *The New Republic,* 10 Dec. 1977, pp. 20–1, at p. 20.
10. Andrew Gordon, "*Close Encounters:* The Gospel According to Steven Spielberg," *Literature/Film Quarterly 8,* no. 3 (1980): 156–64, at pp. 156–7.
11. Edward W. Said, *Orientalism* (New York: Random House, 1978), pp. 4, 3.
12. Gordon, "*Close Encounters:* Gospel." p. 160.
13. Ibid.
14. Mitch Tuchman, "Close Encounter with Steven Spielberg," *Film Comment 14,* no. 1 (1978): 49–55, at p. 49.
15. Gordon, "*Close Encounters:* Gospel." p. 163.
16. Ibid., p. 161.
17. A novelist with a pointedly religious bent, Percy chose a science fiction format for a number of his later books and, in the process, pointed toward

the sort of effective marriage of science fiction and the marvelous that Spielberg works out in *Close Encounters.* The work to which I refer here is his mix of fiction and essay, *Lost in the Cosmos; or, The Last Self-Help Book* (New York: Farrar, Straus, 1983).

18. Pye and Myles, *Movie Brats,* pp. 245–6.
19. Quoted in Joseph McBride's *Steven Spielberg: A Biography* (New York: Da Capo Press, 1999), p. 291.
20. Todorov, *Fantastic,* p. 103.
21. Ibid., p. 139.
22. Ibid., p. 127.

6. The Science Fiction Film as Uncanny Text

1. Rosemary Jackson, *Fantasy: The Literature of Subversion* (London: Methuen, 1981), p. 67.
2. Tzvetan Todorov, *The Fantastic: A Structural Approach to a Literary Genre,* trans. Richard Howard (Ithaca: Cornell University Press, 1975), p. 120.
3. Ibid.
4. Chris Shea and Wade Jennings, "Paul Verhoeven: An Interview," *Post Script 12,* no. 3 (1993): 3–24, at p. 9.
5. Ibid., p. 11
6. Between the studio and the MPAA's ratings board, *RoboCop* was cut, according to Verhoeven, eight times in efforts to obtain a more favorable rating. See his discussion of this process in ibid., p. 14.
7. Ibid.
8. Jackson, *Fantasy,* p. 25.
9. Darko Suvin, *Metamorphoses of Science Fiction: On the Poetics and History of a Literary Genre* (New Haven: Yale University Press, 1979), p. 10.
10. Asimov created his laws of robotics in consultation with the famous science fiction writer and editor Joseph W. Campbell Jr. as he set about writing a series of robot stories in the late 1930s and early 1940s. They are here taken from his collection of robotics stories, *I, Robot* (Greenwich, Conn.: Fawcett Crest, 1950), p. 40.
11. Shea and Jennings, "Paul Verhoeven: An Interview," pp. 18–19. We might recall that Verhoeven's academic training was in mathematics and physics. That scientific background points up both the authority with which he speaks about the reason–science–technology triad and the complexity of his satiric treatment of that world view.
12. Jackson, *Fantasy,* p. 90.
13. Todorov, *Fantastic,* p. 115.
14. Paul Virilio, *War and Cinema: The Logistics of Perception,* trans. Patrick Camiller (London: Verso, 1989), p. 79.
15. Shea and Jennings, "Paul Verhoeven: An Interview," p. 19.
16. Virilio, *War and Cinema,* p. 79.
17. Brian Cronenworth, "Man of Iron," *American Film 13,* no. 1 (1987): 33–5, at p. 35.
18. Shea and Jennings, "Paul Verhoeven: An Interview," p. 19.

19. Barry K. Grant, "*Invaders from Mars* and the Science Fiction Film in the Age of Reagan," *CineAction!* no. 8 (1987): 77–83, at p. 83.
20. Ibid.

7. Crossing Genre Boundaries / Bound by Fantasy

1. Bruce F. Kawin, "Children of the Light," in Barry Keith Grant, ed., *Film Genre Reader II* (Austin: University of Texas Press, 1995), pp. 308–29, at p. 314.
2. Rick Altman, *Film/Genre* (London: BFI Publishing, 1999), p. 59. Altman's theory about genres developing from studio-bred cycles is pointedly tied to the economic character of the Hollywood studio system; as he offers, "Hollywood studios have little interest in anything that must be shared with their competitors," such as full-blown genres (59). He thus argues that, particularly in their early stages, genres are constantly characterized by the sort of boundary blurrings we note here.
3. Kawin, "Children of the Light," p. 322.
4. Caroline Picart, "Re-Birthing the Monstrous: James Whale's (Mis)Reading of Mary Shelley's *Frankenstein*," *Critical Studies in Mass Communication 15,* no. 4 (1998): 383–96, at p. 383.
5. Frank McConnell, "Born in Fire: The Ontology of the Monster," in George E. Slusser and Eric S. Rabkin, eds., *Shadows of the Magic Lamp: Fantasy and Science Fiction in Film* (Carbondale: Southern Illinois University Press, 1985), pp. 231–8, at p. 237.
6. Kawin suggests that the science fiction film's appeal lies in its advocacy of "the creative use of intelligent curiosity," whereas the horror film warns us about the dangers of that same curiosity. See "Children of the Light," p. 321.
7. Chris Rodley, ed., *Cronenberg on Cronenberg* (London: Faber & Faber, 1992), p. 57.
8. Bart Testa, "Technology's Body: Cronenberg, Genre, and the Canadian Ethos," *Post Script 15,* no. 1 (1995): 39–56.
9. Rodley, ed., *Cronenberg on Cronenberg,* p. 59.
10. Ibid., p. 131.
11. Ibid., p. 5.
12. Barbara Creed, "*Alien* and the Monstrous-Feminine," in Annette Kuhn, ed., *Alien Zone: Cultural Theory and Contemporary Science Fiction Cinema* (London: Verso, 1990), pp. 128–41, at p. 137.
13. Tzvetan Todorov, *The Fantastic: A Structural Approach to a Literary Genre,* trans. Richard Howard (Ithaca: Cornell University Press, 1975), p. 139.
14. We might consider in this context the frequent description of the film as a thinly disguised allegory about the issue of AIDS. Indeed, Cronenberg often refers to Seth's problem as a kind of "disease," and notes that what really "fascinated" him about the story was the question of "how does this man deal with his disease: rationalize it, articulate it?" See Rodley, ed., *Cronenberg on Cronenberg,* p. 124.
15. Leonard Heldreth, "Festering in Thebes: Elements of Tragedy and Myth in Cronenberg's Films," *Post Script 15,* no. 2 (1996): 46–61, at p. 59.

16. Harvey Roy Greenberg, "Machine Dreams," *Film and Philosophy*, no. 4 (1997): 111–15, at p. 111.
17. Robert Haas, "Introduction: The Cronenberg Project: Literature, Science, Psychology, and the Monster in Cinema," *Post Script 15*, no. 2 (1996): 3–10, at p. 5.
18. Rodley, ed., *Cronenberg on Cronenberg*, p. 123. Cronenberg here describes *The Fly* as his "biggest financial success; it made more money than all the other films combined" (p. 134). Information on the production background of *The Fly* is drawn from this volume, pp. 122–34.
19. Testa, "Technology's Body," p. 51.
20. Rodley, ed., *Cronenberg on Cronenberg*, p. 90.
21. Altman, *Film/Genre*, p. 59.
22. Ibid., p. 57.

8. Conclusion: A Note on Boundaries

1. Robert D. Romanyshyn, *Technology as Symptom and Dream* (London: Routledge, 1989), p. 114.
2. Janet Wasko, in her study *Hollywood in the Information Age* (Austin: University of Texas Press, 1995), describes how "the number of science fiction or space epics have increased with the evolution of sophisticated effects techniques," and suggests that "it may even be possible that many audience members may reject films without such high-tech adventures and action" (38).
3. See my discussion of the science fiction film's role in the construction of Western culture's attitudes toward the technological: J. P. Telotte, *A Distant Technology: Science Fiction Film and the Machine Age* (Middletown, Conn.: Wesleyan University Press, and Hanover, N.H.: University Press of New England, 1999).
4. Nick Browne, "Preface," in Browne, ed., *Refiguring American Film Genres: Theory and History* (Berkeley: University of California Press, 1998), pp. iii–xiv. at p. xi.
5. Ibid., p. xiv.
6. Rosemary Jackson, *Fantasy: The Literature of Subversion* (London: Methuen, 1981), p. 23.
7. Scott Bukatman, *Terminal Identity: The Virtual Subject in Postmodern Science Fiction* (Durham, N.C.: Duke University Press, 1993), p. 6.
8. Brooks Landon, "Bet On It: Cyber/video/punk/performance," in Larry McCaffery, ed., *Storming the Reality Studio* (Durham, N.C.: Duke University Press, 1991), pp. 239–44, at p. 239.

Bibliography

Altman, Rick. *Film/Genre.* London: BFI Publishing, 1999.
  "A Semantic/Syntactic Approach to Film Genre." In Grant, ed., *Film Genre Reader II,* pp. 26–40.
Ash, Brian, ed. *The Visual Encyclopedia of Science Fiction.* New York: Harmony Books, 1977.
Asimov, Isaac. *I, Robot.* Greenwich, Conn.: Fawcett Crest, 1950.
Barbour, Alan G. *Cliffhanger.* Secaucus, N.J.: Citadel Press, 1977.
Baudrillard, Jean. *The Ecstasy of Communication.* Trans. Bernard and Caroline Schutze. New York: Semiotext(e), 1987.
Baxter, John. *Science Fiction in the Cinema.* New York: Paperback Library, 1970.
Beaver, Harold. "Introduction." In Beaver, ed., *The Science Fiction of Edgar Allan Poe.* New York: Penguin, 1976, pp. vii–xxi.
Biskind, Peter. *Seeing Is Believing: How Hollywood Taught Us to Stop Worrying and Love the Fifties.* New York: Pantheon, 1983.
Brosnan, John. *Movie Magic: The Story of Special Effects in the Cinema.* New York: New American Library, 1976.
Browne, Nick, ed. *Refiguring American Film Genres: Theory and History.* Berkeley: University of California Press, 1998.
Bruno, Guiliana. "Ramble City: Postmodernism and *Blade Runner.*" *October* no. 41 (1987): 61–74. Reprinted in Kuhn, ed., *Alien Zone,* pp. 183–95.
Bukatman, Scott. "The Cybernetic (City)State: Terminal Space Becomes Phenomenal." *Journal of the Fantastic in the Arts 2,* no. 2 (1989): 43–63.
  Terminal Identity: The Virtual Subject in Postmodern Science Fiction. Durham, N.C.: Duke University Press, 1993.
  "Who Programs You? The Science Fiction of the Spectacle." In Kuhn, ed., *Alien Zone,* pp. 196–213.
Buscombe, Edward. "The Idea of Genre in the American Cinema." In Grant, ed., *Film Genre Reader II,* pp. 11–25.
Bywater, Tim, and Thomas Sobchack. *Introduction to Film Criticism: Major Critical Approaches to Narrative Film.* New York: Longman, 1989.
Carter, Paul A. *The Creation of Tomorrow: Fifty Years of Magazine Science Fiction.* New York: Columbia University Press, 1977.
Cawelti, John G. "The Question of Popular Genres." *Journal of Popular Film and Television 13,* no. 2 (1985): 55–61.
Clarens, Carlos. *An Illustrated History of the Horror Film.* New York: Capricorn, 1967.
Cook, David A. *A History of Narrative Film.* 3d ed. New York: W. W. Norton, 1996.

Corn, Joseph J., ed. *Imagining Tomorrow: History, Technology, and the American Future.* Cambridge, Mass.: MIT Press, 1986.

"Introduction." In Corn, ed., *Imagining Tomorrow,* pp. 1–9.

Creed, Barbara. "*Alien* and the Monstrous-Feminine." In Kuhn, ed., *Alien Zone,* pp. 128–41.

Cronenworth, Brian. "Man of Iron." *American Film 13,* no. 1 (1987): 33–5.

Davis, Robert Con, ed. *Lacan and Narration: The Psychoanalytic Difference in Narrative Theory.* Baltimore: Johns Hopkins University Press, 1983.

Doane, Mary Ann. "Technophilia: Technology, Representation, and the Feminine." In Mary Jacobus, Evelyn Fox Keller, and Sally Shuttleworth, eds., *Body/Politics: Women and the Discourse of Science.* London: Routledge, 1990, pp. 163–76.

Dowdy, Andrew. *The Films of the Fifties: The American State of Mind.* New York: Morrow, 1973.

Durgnat, Raymond. *The Crazy Mirror.* New York: Dutton, 1970.

Eagleton, Terry. *Literary Theory: An Introduction.* Minneapolis: University of Minnesota Press, 1983.

Franklin, H. Bruce. *Future Perfect: American Science Fiction of the Nineteenth Century.* Rev. ed. New York: Oxford University Press, 1978.

Fruth, Bryan, et al. "The Atomic Age: Facts and Films from 1945–1965." *Journal of Popular Film and Television 23,* no. 4 (1996): 154–60.

Geduld, Harry. "Return to Méliès: Reflections on the Science Fiction Film." In Johnson, ed., *Focus on the Science Fiction Film,* pp. 142–7.

Gibson, William. *Neuromancer.* New York: Ace Books, 1984.

Gifford, Denis. *Science Fiction Film.* London: Studio Vista, 1971.

Gordon, Andrew. "*Close Encounters:* The Gospel According to Steven Spielberg." *Literature/Film Quarterly 8,* no. 3 (1980): 156–64.

"*The Empire Strikes Back:* Monsters from the Id." *Science-Fiction Studies 7,* no. 3 (1980): 313–18.

"*Return of the Jedi:* The End of the Myth." *Film Criticism 12,* no. 2 (1988): 37–52.

"Science Fiction Film Criticism: The Postmodern Always Rings Twice." *Science-Fiction Studies 14,* no. 3 (1987): 386–91.

Grant, Barry K. "*Invaders from Mars* and the Science Fiction Film in the Age of Reagan." *CineAction!* no. 8 (1987): 77–83.

ed. *Film Genre Reader II.* Austin: University of Texas Press, 1995.

Greenberg, Harvey Roy. "Machine Dreams." *Film and Philosophy,* no. 4 (1997): 111–15.

Gunning, Tom. "The Cinema of Attraction: Early Film, Its Spectator and the Avant-Garde." *Wide Angle 8,* nos. 3–4 (1986): 63–70.

Haas, Robert. "Introduction: The Cronenberg Project: Literature, Science, Psychology, and the Monster in Cinema." *Post Script 15,* no. 2 (1996): 3–10.

Haraway, Donna. "The Actors Are Cyborg, Nature Is Coyote, and the Geography Is Elsewhere: Postscript to 'Cyborgs at Large.'" In Penley and Ross, eds., *Technoculture,* pp. 21–6.

Simians, Cyborgs, and Women: The Reinvention of Nature. New York: Routledge, 1991.

Hardison, O. B., Jr. *Disappearing through the Skylight: Culture and Technology in the Twentieth Century.* New York: Viking, 1989.

Hart, James D. *The Popular Book: A History of America's Literary Taste.* Berkeley: University of California Press, 1963.

Hartwell, David. *Age of Wonders: Exploring the World of Science Fiction.* New York: McGraw–Hill, 1984.

Heldreth, Leonard. "Festering in Thebes: Elements of Tragedy and Myth in Cronenberg's Films." *Post Script 15,* no. 2 (1996): 46–61.

Hollinger, Veronica. "Cybernetic Deconstructions: Cyberpunk and Postmodernism." In McCaffery, ed., *Storming the Reality Studio,* pp. 203–18.

Jackson, Rosemary. *Fantasy: The Literature of Subversion.* London: Methuen, 1981.

James, Edward. *Science Fiction in the Twentieth Century.* Oxford: Oxford University Press, 1994.

Jameson, Fredric. "Progress vs. Utopia; or, Can We Imagine the Future?" *Science-Fiction Studies 9,* no. 2 (1982): 147–58.

"SF Novels/SF Film." *Science-Fiction Studies 7,* no. 3 (1980): 319–22.

Johnson, William. "Journey into Science Fiction." In Johnson, ed., *Focus on the Science Fiction Film,* pp. 1–12.

ed. *Focus on the Science Fiction Film.* Englewood Cliffs, N.J.: Prentice–Hall, 1972.

Kadrey, Richard, and Larry McCaffery. "Cyberpunk 101." In McCaffery, ed., *Storming the Reality Studio,* pp. 17–29.

Kauffmann, Stanley. "Epiphany." *The New Republic,* 10 Dec. 1977, pp. 20–1.

Kawin, Bruce F. "Children of the Light." In Grant, ed., *Film Genre Reader II,* pp. 308–29.

Kline, Sally, ed. *George Lucas: Interviews.* Jackson: University Press of Mississippi, 1999.

Knight, Damon. *In Search of Wonder: Essays on Modern Science Fiction.* Rev. ed. Chicago: Advent, 1967.

Kuhn, Annette, ed. *Alien Zone: Cultural Theory and Contemporary Science Fiction Cinema.* London: Verso, 1990.

La Valley, Albert J. "Traditions of Trickery: The Role of Special Effects in the Science Fiction Film." In Slusser and Rabkin, eds., *Shadows of the Magic Lamp,* pp. 141–58.

Landon, Brooks. "Bet On It: Cyber/video/punk/performance." In McCaffery, ed., *Storming the Reality Studio,* pp. 239–44.

"Cyberpunk." *Cinefantastique 18,* no. 1 (1987): 27–31, 58.

"Rethinking Science Fiction in the Age of Electronic (Re)production: On a Clear Day You Can See the Horizon of Invisibility." *Post Script 10,* no. 1 (1990): 60–71.

Lavery, David. *Late for the Sky: The Mentality of the Space Age.* Carbondale: Southern Illinois University Press, 1992.

Lucanio, Patrick. *Them or Us: Archetypal Interpretations of Fifties Alien Invasion Films.* Bloomington: Indiana University Press, 1987.

Lyons, Mike. "Cyber-Cinema." *Cinefantastique 28,* no. 8 (1997): 40–3, 62.

Lyotard, Jean-François. *The Postmodern Condition: A Report on Knowledge.* Trans. Geoff Bennington and Brian Massumi. Minneapolis: University of Minnesota Press, 1984.

McBride, Joseph. *Steven Spielberg: A Biography.* New York: Da Capo Press, 1999.

McCaffery, Larry. "Introduction: The Desert of the Real." In McCaffery, ed., *Storming the Reality Studio,* pp. 1–16.

——— ed. *Storming the Reality Studio.* Durham, N.C.: Duke University Press, 1991.

McConnell, Frank. "Born in Fire: The Ontology of the Monster." In Slusser and Rabkin, eds., *Shadows of the Magic Lamp,* pp. 231–8.

McDermott, Mary, and W. R. Robinson. "*2001* and the Literary Sensibility." *The Georgia Review,* no. 26 (1972): 21–37.

McHale, Brian. "POSTcyberMODERNpunkISM." In McCaffery, ed., *Storming the Reality Studio,* pp. 308–23.

Mumford, Lewis. *The Story of Utopias.* New York: Viking, 1962.

Murray, Janet H. *Hamlet on the Holodeck: The Future of Narrative in Cyberspace.* Cambridge, Mass.: MIT Press, 1997.

Newitz, Annalee. "Magical Girls and Atomic Bomb Sperm: Japanese Animation in America." *Film Quarterly 49,* no. 1 (1995): 2–15.

Penley, Constance. "Time Travel, Primal Scene and the Critical Dystopia." In Kuhn, ed., *Alien Zone,* pp. 116–27.

Penley, Constance, and Andrew Ross. "Cyborgs at Large: Interview with Donna Haraway." In Penley and Ross, eds., *Technoculture,* pp. 1–20.

——— eds. *Technoculture.* Minneapolis: University of Minnesota Press, 1991.

Percy, Walker. *Lost in the Cosmos; or, The Last Self–Help Book.* New York: Farrar, Straus, 1983.

Picart, Caroline. "Re-Birthing the Monstrous: James Whale's (Mis)Reading of Mary Shelley's *Frankenstein.*" *Critical Studies in Mass Communication 15,* no. 4 (1998): 383–96.

Poster, Mark, ed. *Jean Baudrillard: Selected Writings.* Stanford, Calif.: Stanford University Press, 1988.

Pye, Michael, and Lynda Myles. *The Movie Brats: How the Film Generation Took Over Hollywood.* New York: Holt, Rinehart, 1979.

Ramsaye, Terry. *A Million and One Nights: A History of the Motion Picture.* New York: Simon & Schuster, 1926; rpt., New York: Touchstone, 1986.

Ricoeur, Paul. "Ideology and Utopia as Cultural Imagination." Donald M. Borchert and David Stewart, eds. *Being Human in a Technological Age.* Athens: Ohio University Press, 1979, pp. 107–25.

Rodley, Chris. *Cronenberg on Cronenberg.* London: Faber & Faber, 1992.

Romanyshyn, Robert D. *Technology as Symptom and Dream.* London: Routledge, 1989.

Ross, Andrew, ed. *Science Wars.* Durham, N.C.: Duke University Press, 1996.

Ruppert, Peter. *Reader in a Strange Land: The Activity of Reading Literary Utopias.* Athens: University of Georgia Press, 1986.

Ryan, Michael, and Douglas Kellner. "Technophobia." In Kuhn, ed., *Alien Zone,* pp. 58–65.

Said, Edward W. *Orientalism.* New York: Random House, 1978.

Schelde, Per. *Androids, Humanoids, and Other Science Fiction Monsters: Science and Soul in Science Fiction Film.* New York: New York University Press, 1993.

Segal, Howard P. "The Technological Utopians." In Corn, ed., *Imagining Tomorrow,* pp. 119–36.

Shea, Chris, and Wade Jennings. "Paul Verhoeven: An Interview." *Post Script 12,* no. 3 (1993): 3–24.

Slusser, George E., and Eric S. Rabkin, eds. *Shadows of the Magic Lamp: Fantasy and Science Fiction in Film.* Carbondale: Southern Illinois University Press, 1985.

Sobchack, Vivian. *Screening Space: The American Science Fiction Film.* 2d ed. New York: Ungar, 1987.

"The Virginity of Astronauts: Sex and the Science Fiction Film." In Kuhn, ed., *Alien Zone,* pp. 103–15.

Sontag, Susan. *Against Interpretation and Other Essays.* New York: Dell, 1966.

Springer, Claudia. *Electronic Eros: Bodies and Desire in the Postindustrial Age.* Austin: University of Texas Press, 1996.

Stern, Michael. "Making Culture into Nature." In Kuhn, ed., *Alien Zone,* pp. 66–72.

Stewart, Garrett. "The 'Videology' of Science Fiction." In Slusser and Rabkin, eds., *Shadows of the Magic Lamp,* pp. 159–207.

Suvin, Darko. *Metamorphoses of Science Fiction: On the Poetics and History of a Literary Genre.* New Haven: Yale University Press, 1979.

Tarratt, Margaret. "Monsters from the Id." In Grant, ed., *Film Genre Reader II,* pp. 330–49.

Telotte, J. P. *A Distant Technology: Science Fiction Film and the Machine Age.* Middletown, Conn.: Wesleyan University Press, and Hanover, N.H.: University Press of New England, 1999.

Replications: A Robotic History of the Science Fiction Film. Urbana: University of Illinois Press, 1995.

Voices in the Dark: The Narrative Strategies of Film Noir. Urbana: University of Illinois Press, 1989.

Testa, Bart. "Technology's Body: Cronenberg, Genre, and the Canadian Ethos." *Post Script 15,* no. 1 (1995): 39–56.

Tichi, Cecelia. *Shifting Gears: Technology, Literature, Culture in Modernist America.* Chapel Hill: University of North Carolina Press, 1987.

Todorov, Tzvetan. *The Fantastic: A Structural Approach to a Literary Genre.* Trans. Richard Howard. Ithaca: Cornell University Press, 1975.

Tuchman, Mitch. "Close Encounter with Steven Spielberg." *Film Comment 14,* no. 1 (1978): 49–55.

Tudor, Andrew. *Monsters and Mad Scientists: A Cultural History of the Horror Movie.* Oxford: Blackwell, 1991.

Virilio, Paul. "The Last Vehicle." In Dietmar Kamper and Christoph Wulf, eds., *Looking Back on the End of the World.* New York: Semiotext(e), 1989, pp. 106–19.

The Vision Machine. Trans. Julie Rose. Bloomington: Indiana University Press, 1994.

War and Cinema: The Logistics of Perception. Trans. Patrick Camiller. London: Verso, 1989.

Wasko, Janet. *Hollywood in the Information Age.* Austin: University of Texas Press, 1995.

Wilson, Louise. "Cyberwar, God and Television: Interview with Paul Virilio." *CTheory.* www.ctheory.com/a-cyberwar_god.html.

Wilson, Richard Guy, Dianne H. Pilgrim, and Dickran Tashjian. *The Machine Age in America: 1918–1941.* New York: Abrams, 1986.

Wolfe, Gary. *The Known and the Unknown: The Iconography of Science Fiction.* Kent: Kent State University Press, 1979.

Wright, Judith Hess. "Genre Films and the Status Quo." In Grant, ed., *Film Genre Reader II,* pp. 41–9.

Wright, Will. *Sixguns and Society: A Structural Study of the Western.* Berkeley: University of California Press, 1975.

Select Filmography of the American Science Fiction Film

The listing that follows is by no means a complete – or even nearly complete – catalog of American science fiction films; rather, it represents a starting point for study. It includes many of those films that are mentioned in the text, works that have gained a classic or even a cult status, and others that for various reasons represent important trends in the American development of this genre. Some of the films listed here might arguably be included in a catalog of other film genres – horror, comedy, even the musical. Many that I have chosen to omit – including some rather unremarkable sequels to significant science fiction films – deserve listing and viewing. However, I have tried to make this a *useful* catalog, one that *represents* the scope, variety, and quality of the American science fiction film, but one that also refrains from cataloging works simply for the sake of numbers. For additional entries and information, one might consult the more specialized filmographies in my *Replications: A Robotic History of the Science Fiction Film* and *A Distant Technology: Science Fiction Film and the Machine Age,* as well as various Internet resources, such as the Internet Movie Database (www.us.imdb.com).

The Abyss (1989)
Lightstorm Entertainment / Pacific Western / 20th Century–Fox. DIR.: James Cameron. PROD.:Gale Anne Hurd. SCR.: Cameron. PHOTOG.: Mikael Salomon, Dennis Skotak. DESIGN: Leslie Dilley. CAST: Ed Harris, Mary Elizabeth Mastrantonio, Michael Biehn. 140 min. (Extended version, 171 min.)

Alien (1979)
Brandywine / 20th Century–Fox. DIR.: Ridley Scott. PROD.: Gordon Carroll. SCR.: Dan O'Bannon. PHOTOG.: Derek Vanlint. ED.: Terry Rawlings, Peter Weatherley. MUSIC: Jerry Goldsmith. CAST: Tom Skerritt, Sigourney Weaver, Ian Holm, John Hurt. 116 min.

Aliens (1986)
Brandywine / 20th Century–Fox. DIR.: James Cameron. PROD.: Gale Anne Hurd. SCR.: Cameron. PHOTOG.: Adrian Biddle. DESIGN: Peter Lamont. ED.: Ray Lovejoy. SFX: Stan Winston. MUSIC: James Horner. CAST: Sigourney Weaver, Michael Biehn, Paul Reiser, Carrie Henn. 138 min. (Extended version, 154 min.)

Altered States (1980)
Warner Bros. DIR.: Ken Russell. PROD.:Howard Gottfried. SCR.: Sidney Aaron, Paddy Chayefsky. PHOTOG.: Jordan S. Cronenweth. ED.: Stuart Baird, Eric Jenkins. DESIGN: Richard Macdonald. CAST: William Hurt, Bob Balaban, Blair Brown, Dori Brenner. 103 min.

Android (1982)
Island Alive/New World. DIR.: Aaron Lipstadt. SCR.: James Reigle, Don Opper. PHOTOG.: Tim Suhrstedt. ED.: Andy Horvitch. CAST: Klaus Kinski, Norbert Weisser, Don Opper, Brie Howard. 80 min.

The Andromeda Strain (1971)
MCA/Universal. DIR.: Robert Wise. PROD.: Wise. SCR.: Nelson Gidding (based on the Michael Crichton novel). PHOTOG.: Richard H. Kline. ED.: Stuart Gilmore, John W. Holmes. CAST: Arthur Hill, David Wayne, Paula Kelly, Kate Reid. 131 min.

Armageddon (1998)
Jerry Bruckheimer Films/Touchstone/Valhalla. DIR.: Michael Bay. PROD.: Jerry Bruckheimer, Gale Anne Hurd. SCR.: J. J. Abrams. PHOTOG.: John Schwartzman. ED.: Mark Goldblatt, Chris Lebenzon. CAST: Bruce Willis, Billy Bob Thornton, Liv Tyler, Ben Affleck, Will Patton. 150 min.

The Arrival (1996) [aka *Shockwave*]
Live Ent./Steelwork/Orion. DIR.: David N. Twohy. PROD.: Thomas G. Smith. SCR.: Twohy. PHOTOG.: Hiro Narita. ED.: Martin Hunter. CAST: Charlie Sheen, Lindsey Crouse, Ron Silver. 109 min.

Back to the Future (1985)
Amblin Ent./MCA/Universal. DIR.: Robert Zemeckis. PROD.: Neil Canton and Bob Gale. SCR.: Zemeckis, Bob Gale. PHOTOG.: Dean Cundey. ED.: Harry Keramidas, Arthur Schmidt. DESIGN: Lawrence G. Paull. CAST: Michael J. Fox, Christopher Lloyd, Crispin Glover, Lea Thompson. 116 min.

Barbarella (1968) [aka *Barbarella: Queen of the Galaxy*]
Dino de Laurentiis Cinematografica/Marianne Prods./Paramount. DIR.: Roger Vadim. PROD.: Dino de Laurentiis. SCR.: Terry Southern, Vadim, et al. PHOTOG.: Claude Renoir. DESIGN: Mario Garbuglia. CAST: Jane Fonda, John Phillip Law, Milo O'Shea, David Hemmings. 98 min.

The Beast from 20,000 Fathoms (1953)
Mutual/Warner Bros. DIR.: Eugène Lourié. PROD.: Jack Dietz. SCR.: Fred Freiberger, Louis Morheim, Lourié (based on a Ray Bradbury story). PHOTOG.: Jack Russell. ED.: Bernard W. Burton. ANIMATION: Ray Harryhausen. CAST: Steve Brodie, Cecil Kellaway, Kenneth Tobey, Paula Raymond. 80 min.

Beginning of the End (1957)
AB–PT Pictures. DIR.: Bert I. Gordon. PROD.: Gordon. SCR.: Fred
Freiberger, Lester Gorn. PHOTOG.: Jack A. Marta. ED.: Aaron Stell.
CAST: Peter Graves, Peggie Castle, Morris Ankrum. 73 min.

The Black Hole (1979)
Walt Disney Prods. DIR.: Gary Nelson. PROD.: Ron Miller. SCR.: Jeb
Rosebrook, Gerry Day. DESIGN/SFX: Peter Ellenshaw. CAST: Maximilian
Schell, Anthony Perkins, Robert Forster, Yvette Mimieux. 97 min.

Blade Runner (1982)
Ladd Co./Warner Bros. DIR.: Ridley Scott. SCR.: Hampton Fanchen,
David Peoples (based on Philip K. Dick's story "Do Androids Dream of
Electric Sheep?"). PHOTOG.: Jordan Cronenweth. DESIGN: Lawrence G.
Paull. CAST: Harrison Ford, Rutger Hauer, Sean Young. 124 min.

The Blob (1958)
Fairview Prods./Tonylyn Prods./Allied Artists. DIR.: Irwin S.
Yeaworth Jr. PROD.: Jack H. Harris. SCR.: Kate Phillips, Theodore
Simonson. PHOTOG.: Thomas E. Spalding. ED.: Alfred Hillmann. CAST:
Steven McQueen, Anita Corsaut, Earl Rowe, Olin Howlin. 86 min.

A Boy and His Dog (1975)
LQ/JAF. DIR.: L. Q. Jones. PROD.: Alvy Moore. SCR.: L. Q. Jones (based
on the Harlan Ellison story). PHOTOG.: John Arthur Morrill. ED.: Scott
Conrad. DESIGN: Ray Boyle. CAST: Don Johnson, Jason Robards Jr.,
Susanne Benton. 91 min.

The Bride of Frankenstein (1935)
Universal. DIR.: James Whale. PROD.:Carl Laemmle Jr. SCR.: John L.
Balderston, William Hurlbut. PHOTOG.: John D. Mescall. MUSIC: Franz
Waxman. CAST: Boris Karloff, Colin Clive, Ernest Thesiger, Elsa
Lanchester. 75 min.

The Bubble (1967) [aka *The Zoo* (3D)]
Arch Oboler Prods. DIR.: Arch Oboler. PROD.: Oboler. SCR.: Oboler.
ED.: Igo Kantor. CAST: Michael Cole, Deborah Walley, Johnny
Desmond. 112 min.

Buck Rogers (1939) [aka *Buck Rogers Conquers the Universe*]
Universal. DIR.: Ford I. Beebe, Saul A. Goodkind. PHOTOG.: Jerome
Ash. ED.: Joseph Gluck, Louis Sackin, Alvin Todd. CAST: Larry "Buster"
Crabbe, Jackie Moran, Constance Moore, Anthony Warde, Jack Mulhall.
SERIAL: 12 episodes. Condensed compilation (1940), *Desination Saturn.*

A Clockwork Orange (1972)
Hawk Films/Polaris Prods./Warner Bros. DIR.: Stanley Kubrick.
PROD.: Kubrick. SCR.: Kubrick (based on the Anthony Burgess novel).

PHOTOG.: John Alcott. ED.: William Butler. DESIGN: John Barry. CAST: Malcolm McDowell, Patrick McGee, Warren Clark. 137 min.

Close Encounters of the Third Kind (1977)
EMI/Columbia. DIR.: Steven Spielberg. PROD.: Julia and Michael Phillips. SCR.: Spielberg (with Paul Schrader). PHOTOG.: Vilmos Zsigmond. ED.: Michael Kahn. DESIGN: John Alves. MUSIC: John Williams. CAST: Richard Dreyfuss, Teri Garr, François Truffaut, Bob Balaban. 132 min. (Special edition, 1980, 135 min.)

Cocoon (1985)
Zanuck/Brown Prods./20th Century–Fox. DIR.: Ron Howard. SCR.: Tom Benedek, David Saperstein. PHOTOG.: Donald Peterman. ED.: Daniel P. Hanley, Michael J. Hill. DESIGN: Jack T. Collis. CAST: Don Ameche, Wilford Brimley, Hume Cronyn, Jessica Tandy, Brian Dennehy, Steve Guttenberg. 117 min.

The Colossus of New York (1958)
Paramount. DIR.: Eugène Lourié. PROD.: William Alland. SCR.: Thelma Schnee. PHOTOG.: John F. Warren. DESIGN: Hal Pereira, John Goodman. ED.: Floyd Knudtson. CAST: Ross Martin, Mala Powers, Otto Kruger. 70 min.

Coma (1978)
MGM/UA. DIR.: Michael Crichton. PROD.: Martin Erlichman. SCR.: Crichton. PHOTOG.: Victor J. Kemper, Gerald Hirschfeld. ED.: David Britherton. DESIGN: Albert Brenner. CAST: Genevieve Bujold, Michael Douglas, Elizabeth Ashley, Richard Widmark. 104 min.

The Conquest of Space (1955)
Paramount. DIR.: Byron Haskin. PROD.: George Pal. SCR.: Philip Yordan, Barré Lyndon, George Worthing Yates, James O'Hanlon. PHOTOG.: Lionel Linden. ED.: Everett Douglas. CAST: Walter Brooke, Eric Fleming, Mickey Shaughnessy, Phil Foster. 81 min.

Cyborg (1989)
Golan–Globus. DIR.: Albert Pyun. PROD.: Menahem Golan, Yoram Globus. SCR.: Kitty Chalmers. PHOTOG.: Philip Alan Waters. DESIGN: Douglas Leonard. MUSIC: Kevin Bassinson. CAST: Jean-Claude Van Damme, Deborah Richter, Vincent Klyn, Alex Daniels. 86 min.

Dark City (1998)
Mystery Clock/New Line. DIR.: Alex Proyas. PROD.: Proyas. SCR.: Proyas and Lem Dobbs. PHOTOG.: Dariusz Wolski. ED.: Dov Hoenig. CAST: Rufus Sewell, William Hurt, Kiefer Sutherland, Jennifer Connelly. 100 min.

Dark Star (1973)
> Jack H. Harris Ent. DIR.: John Carpenter. PROD.: Carpenter. SCR.: Carpenter, Dan O'Bannon. PHOTOG.: Douglas H. Knapp. ED.: O'Bannon. MUSIC: Carpenter. CAST: Brian Narelle, Dan O'Bannon, Jeanna Fine. 91 min.

D.A.R.Y.L. (1985)
> Columbia/Paramount/World Film. DIR.: Simon Wincer. PROD.: John Heyman. SCR.: David Ambrose, Allan Scott, Jeffrey Ellis. MUSIC: Marvin Hamlisch. CAST: Barret Oliver, Mary Beth Hurt, Michael McKean. 100 min.

The Day the Earth Stood Still (1951)
> 20th Century–Fox. DIR.: Robert Wise. PROD.: Julian Blaustein. SCR.: Edmund North. PHOTOG.: Leo Tover. MUSIC: Bernard Herrmann. ED.: William Reynolds. DESIGN: Lyle Wheeler, Addison Hehr. CAST: Michael Rennie, Patricia Neal, Sam Jaffe, Billy Gray. 92 min.

The Day the World Ended (1956)
> Golden State/ARC. DIR.: Roger Corman. PROD.: Corman. SCR.: Lou Russoff. PHOTOG.: Jackey A. Feindel. ED.: Ronald Sinclair. SFX: Paul Blaisdell. CAST: Richard Denning, Adele Jergens, Lori Nelson, Paul Birch. 79 min.

Deep Impact (1998)
> DreamWorks SKG/Paramount/Zanuck/Brown Prods. DIR.: Mimi Leder. PROD.: Richard D. Zanuck. SCR.: Bruce Joel Rubin, Michael Tolkin. PHOTOG.: Dietrich Lohmann. ED.: Paul Cichoki, David Rosenbloom. CAST: Robert Duvall, Téa Leoni, Elijah Wood, Vanessa Redgrave, Morgan Freeman. 120 min.

Demon Seed (1977)
> MGM. DIR.: Donald Cammell. PROD.: Herb Joffe. SCR.: Robert Jaffe, Roger O. Hirson (based on Dean R. Koontz's novel). PHOTOG.: Bill Butler. ED.: Frank Mazzola. CAST: Julie Christie, Fritz Weaver, Gerrit Graham. 97 min.

Destination Moon (1950)
> George Pal Prods./Eagle-Lion. DIR.: Irving Pichel. PROD.: George Pal. SCR.: James O'Hanlon, Robert A. Heinlein, Rip Van Ronkel. PHOTOG.: Lionel Lindon. ED.: Duke Goldstone. CAST: John Archer, Warner Anderson, Tom Powers, Dick Wesson. 91 min.

Dr. Cyclops (1940)
> Paramount. DIR.: Ernest B. Schoedsack. PROD.: Merian C. Cooper. SCR.: Tom Kilpatrick. PHOTOG.: Henry Sharp. ED.: Wellsworth Hoagland. CAST: Albert Dekker, Thomas Coley, Paul Fix, Janice Logan. 76 min.

Dr. Strangelove, or How I Learned to Stop Worrying and Love the Bomb (1964)
Hawk Films/Columbia. DIR.: Stanley Kubrick. PROD.: Kubrick. SCR.: Kubrick, Terry Southern, Peter George. PHOTOG.: Gilbert Taylor. DESIGN: Ken Adam. ED.: Anthony Harvey. CAST: Peter Sellers, George C. Scott, Sterling Hayden, Slim Pickens. 102 min.

Doctor X (1932)
Warner Bros. DIR.: Michael Curtiz. SCR.: Earl W. Baldwin, Robert Tasker. PHOTOG.: Ray Rennahan, Richard Tower. ED.: George J. Amy. CAST: Lionel Atwill, Faye Wray, Preston Foster, Lee Tracy. 77 min.

Dune (1984)
De Laurentiis/Universal. DIR.: David Lynch. PROD.: Dino de Laurentiis. SCR.: Lynch (based on the Frank Hebert novel). PHOTOG.: Freddie Francis. ED.: Antony Gibbs. DESIGN: Anthony Masters. CAST: Francesca Annis, Kyle MacLaughlan, Jurgen Prochnow, Brad Dourif. 137 min.

E.T. the Extra-Terrestrial (1982)
Universal. DIR.: Steven Spielberg. PROD.: Kathleen Kennedy, Spielberg. PHOTOG.: Allen Daviau. ED.: Carol Littleton. DESIGN: James D. Bissell. CAST: Dee Wallace, Henry Thomas, Peter Coyote, Robert MacNaughton, Drew Barrymore. 115 min.

Earth vs. the Flying Saucers (1956)
Clover/Columbia. DIR.: Fred F. Sears. SCR.: George Worthing Yates, Raymond T. Marcus. PHOTOG.: Fred Jackman Jr. DESIGN: Paul Palmentola. ED.: Danny B. Landres. SFX/ANIMATION: Ray Harryhausen. CAST: Hugh Marlowe, Joan Taylor, Donald Curtis. 83 min.

The Empire Strikes Back (1980) [aka *Star Wars Episode V*]
Lucasfilm/20th Century–Fox. DIR.: Irvin Kershner. PROD.: Gary Kurtz. SCR.: Leigh Brackett, Lawrence Kasdan. STORY: George Lucas. PHOTOG.: Peter Suschitzky. DESIGN: Norman Reynolds. ED.: Paul Hirsch. MUSIC: John Williams. CAST: Mark Hamill, Harrison Ford, Carrie Fisher, Billy Dee Williams. 124 min.

Escape from New York (1981)
AVCO Embassy. DIR.: John Carpenter. PROD.: Larry J. Franco and Debra Hill. SCR.: Carpenter, Nick Castle. PHOTOG.: Dean Cundey, Jim Lucas. DESIGN: John Alves. ED.: Todd C. Ramsey. CAST: Kurt Russell, Lee Van Cleef, Adrienne Barbeau, Ernest Borgnine. 99 min.

Eve of Destruction (1991)
Interscope Commun./Nelson Ent./Orion. DIR.: Duncan Gibbins. PROD.: David Madden. SCR.: Duncan Gibbins, Yale Udoff. PHOTOG.: Alan Hume. ED.: Caroline Biggerstaff. DESIGN: Peter Lamont. CAST: Gregory Hines, Renee Soutendjik. 101 min.

Fantastic Voyage (1966)
20th Century–Fox. DIR.: Richard Fleischer. PROD.: Saul David. SCR.:
David Duncan, Harry Kleiner. PHOTOG.: Ernest Laszlo. ED.: William B.
Murphy. CAST: Stephen Boyd, Raquel Welch, Edmond O'Brien, Donald
Pleasence. 100 min.

The Fifth Element (1997)
Gaumont/Columbia. DIR.: Luc Besson. PROD.: Iain Smith and Patrice
Ledoux. SCR.: Besson and Robert Mark Kamen. PHOTOG.: Thierry
Arbogast. ED.: Sylvie Landen. DESIGN: Dan Weil. CAST: Bruce Willis,
Gary Oldman, Ian Holm, Milla Jovovich. 126 min.

Five (1951)
Arch Oboler Prods./Columbia. DIR.: Arch Oboler. PROD.: Oboler. SCR.:
Oboler. PHOTOG.: Louis Clyde Stouman. ED.: Sid Lubow. CAST: William
Phipps, James Anderson, Susan Douglas, Earl Lee, Charles Lampkin.
93 min.

Flash Gordon (1936)
Universal. DIR.: Frederick Stephani, Ray Taylor. PROD.: Henry MacRae.
SCR.: Stephani, George Plympton, Basil Dickey, Ella O'Neill (based on
Alex Raymond's comic strip). PHOTOG.: Jerome H. Ash, Richard Fryer.
ART DIR.: Ralph Berger. CAST: Larry "Buster" Crabbe, Jean Rogers,
Charles Middleton, Frank Shannon. SERIAL: 13 episodes. Condensed
compilation (1936), *Spaceship to the Unknown: Space Soldiers* [aka
Flash Gordon: Rocketship]

Flight of the Navigator (1986)
New Star/PSO/Viking/Walt Disney Prods. DIR.: Randal Kleiser. SCR.:
Mark H. Baker, Michael Burton, Matt McManus. PHOTOG.: James
Glennon. DESIGN: William J. Creber. ED.: Jeff Gourson. CAST: Joey
Cramer, Paul Reubens, Veronica Cartwright. 90 min.

The Fly (1958)
20th Century–Fox. DIR.: Kurt Neumann. PROD.: Kurt Neumann. SCR.:
James Cavell. PHOTOG.: Karl Struss. ED.: Merril G. White. DESIGN: Lyle
R. Wheeler, Theobold Holsopple. CAST: Al (David) Hedison, Patricia
Owens, Vincent Price. 94 min.

The Fly (1986)
Brooksfilms/20th Century–Fox. DIR.: David Cronenberg. PROD.: Stuart
Cornfeld. SCR.: Charles Edward Pogue. PHOTOG.: Mark Irwin. ED.:
Ronald Sanders, Steve Weslak. CAST: Jeff Goldblum, Geena Davis, John
Getz. 100 min.

Forbidden Planet (1956)
MGM. DIR.: Fred McLeod Wilcox. PROD.: Nicholas Nayfack. SCR.: Cyril
Hume. PHOTOG.: George Folsey. DESIGN: Cedric Gibbons, Arthur

Lonergan. CAST: Walter Pidgeon, Leslie Nielsen, Anne Francis, Warren Stevens. 98 min.

Frankenstein (1931)
Universal. DIR.: James Whale. PROD.: Carl Laemmle Jr. SCR.: Garrett Fort, Francis Edward Farough (based on the Mary Shelley novel). PHOTOG.: Arthur Edeson. CAST: Boris Karloff, Colin Clive, Mae Clark, Edward Van Sloan. 71 min.

From the Earth to the Moon (1958)
Warner Bros. DIR.: Byron Haskin. PROD.: Benedict E. Bogeaus. SCR.: Robert Blees. PHOTOG.: Edwin DuPar. ED.: James Leicester. CAST: Joseph Cotton, George Sanders, Debra Paget. 100 min.

Futureworld (1976)
American International. DIR.: Richard T. Heffron. PROD.: Paul Lazarus III. SCR.: Mayo Simon, George Schenck. PHOTOG.: Howard Schwartz, Gene Polito. ED.: James Mitchell. CAST: Peter Fonda, Blythe Danner, Arthur Hill, Yul Brynner. 104 min.

Gattaca (1997)
Columbia/Jersey. DIR.: Andrew Niccol. SCR.: Niccol. PHOTOG.: Slavomir Idziak. ED.: Lisa Zeno Churgin. CAST: Ethan Hawke, Uma Thurman, Gore Vidal, Xander Berkeley. 101 min.

The Giant Claw (1957)
Clover/Columbia. DIR.: Fred F. Sears. PROD.: Sam Katzman. SCR.: Paul Ganglin, Samuel Newman. PHOTOG.: Benjamin H. Kline. ED.: Anthony DiMarco, Saul A. Goodkind. CAST: Jeff Morrow, Mara Corday, Louis Merrill. 75 min.

The Guyver (1991) [aka *Mutronics*]
Imperial Ent./New Line (U.S.–Japan). DIR.: Screaming Mad George, Steve Wang. PROD.: Brian Yuzma. PHOTOG.: Levie Isaacks. ED.: Andy Horvitch. DESIGN: Matthew C. Jacobs. CAST: Mark Hamill, Vivian Wu, Jack Armstrong. 92 min.

The Hidden (1987)
Heron/New Line/Third Elm Street Venture. DIR.: Jack Sholder. SCR.: Bob Hunt. PHOTOG.: Jacques Haitkin. ED.: Michael Knue. MUSIC: Michael Convertino. CAST: Michael Nouri, Kyle MacLachlan. 98 min.

I Married a Monster from Outer Space (1958)
Paramount. DIR.: Gene Fowler Jr. SCR.: Louis Vittes. PHOTOG.: Haskell Boggs. ED.: George Tomasini. DESIGN: Jal Pereira, Henry Bumstead. CAST: Tom Tryon, Gloria Talbott, Ken Lynch. 78 min.

The Illustrated Man (1969)
SKM /Warner Bros. DIR.: Jack Smight. PROD.: Howard B. Kreitsek and
Ted Mann. SCR.: Ray Bradbury (based on his novel) and Howard B.
Kreitsek. PROD.: Kreitsek and Ted Mann. PHOTOG.: Philip H. Lathrop.
CAST: Rod Steiger, Claire Bloom, Robert Drivas. 100 min.

The Incredible Shrinking Man (1957)
Universal–International. DIR.: Jack Arnold. PROD.: Albert Zugsmith.
SCR.: Richard Alan Simmons, Richard Matheson (based on Matheson's
novel). PHOTOG.: Willis W. Carter. ED.: Albrecht Joseph. CAST: Grant
Williams, Randy Stuart, April Kent. 81 min.

Invaders from Mars (1953)
National /20th Century–Fox. DIR.: William Cameron Menzies. PROD.:
Edward L. Alperson. SCR.: Richard Blake (and John Tucker Battle).
PHOTOG.: John Seitz. ED.: Arthur Roberts. DESIGN: Menzies. CAST:
Helena Carter, Arthur Franz, Jimmy Hunt. 78 min.

Invasion of the Body Snatchers (1956) [aka *Sleep No More*]
Allied Artists /Walter Wanger Prods. DIR.: Don Siegel. PROD.: Walter
Wanger. SCR.: Daniel Mainwaring. PHOTOG.: Ellsworth Fredericks.
DESIGN: Edward Haworth. CAST: Kevin McCarthey, Dana Wynter, King
Donovan, Carolyn Jones. 80 min.

Invasion of the Body Snatchers (1978)
Solofilm /United Artists. DIR.: Philip Kaufman. PROD.: Robert H. Solo.
SCR.: W. D. Richter (and Kaufman). PHOTOG.: Michael Chapman. ED.:
Douglas Stewart. DESIGN: Charles Rosen. CAST: Donald Sutherland,
Brooke Adams, Leonard Nimoy, Jeff Goldblum, Veronica Cartwright.
115 min.

Invasion, U.S.A. (1952)
American /Columbia. DIR.: Alfred E. Green. SCR.: Franz Schulz, Robert
Smith. PHOTOG.: John L. Russell. ED.: W. Donn Hayes. SFX: Jack Rabin.
CAST: Gerald Mohr, Peggie Castle, Dan O'Herlihy. 73 min.

The Invisible Boy (1957) [aka *S.O.S. Spaceship*]
MGM /Pan. DIR.: Herman Hoffman. PROD.: Nicholas Nayfack. SCR.:
Cyril Hume. PHOTOG.: Harold Wellman. ED.: John Faure. DESIGN:
Merrill Pye. CAST: Richard Eyer, Diane Brewster, Philip Abbot.
90 min.

The Invisible Man (1933)
Universal. DIR.: James Whale. PROD.: Carl Laemmle Jr. SCR.: R. C.
Sherriff (based on the H. G. Wells novel). PHOTOG.: Arthur Edeson.
ED.: Ted J. Kent. CAST: Claude Rains, Gloria Stuart, Henry Travers,
E. E. Clive. 71 min.

The Invisible Ray (1936)
  Universal. DIR.: Lambert Hillyer. PROD.: Edmund Grainger. SCR.: John
  Colton. PHOTOG.: George Robinson, John P. Fulton. CAST: Boris Karloff,
  Bela Lugosi, Frances Drake. 81 min.

Island of Lost Souls (1933) [aka *The Island of Dr. Moreau*]
  Paramount. DIR.: Erle C. Kenton. SCR.: Waldemar Young, Philip Wylie
  (based on the H. G. Wells novel *The Island of Dr. Moreau*). PHOTOG.:
  Karl Struss. CAST: Charles Laughton, Richard Arlen, Leila Hyams.
  70 min.

It! The Terror from Beyond Space (1958)
  Vogue Pictures /United Artists. DIR.: Edward L. Cahn. PROD.: Robert
  Kent. SCR.: Jerome Bixby. PHOTOG.: Kenneth Peach. ED.: Grant
  Whytock. CAST: Marshall Thompson, Shawn Smith, Ann Doran,
  Richard Benedict, Ray "Crash" Corrigan. 68 min.

It Came from Outer Space (1953)
  Universal–International. DIR.: Jack Arnold. SCR.: Harry Essex. PHOTOG.:
  Clifford Stine. DESIGN: Bernard Herzbrun, Robert Boyle. ED.: Paul
  Weatherwax. CAST: Richard Carlson, Barbara Rush, Charles Drake, Joe
  Sawyer. 81 min.

Journey to the Center of the Earth (1959) [aka *Trip to the Center of the
Earth*]
  20th Century–Fox. DIR.: Henry Levin. SCR.: Charles Brackett, Robert
  Gunter (based on the Jules Verne novel). PHOTOG.: Leo Tover. ED.:
  Stuart Gilmore, Jack W. Holmes. MUSIC: Bernard Herrmann. CAST:
  James Mason, Arlene Dahl, Pat Boone. 132 min.

Jurassic Park (1993)
  Amblin /Universal. DIR.: Steven Spielberg. PROD.: Kathleen Kennedy
  and Gerald R. Molen. SCR.: Michael Crichton, David Koepp (based on
  Crichton's novel). PHOTOG.: Dean Cundey. ED.: Michael Kahn. MUSIC:
  John Williams. CAST: Sam Neill, Laura Dern, Jeff Goldblum, Richard
  Attenborough. 127 min.

Just Imagine (1930)
  Fox. DIR.: David Butler. SCR.: Butler (from story by Buddy DeSylva,
  Lew Brown, Ray Henderson). MUSIC: DeSylva, Brown, and Henderson.
  PHOTOG.: Ernest Palmer. ED.: Irene Morra. CAST: John Garrick, El
  Brendel, Maureen O'Sullivan. 107 min.

The Last Starfighter (1984)
  Lorimar /Universal. DIR.: Nick Castle Jr. PROD.: Garry Adelson and
  Edward O. Denault. SCR.: Jonathan R. Betuel. PHOTOG.: King Baggot.
  ED.: Carroll Timothy O'Meara. CAST: Dan O'Herlihy, Robert Preston,
  Catherine Stewart, Lance Guest. 100 min.

The Lawnmower Man (1992)
Allied Vision / Fuji 8 / New Line. DIR.: Brett Leonard. PROD.: Gimel Everett. PHOTOG.: Russell Carpenter. ED.: Alan Baumgarten. DESIGN: Alex McDowell. CAST: Jeff Fahey, Pierce Brosnan, Jenny Wright. 108 min.

Logan's Run (1976)
MGM–UA. DIR.: Michael Anderson. PROD.: Saul David. SCR.: David Zelag Goodman (based on William F. Nolan and George Clayton Johnson's novel). PHOTOG.: Ernest Laszlo. ED.: Bob Wyman. CAST: Michael York, Jenny Agutter, Peter Ustinov. 118 min.

Mad Love (1935) [aka *The Hands of Orlac*]
MGM. DIR.: Karl Freund. SCR.: Guy Endore, P. J. Wolfson, John Balderston. PHOTOG.: Chester Lyons, Gregg Toland. CAST: Colin Clive, Peter Lorre, Frances Drake. 83 min.

Making Mr. Right (1987)
Barry Enright Film / Orion. DIR.: Susan Seidelman. SCR.: Floyd Byars, Laurie Frank. PHOTOG.: Edward Lachman. DESIGN: Barbara Ling. CAST: John Malkovich, Ann Magnuson, Glenne Headly. 98 min.

Man Made Monster (1941) [aka *Atomic Monster*]
Universal. DIR.: George Waggner. SCR.: Joseph West (George Waggner). PHOTOG.: Elwood Bredell. ED.: Arthur Hilton. CAST: Lionell Atwil, Lon Chaney Jr., Anne Nagel. 68 min.

Marooned (1969) [aka *Space Travelers*]
Columbia. DIR.: John Sturges. PROD.: M. J. Frankovich. SCR.: Mayo Simon and Martin Caidin. PHOTOG.: Daniel Fapp. ED.: Walter Thompson. CAST: Gregory Peck, Richard Crenna, David Janssen. 134 min.

The Matrix (1999)
Groucho II Film Ptnrshp / Silver / Village Roadshow / Warner Bros. DIR.: Andy and Larry Wachowski. PROD.: Joel Silver. SCR.: Andy and Larry Wachowski. PHOTOG.: Bill Pope. ED.: Zach Staenberg. PROD. DES.: Owen Patterson. CAST: Keanu Reeves, Laurence Fishburne, Carrie-Anne Moss, Hugo Weaving, Joe Pantoliano. 136 min.

The Mysterious Island (1929)
MGM. DIR.: Lucien Hubbard, [Benjamin Christensen, and Maurice Tourneur]. PROD.: J. Ernest Williamson. SCR.: Lucien Hubbard, Carl L. Pierson (based on the Jules Verne novel). PHOTOG.: Percy Hilburn. ART DIR.: Cedric Gibbons. MUSIC: Martin Broones, Arthur Lange. CAST: Lionel Barrymore, Jane Daly, Harry Gribbon, Montague Love. 95 min.

The Omega Man (1971)
Warner Bros. DIR.: Boris Sagal. PROD.: Walter Seltzer. SCR.: John
William Corrington and Joyce H. Corrington (based on Richard
Matheson [as Logan Swanson] novel *I Am Legend*). PHOTOG.: Russell
Metty. ED.: William H. Ziegler. CAST: Charlton Heston, Anthony Zerbe,
Rosalind Cash. 98 min.

On the Beach (1959)
Lomitas /United Artists. DIR.: Stanley Kramer. PROD.: Kramer. SCR.:
John Paxton. PHOTOG.: Guiseppe Rotunno. DESIGN: Rudolph Steinrad.
ED.: Cliff Bell. CAST: Gregory Peck, Ava Gardner, Fred Astaire, Anthony
Perkins. 134 min.

Outland (1981)
Outland Prods. /The Ladd Co. DIR.: Peter Hyams. SCR.: Hyams.
PHOTOG.: Stephen Goldblatt. ED.: Stuart Baird. CAST: Peter Boyle,
Sean Connery, Frances Sternhagen. 109 min.

Panic in the Year Zero (1962) [aka *End of the World*]
American International. DIR.: Ray Milland. SCR.: John Morton, Jay
Simms. PHOTOG.: Gilbert Warrenton. ED.: William Austin. CAST: Ray
Milland, Frankie Avalon, Jean Hagan, Joan Freeman. 95 min.

The Phantom Creeps (1939) [aka *The Shadow Creeps*]
Universal. DIR.: Ford Beebe, Saul A. Goodkind. SCR.: Mildred Barish,
Willis Cooper, Basil Dickey, George Plympton. PHOTOG.: Jerry Ash,
William Sickner. CAST: Bela Lugosi, Robert Kent, Dorothy Arnold.
SERIAL: 12 episodes.

The Phantom Empire (1935) [aka *Gene Autry and the Phantom
Empire*]
Mascot. DIR.: Otto Brower, B. Reeves Eason. PROD.: Armand Schaefer.
SCR.: Wallace MacDonald, Gerald Geraghty, H. Freedman. CAST: Gene
Autry, Smiley Burnette, Frankie Darro, Betsy Ross King. SERIAL: 12
episodes.

The Philadelphia Experiment (1984)
Cinema Group Venture /New Pictures. DIR.: Stewart Raffill. PROD.:
Douglas Curtis and Joel B. Michaels. SCR.: William Gray, Michael
Janover. PHOTOG.: Dick Bush. ED.: Neil Travis. CAST: Michael Paré,
Nancy Allen, Bobby DiCicco, Louise Latham. 102 min.

Plan 9 from Outer Space (1956)
DCA. DIR.: Edward D. Wood Jr. SCR.: Wood. ED.: Wood. PHOTOG.:
William C. Thompson. SFX: Charles Duncan. CAST: John Breckinridge,
Tor Johnson, Bela Lugosi. 78 min.

Planet of the Apes (1968)
APJAC/20th Century–Fox. DIR.: Franklin J. Schaffner. PROD.: Arthur P. Jacobs. SCR.: Rod Serling, Michael Wilson (based on the Pierre Boulle novel). PHOTOG.: Leon Shamroy. ED.: Hugh S. Fowler. CAST: Charlton Heston, Roddy McDowell, Kim Hunter, Maurice Evans. 112 min.

Predator (1987)
Amercent/American Entertainment Partners/20th Century–Fox. DIR.: John McTiernan. SCR.: James E. and John C. Thomas. PHOTOG.: Donald McAlpine. ED.: Mark Helfrich, John F. Link. CAST: Arnold Schwarzenegger, Jesse Ventura, Carl Weathers. 106 min.

The Purple Monster Strikes (1945) [aka *The Purple Shadow Strikes*]
Republic. DIR.: Spencer Gordon Bennet, Fred C. Brannon. SCR.: Royal K. Cole et al. PHOTOG.: Bud Thackery. ED.: Cliff Bell, Harold Minter. CAST: Dennis Moore, Linda Stirling, Roy Barcroft. SERIAL: 15 episodes.

The Questor Tapes (1974)
Jeffrey Hayes Prod./Universal. DIR.: Richard A. Colla. PROD.: Howie Horwitz. SCR.: Gene Roddenberry, Gene L. Coon. PHOTOG.: Michael Margulies. ED.: Robert L. Kimble, J. Terry Wiliams. MUSIC: Gil Melle. CAST: Robert Foxworth, Mike Farrell, Lew Ayres, Dana Wynter. 97 min., TV movie.

Radar Men from the Moon (1951)
Republic. DIR.: Fred C. Brannon. SCR.: Ronald Davidson. PHOTOG.: John MacBurnie. ED.: Cliff Bell. CAST: George Wallace, Roy Barcroft, Clayton Moore. SERIAL: 12 episodes.

The Return of the Fly (1959)
20th Century–Fox. DIR.: Edward L. Bernds. PROD.: Bernard Glasser. SCR.: Bernds. PHOTOG.: Brydon Baker. ED.: Richard C. Meyer. DESIGN: Lyle R. Wheeler, John Mansbridge. CAST: Vincent Price, Brett Halsey, David Frankham. 78 min.

Return of the Jedi (1983) [aka *Star Wars Episode VI*]
Lucasfilm/20th Century–Fox. DIR.: Richard Marquand. PROD.: Jim Bloom and Robert Watts. SCR.: Lawrence Kasdan, George Lucas. PHOTOG.: Alan Hume. ED.: Sean Barton, Marcia Lucas, Duwayne Dunham. DESIGN: Norman Reynolds. MUSIC: John Williams. CAST: Mark Hamill, Harrison Ford, Carrie Fisher, Billy Dee Williams. 133 min.

Riders to the Stars (1954)
A-men Prods./United Artists. DIR.: Richard Carlson [and Herbert L. Strock]. PROD.: Ivan Tors. SCR.: Curt Siodmak. PHOTOG.: Stanley Cortez. ED.: Herbert L. Strock. CAST: Richard Carlson, Martha Hyer, Herbert Marshall, Dawn Addams. 81 min.

Robinson Crusoe on Mars (1964)
Devonshire/Paramount. DIR.: Byron Haskin. PROD.: Aubrey Schenck.
SCR.: John C. Higgins. PHOTOG.: Winton C. Hoch. ED.: Terry O. Morse.
MUSIC: Van Cleave. CAST: Paul Mantee, Victor Lundin, Adam West.
110 min.

RoboCop (1987)
Orion. DIR.: Paul Verhoeven. PROD.: Edward Neumeier and Arne
Schmidt. SCR.: Edward Neumeier, Michael Miner. PHOTOG.: Jost Vacaro.
DESIGN: William Sandell. SFX: Peter Kuran. CAST: Peter Weller, Nancy
Allen, Ronny Cox, Daniel O'Herlihy. 105 min.

RoboCop 2 (1990)
Orion. DIR.: Irvin Kershner. PROD.: Jon Davison. SCR.: Frank Miller,
Walon Green. PHOTOG.: Mark Irwin. ED.: Deborah Zeitman, Lee Smith,
Armen Minasian. DESIGN: Peter Jamison. MUSIC: Leonard Rosenman.
CAST: Peter Weller, Nancy Allen, Daniel O'Herlihy, Tom Noonan,
Belinda Bauer. 116 min.

Robot Jox (1990)
Altar Prods./Empire Pictures. DIR.: Stuart Gordon. PROD.: Albert Ball.
SCR.: Joe Haldeman, from story by Stuart Gordon. PHOTOG.: Marc
Ahlberg. ED.: Ted Nicolaou, Lori Scott Bal. DESIGN: Giovanni Natalucci.
MUSIC: Frederic Talgorn. CAST: Gary Graham, Anne-Marie Johnson,
Paul Koslo, Michael Alldredge. 84 min.

Robot Monster (1953) [aka *Monster from Mars; Monsters from
the Moon*]
Astor Pictures. DIR.: Phil Tucker. PROD.: Phil Tucker. SCR.: Wyott
Ordung. PHOTOG.: Jack Greenhalgh. ED.: Merrill White. MUSIC: Elmer
Bernstein. CAST: George Nader, Claudia Barrett, Selena Royale, John
Mylong, George Barrows. 63 min.

The Rocketeer (1991)
Gordon Co./Silver Screen Partners/Touchstone/Walt Disney Prods.
DIR.: Joe Johnston. SCR.: Danny Bilson, Paul De Meo. PHOTOG.: Hiro
Narita. ED.: Arthur Schmidt. DESIGN: James D. Bissell. CAST: Alan
Arkin, Timothy Dalton, Bill Campbell, Jennifer Connelly. 109 min.

Rocketship X-M (1950)
Lippert. DIR.: Kurt Neumann. PROD.: Neumann. SCR.: Neumann.
PHOTOG.: Karl Struss. ED.: Harry W. Gerstad. MUSIC: Ferde Grofe Sr. SFX:
Don Stewart. CAST: John Emery, Lloyd Bridges, Osa Massen. 77 min.

Saturn 3 (1980)
ITC/Transcontinental (Britain). DIR.: Stanley Donen [and John Barry].
PROD.: Donen. SCR.: Martin Amis. PHOTOG.: Billy Williams. MUSIC: Elmer
Bernstein. CAST: Kirk Douglas, Farrah Fawcett, Harvey Keitel. 88 min.

Scanners (1981)
CFDC/Filmplan (Canada). DIR.: David Cronenberg. PROD.: Claude Heroux. SCR.: Cronenberg. PHOTOG.: Mark Irwin. ED.: Ronald Sanders. MUSIC: Howard Shore. CAST: Patrick McGoohan, Stephen Lack, Jennifer O'Neill. 102 min.

Seconds (1966)
Joel Prods./John Frankenheimer Prods./Paramount. DIR.: John Frankenheimer. PROD.: Edward Lewis. SCR.: Lewis John Carlino. PHOTOG.: James Wong Howe. DESIGN: Ted Haworth. MUSIC: Jerry Goldsmith. CAST: Rock Hudson, John Randolph, Salmoe Jens, Will Geer. 106 min.

Short Circuit (1986)
PSO/TriStar. DIR.: John Badham. PROD.: David Foster, Lawrence Turman. SCR.: S. S. Wilson, Brent Maddock. ED.: Frank Moriss. CAST: Steven Guttenberg, Ally Sheedy, Fisher Stevens. 98 min.

Silent Running (1972)
Michael Gruskoff Prods./Universal. DIR.: Douglas Trumbull. PROD.: Michael Gruskoff and Douglas Trumbull. SCR.: Deric Washburn, Michael Cimino, Steve Bochco. PHOTOG.: Charles F. Wheeler. MUSIC: Peter Schickele. CAST: Bruce Dern, Cliff Potts, Ron Rifkin. 89 min.

Six Hours to Live (1932)
Fox. DIR.: William Dieterle. SCR.: Bradley King. PHOTOG.: George F. Seitz. CAST: Warner Baxter, Irene Ware, John Boles, George Marion. 78 min.

Sleeper (1973)
Rollins–Joffe/UA. DIR.: Woody Allen. PROD.: Charles H. Joffe. SCR.: Allen, Marshall Brickman. PHOTOG.: David M. Walsh. ED.: Ron Kalish, Ralph Rosenblum. CAST: Woody Allen, Diane Keaton, John Beck, Mary Gregory. 88 min.

Soylent Green (1973)
MGM. DIR.: Richard Fleischer. PROD.: Walter Seltzer and Russell Thacher. SCR.: Stanley G. Greenberg. PHOTOG.: Richard Kline. ED.: Samuel E. Bentley. DESIGN: Edward C. Carfagno. CAST: Charlton Heston, Edward G. Robinson, Whit Bissell, Leigh Taylor-Young. 95 min.

Species (1995)
MGM. DIR.: Roger Donaldson. PROD.: Denis Feldman and Frank Mancuso Jr. SCR.: Dennis Feldman. PHOTOG.: Andrzej Bartkowick. ED.: Conrad Buff IV, Randy Thom. DESIGN: John Muto. CAST: Ben Kingsley, Michael Madsen, Marge Helgenberger. 108 min.

Star Trek – The Motion Picture (1979)
Century Assoc./Paramount. DIR.: Robert Wise. PROD.: Gene Roddenberry. SCR.: Harold Livingstone. CAST: William Shatner, Leonard

Nimoy, DeForest Kelley, James Doohan, Nichelle Nichols, Persis Khambatta, Stephen Collins. 132 min.

Star Trek [II]: The Wrath of Khan (1982)
Paramount. DIR.: Nicholas Meyer. SCR.: Jack B. Sowards. PHOTOG.: Gayne Rescher. ED.: William P. Dornisch. CAST: William Shatner, Leonard Nimoy, DeForest Kelley, James Doohan, Nichelle Nichols, Ricardo Montalban. 113 min.

Star Wars (1977) [aka *Star Wars Episode IV – A New Hope*]
20th Century–Fox. DIR.: George Lucas. PROD.: Gary Kurtz. SCR.: Lucas. PHOTOG.: Gilbert Taylor. ED.: Paul Hirsch, Marcia Lucas, Richard Chew. DESIGN: John Barry. SFX: John Dykstra. MUSIC: John Williams. CAST: Mark Hamill, Harrison Ford, Carrie Fisher, Alec Guiness. 121 min.

Star Wars: Episode I – The Phantom Menace (1999)
Lucasfilm/20th Century–Fox. DIR.: George Lucas. PROD.: Rick McCallum. SCR.: Lucas. MUSIC: John Williams. PHOTOG.: David Tattersall. ED.: Ben Burtt and Paul Martin Smith. CAST: Liam Neeson, Ewan McGregor, Natalie Portman, Jake Lloyd. 136 min.

Stargate (1994)
Carolco/Centropolis. DIR.: Roland Emmerich. SCR.: Emmerich, Dean Devlin. PHOTOG.: Karl Walter Lindenlaub. ED.: Derek Brechin, Michael J. Duthie. CAST: Kurt Russell, James Spader, Jaye Davidson. 121 min.

Starship Troopers (1997)
Big Bug/Touchstone/TriStar. DIR.: Paul Verhoeven. SCR.: Ed Neumeier (based on the Robert A. Heinlein novel). PHOTOG.: Jost Vacaro. ED.: Mark Goldblatt, Caroline Ross. DESIGN: Allen Cameron. CAST: Casper Van Dien, Dina Meyer, Denise Richards, Neil Patrick Harris. 129 min.

The Stepford Wives (1975)
Fadsin Cinema Assoc./Paloma/Columbia. DIR.: Bryan Forbes. PROD.: Edgar J. Scherick. SCR.: William Goldman (based on Ira Levin's novel). PHOTOG.: Owen Roizman. DESIGN: Gene Callahan. MUSIC: Michael Small. CAST: Katherine Ross, Paula Prentiss, Peter Masterson, Tina Louise, William Prince. 114 min.

The Terminal Man (1974)
Warner Bros. DIR.: Mike Hodges. PROD.: Hodges. SCR.: Hodges (based on Michael Crichton's novel). CAST: George Segal, Joan Hackett, Richard Dysart. 107 min.

The Terminator (1984)
Hemdale. DIR.: James Cameron. PROD.: Gale Anne Hurd. SCR.: Cameron, Hurd. PHOTOG.: Adam Greenberg. SFX: Stan Winston.

CAST: Linda Hamilton, Michael Biehn, Arnold Schwarzenegger.
108 min.

Terminator 2: Judgment Day (1991) [aka *T2*]
Carolco/Le Studio Canal/Lightstorm Entertainment/Pacific Western.
DIR.: James Cameron. PROD.: Cameron. SCR.: Cameron, William Wisher.
CAST: Linda Hamilton, Arnold Schwarzenegger, Edward Furlong,
Robert Patrick. 135 in.

Them! (1954)
Warner Bros. DIR.: Gordon Douglas. PROD.: David Weisbart. SCR.: Russell S. Hughes, Ted Sherdeman. PHOTOG.: Sidney Hickox. ED.: Thomas
Reilly. CAST: James Whitmore, James Arness, Joan Weldon, Edmund
Gwenn. 93 min.

The Thing (1982)
Turman-Foster Co./Universal. DIR.: John Carpenter. PROD.: Stuart
Cohen and David Foster. SCR.: Bill Lancaster (based on John W.
Campbell Jr.'s story "Who Goes There?"). SFX: Rob Bottin (and Stan
Winston). CAST: Kurt Russell, Wilford Brimley, Richard Dysart,
Richard Masur. 127 min.

The Thing from Another World (1951) [aka *The Thing*]
RKO/Winchester. DIR.: Christian Nyby [and Howard Hawks]. PROD.:
Howard Hawks. SCR.: Charles Lederer (based loosely on John W.
Campbell Jr.'s story "Who Goes There?"). PHOTOG.: Russell Harlan.
ED.: Roland Gross. CAST: Kenneth Tobey, James Arness, Margaret
Sheridan, Robert Cornthwaite, Dewey Martin. 87 min.

This Island Earth (1955)
Sabre Prods./Universal–International. DIR.: Joseph M. Newman [and
Jack Arnold]. PROD.: William Alland. SCR.: Franklin Coen, Edward G.
O'Callaghan. PHOTOG.: Clifford Stine. ED.: Virgil Vogel. CAST: Jeff
Morrow, Rex Reason, Faith Domergue. 87 min.

THX 1138 (1971)
Warner Bros. DIR.: George Lucas. PROD.: Lawrence Sturhahn. SCR.:
Lucas, Walter Murch. PHOTOG.: Dave Meyers, Albert Kihn. DESIGN:
Michael Haller. CAST: Robert Duvall, Donald Pleasence, Maggie
McOmie. 88 min. (Based on Lucas's earlier short film *Electronic
Labyrinth: THX 1138: 4EB.*)

Time After Time (1979)
Warner Bros./Zoetrope. DIR.: Nicholas Meyer. PROD.: Herb Jaffe. SCR.:
Meyer. PHOTOG.: Paul Lohmann. ED.: Don Cambern. MUSIC: Miklos
Rosza. CAST: Malcolm McDowell, Mary Steenburgen, David Warner,
Shelley Hack. 112 min.

The Time Machine (1960)

Galaxy/MGM. DIR.: George Pal. PROD.: Pal. SCR.: David Duncan (based on the H. G. Wells novel). PHOTOG.: Paul C. Vogel. ED.: George Tomassini. CAST: Rod Taylor, Alan Young, Yvette Mimieux. 103 min.

Timecop (1994)

Dark Horse Ent./JVC Ent./Largo Ent./Renaissance/Signature/Universal. DIR.: Peter Hyams. SCR.: Mark Verheiden. PHOTOG.: Peter Hyams. ED.: Steven Kemper. DESIGN: Philip Harrison. CAST: Jean-Claude Van Damme, Mia Sara, Ron Silver. 98 min.

Total Recall (1990)

TriStar/Carolco. DIR.: Paul Verhoeven. PROD.: Ronald Shusett, Buzz Feitshans. SCR.: Ronald Shusett, Dan O'Bannon, Garry Goldman (based on Philip K. Dick's story "We Can Remember It for You Wholesale"). PHOTOG.: Jost Vacano. ED.: Frank J. Urioste. DESIGN: William Sandell. MUSIC: Gerry Goldsmith. CAST: Arnold Schwarzenegger, Rachel Ticotin, Sharon Stone, Michael Ironside, Ronny Cox. 114 min.

Tron (1982)

Lisberger/Kushner/Walt Disney Prods. DIR.: Steven Lisberger. PROD.: Donald Kushner. SCR.: Lisberger. PHOTOG.: Bruce Logan. ED.: Jeff Gourson. DESIGN: Dean Edward Mitzner. MUSIC: Wendy Carlos. CAST: Jeff Bridges, Bruce Boxleitner, David Warner, Cindy Morgan. 96 min.

Twelve Monkeys (1996)

Atlas Ent./Classico/Universal. DIR.: Terry Gilliam. PROD.: Lloyd Phillips and Charles Roven. SCR.: David and Janet Peoples. PHOTOG.: Roger Pratt. ED.: Mick Andsley. DESIGN: Jeffrey Beecroft. ART DIR.: Wm. Ladd Skinner. CAST: Bruce Willis, Brad Pitt, Madeleine Stowe, Christopher Plummer. 131 min.

Twenty Million Miles to Earth (1957) [aka *The Beast from Space; The Giant Ymir*]

Morningside Movies/Columbia. DIR.: Nathan Juran. PROD.: Charles H. Schneer. SCR.: Christopher Knopf, Robert Creighton Williams. PHOTOG.: Irving Lippman. SFX: Ray Harryhausen. CAST: William Hopper, Joan Taylor, Frank Puglia. 82 min.

20,000 Leagues Under the Sea (1954)

Walt Disney Prods. DIR.: Richard Fleischer. SCR.: Earl Felton (based on the Jules Verne novel). PHOTOG.: Franz Planer. ED.: Elmo Williams. CAST: Kirk Douglas, Paul Lukas, Peter Lorre, James Mason. 127 min.

2001: A Space Odyssey (1968)

MGM/Polaris. DIR.: Stanley Kubrick. PROD.: Kubrick. SCR.: Kubrick, Arthur C. Clarke (based on Clarke's short story "The Sentinel").

PHOTOG.: Geoffrey Unsworth, John Alcott. ED.: Ray Lovejoy. SFX: Wally Veevers, Douglas Trumbull, Con Pederson, Tom Howard. CAST: Keir Dullea, Gary Lockwood, William Sylvester. 141 min.

The Twonky (1953)
Arch Oboler Prods. DIR.: Arch Oboler. PROD.: Oboler. SCR.: Oboler. PHOTOG.: Joseph F. Biroc. ED.: Betty Steinberg. CAST: Hans Conreid, Janet Warren, Billy Lynn. 84 min.

The Undersea Kingdom (1936)
Republic. DIR.: Joseph Kane, B. Reeves Eason. PROD.: Barney Sarecky. SCR.: John Rathmell, Maurice Geraghty, Oliver Drake. CAST: Ray "Crash" Corrigan, Monte Blue, Lon Chaney Jr. SERIAL: 12 episodes.

Universal Soldier (1992)
Carolco/Centropolis/IndieProd. DIR.: Roland Emmerich. SCR.: Dean Devlin, Christopher Leitch, and Richard Rothstein. PHOTOG.: Karl Walter Lindenlaub. ED.: Michael J. Duthie. DESIGN: Nelson Coates. CAST: Jean-Claude Van Damme, Dolph Lundgren, Ally Walker. 102 min.

Videodrome (1982)
Famous Players/Filmplan (Canada). DIR.: David Cronenberg. PROD.: Claude Héroux. SCR.: Cronenberg. PHOTOG.: Mark Irwin. ED.: Ron Sanders. CAST: James Woods, Sonja Smits, Deborah Harry, Peter Dvorsky. 87 min.

Voyage to the Bottom of the Sea (1961)
20th Century–Fox/Windsor. DIR.: Irwin Allen. PROD.: Allen. SCR.: Allen, Charles Bennett. PHOTOG.: Winton C. Hoch, John Lamb. ED.: George Boemler. CAST: Walter Pidgeon, Joan Fontaine, Barbara Eden, Peter Lorre. 105 min.

War of the Worlds (1953)
Paramount. DIR.: Byron Haskin. PROD.: George Pal. SCR.: Barré Lyndon (based on the H. G. Wells novel). PHOTOG.: George Barnes. ED.: Everett Douglas. CAST: Gene Barry, Ann Robinson, Les Tremayne. 85 min.

Westworld (1973)
MGM. DIR.: Michael Crichton. PROD.: Paul N. Lazarus III. SCR.: Crichton. PHOTOG.: Gene Polito. DESIGN: Herman Blumenthal. ED.: David Bretherton. CAST: Richard Benjamin, Yul Brynner, James Brolin. 88 min.

When Worlds Collide (1951)
Paramount. DIR.: Rudolph Maté. PROD.: George Pal. SCR.: Sydney Boehm (from the novel by Edwin Balmer and Philip Wylie). PHOTOG.: W. Howard Greene, John F. Seitz. ED.: Arthur P. Schmidt. CAST: Richard Dere, Barbara Rush, Peter Hanson. 83 min.

X: The Man with X-Ray Eyes (1963)
Alta Vista Prods./American International. DIR.: Roger Corman. PROD.:
Corman. SCR.: Robert Dillon, Ray Russell. PHOTOG.: Floyd Crosby.
CAST: Ray Milland, Harold Stone, Diana Van der Vlis. 76 min.

Zardoz (1974)
20th Century–Fox/John Boorman Prods. (Britain). DIR.: John
Boorman. PROD.: Boorman. SCR.: Boorman. PHOTOG.: Geoffrey
Unsworth. ED.: John Merrill. DESIGN: Anthony Pratt. CAST: Sean
Connery, Charlotte Rampling, John Alderton. 102 min.

Zombies of the Stratosphere (1952)
Republic. DIR.: Fred C. Brannon. SCR.: Ronald Davidson. PHOTOG.:
John McBurnie. ED.: Cliff Bell. CAST: Judd Holdren, Aline Towne,
Wilson Wood, Leonard Nimoy. SERIAL: 12 episodes.

Index

interested not so much
in the 'realist' type of
sfx, but the expressive,
abstract – will have to say
why though?

on intertextual approach